SIMPLY SPEAKING...
SIMPLE ANSWERS TO COMPLEX QUESTIONS

DR. GEORGE N. FORBES

Copyright © 2009 by Dr. George N. Forbes

Simply Speaking. . .
Simple Answers To Complex Questions
by Dr. George N. Forbes

Printed in the United States of America

ISBN 9781607910244

All rights reserved solely by the author. The author guarantees all contents are original and do not infringe upon the legal rights of any other person or work. No part of this book may be reproduced in any form without the permission of the author. The views expressed in this book are not necessarily those of the publisher.

Unless otherwise indicated, Bible quotations are taken from The NIV of the Bible. Copyright © 1988 by Zondervan.

www.xulonpress.com

DEDICATION

To my son, Bryan, a preacher of the Word and my pride and joy; and to the memory of my daughter, Katherine Brooke, who left us much too early.

To my dearest friend, Gene Welsh. Thank you Gene for being such a mentor and good friend.

To the First Christian Church, Aberdeen, Mississippi for giving me a "second chance."

Finally, to my "editor," Pam Ross. Thank you Pam for your hard work in preparing this work for publication and for being so important to me.

CONTENTS

Chapter one	WHAT ARE THE CHRISTIAN CHURCHES AND WHAT DO WE BELIEVE?......................11
Chapter two	WHAT IS THE CHURCH OF THE NEW TESTAMENT?..........34
Chapter three	BUT WHICH CHURCH IS THE RIGHT CHURCH?..............41
Chapter four	WHAT IS THE MISSION OF THE CHURCH TODAY?......50
Chapter five	WHY THE BIBLE?.......................53
Chapter six	WHEN, WHERE, AND WHY DO I WORSHIP?...............59
Chapter seven	WHAT DO WE DO WITH SIN?..65
Chapter eight	WHAT MUST I DO TO BE SAVED?..73

Simply Speaking...

Chapter nine	WHAT'S IN IT FOR ME?...........80
Chapter ten	HOW CAN I KNOW I AM SAVED?..94
Chapter eleven	WHAT IS THIS "LORD'S SUPPER" ANYWAY?................105
Chapter twelve	HOW CAN I KNOW THE WILL OF GOD?........................111
Chapter thirteen	WHAT IS THE POINT AND PURPOSE OF BAPTISM?........123
Chapter fourteen	WHY IS THE "ONCE IN GRACE, ALWAYS IN GRACE DOCTRINE" WRONG?............129
Chapter fifteen	WHY PRAY?..............................134
Chapter sixteen	WHAT DO WE DO WITH THE HOLY SPIRIT?..................140
Chapter seventeen	WHAT ABOUT SPIRITUAL GIFTS?.......................................149
Chapter eighteen	WHAT CAN I DO TO SERVE?......................................163
Chapter nineteen	DO I HAVE TO GIVE MY MONEY?....................................169
Chapter twenty	WHAT PLACE DOES LOVE HAVE IN THE CHRISTIAN LIFE?..178

Chapter twenty-one	WHAT ABOUT SUFFERING AND THE CHRISTIAN?	189
Chapter twenty-two	WHAT ARE ELDERS AND DEACONS?	202
Chapter twenty-three	WHAT ARE THE ROLES OF ELDERS AND DEACONS?	217
Chapter twenty-four	WHAT IS THE ROLE OF WOMEN IN THE CHURCH?	229
Chapter twenty-five	HOW SHOULD WE VIEW MARRIAGE, DIVORCE AND REMARRIAGE?	246
Chapter twenty-six	WHAT ABOUT JUDGMENT?	278
Chapter twenty-seven	WHAT ABOUT THE MILLENNIUM?	287

CHAPTER ONE

WHAT ARE THE CHRISTIAN CHURCHES, AND WHAT DO WE BELIEVE?

ORIGIN AND HISTORY

The membership of the Christian Churches in America was originally called "The disciples of Christ." In some areas we are known as "Churches of Christ." We number, at last count, about six million strong. We are often confused with the a cappella movement, and we were divided over the keyboard in the 1906 census. We are, however, doctrinally unified, and we are attempting some form of reconciliation between the two groups with a number of forward thinking people on both sides involved. Another false idea is that we believe in baptismal regeneration—a belief that baptism into water has some magical effect on the person being baptized.

The Christian Church movement is best characterized today as an independent movement attempting to "RESTORE" a New Testament form of worship and salvation. Our movement has no "creed" but Christ and we "speak only where the Bible speaks." Our motto is "In matters of doctrine, unity; in matters of opinion, liberty; and in all things love." We practice immersion as the only form of baptism and it is for the remission of sins. We also put Christ as the center of our lives and our worship experience by making the focal point of our worship the partaking of the Lord's Supper. We use the Bible as our only source of authority and do not rely upon the teachings of men as having any authority over us.

OUR ORIGIN

To understand the Christian Church/ Church of Christ, we must trace our origins on American soil. These churches were seeded in strong personalities and rooted in movements urging Christian unity on a simple New Testament basis. We began in the early nineteenth century primarily by Scottish Presbyterian preachers who read the Bible and discovered errors in the faith and practices of their denomination. We also find origins in Methodism in Virginia and North Carolina; Presbyterians in Kentucky and what is now West Virginia; and Baptists in New England and on the western frontier. There were large numbers of converts on the western frontier, which, at that time, consisted of Kentucky, Ohio and Tennessee. The "big names" in the movement were Barton W. Stone, Thomas and Alexander Campbell, Raccoon John Smith, Walter Scott and other pioneers of the movement.

THE O'KELLY-HAGGARD MOVEMENT

One movement arose in Virginia when James O'Kelly, Rice Haggard, and other Methodists rebelled against the authority of Bishop Asbury in 1792. A year later, they organized the "Republican Methodist Church." Taking the Bible as their creed, their main dissent from the Methodist

Church was based on their belief that "primitive church government" was a republic by nature. Many Christian Churches in Virginia and North Carolina originated from this movement. Some of them later joined forces with the people associated with Thomas and Alexander Campbell and Barton W. Stone. Others finally united with the Congregationalists in 1931.

THE CHRISTIAN CONNECTION MOVEMENT

Another movement began in New England when two young men revolted against Calvinism in the Baptist churches there. One was Elias Smith, a Baptist who was born in 1769 in Lyme Connecticut, but who grew up on the frontier in Vermont. The other was Abner Jones, born in 1772 in Royalton, Massachusetts. As did Smith, Jones grew up on the frontier in Vermont. Both men renounced Calvinism and sought to abandon existing "ecclesiastical systems." They attempted to establish a simpler faith and practice of the New Testament. Smith and Jones worked together; and soon dozens of "Christian Churches," resulting from their work, sprang up in New England.

THE STONE MOVEMENT

Another movement of even greater significance originated in Kentucky. Barton W. Stone, born in 1772 at Port Tobacco, Maryland, was its primary leader. Stone received his education in Pittsylvania County Virginia and at David Caldwell's famous "log" college located near the present city of Greensboro, North Carolina. Ordained to the Presbyterian ministry, he later followed the route of Daniel Boone's "Wilderness Trail" to the West and eventually accepted ministries at Concord and Cane Ridge, Kentucky. With a few fellow Presbyterian ministers who wanted to

Simply Speaking...

escape from an ironclad type of Calvinism, Stone withdrew from the jurisdiction of the Synod of Kentucky.

Stone and his fellow ministers, under supervision from the synod, organized an independent Springfield Presbytery in 1803. Less than a year later in 1804, they dissolved the Presbytery they had created. They published a "Last Will and Testament of the Springfield Presbytery" in which they argued for more lay rule in church matters, a firmer reliance on the Bible as a guide, and "union with the body of Christ" at large. They adopted the name "Christian" at the suggestion of Rice Haggard who had come to Kentucky from Virginia. The movement spread rapidly in Kentucky, Ohio, Indiana, and Tennessee. Then it invaded Illinois, Iowa, and Missouri. Stone published a magazine entitled the *Christian Messenger* in which he expressed his views and pleaded for unity of all the followers of Christ in every church on a simple Bible base.

Naturally, some Presbyterians opposed the "Stoneites" or "New-Light" schism. This led to tension between the Presbyterians and Stone and his followers over doctrinal matters.

Stone, however, not much of a controversialist himself realized that rigid Calvinism had softened in Kentucky by about 1825. Thereafter, he gave his primary emphasis to the unity of all believers in Christ. *The basis of this unity*, he always maintained, *was neither doctrine nor dogmas, but love and good will.* Stone maintained that *no doctrines, however true, ought to be forced on the Christian believer.* This gentle and tolerant man *favored freedom of belief, not only in theory, but also in practice.*

He raised his voice in Christian unity in a day when few others believed in unity. The basis of unity, he taught, was Christian love. Christian unity, for him, was a "divine imperative" necessary for the conversion of the world, for effective Christian witnessing, and for fulfilling Jesus prayer in John 17, "My prayer is not for them alone. I pray also for those who will believe in Me through their message, for that all of them may be one, Father, just as you are in Me and I am in You" (Vs. 20-21).

Stone was one of the first religious leaders in America not only to preach theoretical Christian unity but also to practice it in his own personal life, as well as in contact with his fellow-Christians.

THE CAMPBELLS, FATHER AND SON

Thomas Campbell and his son, Alexander led the most significant movement in behalf of Christian unity by restoring New Testament Christianity. Thomas Campbell was born in Ireland in 1763, and reared in the Church of England. He "schooled" at the University of Glasgow and trained for the ministry in the Seceder Divinity Hall. He became a Seceder Presbyterian minister. In 1804-05, he tried in vain to help unite the Seceder Synods of Ireland. (The union finally took place in 1820.) He came to The United States in 1807 and became the minister of several small Seceder Presbyterian Churches in Washington County, Pennsylvania. Due to his Catholic upbringing, he invited some non-Presbyterians to join in the communion service. He was officially accused of departing from the standards of his church, and because of the aroused feeling, he withdrew from the Seceder Synod.

Before Thomas Campbell left the Seceder Presbyterian ministry, a group of friends met with him to form the "Christian Association of Washington" on August 17, 1809. The group adopted the motto: "Where the Scriptures speak, we speak; where they are silent, we are silent." Thomas Campbell drew up an important document called "The Declaration and Address." Its most significant statement was that "the Church of Christ upon earth is essentially, intentionally, and constitutionally one." The document expressed the "awful consequences of division among Christians" and sounded an impassioned plea for unity. The address declared that divisions had been caused by the neglect of the revealed will of God, by human opinions and introduction of "human inventions into the faith and practice of the Church." Thomas Campbell also held that faith in Jesus Christ and obedience to His Word was all that was "absolutely necessary to qualify them for admission into His Church." The address also stated that the New Testament was a perfect constitution for the "worship, discipline and government of the New Testament Church."

Alexander Campbell arrived in America in 1809 and agreed with his father's position. When the regular Presbyterian Church rejected Thomas Campbell's application for admission, the Christian Association of Washington, Pennsylvania, organized itself into a church on May 4, 1811. A simple church was erected near Bethany, Virginia (currently West Virginia), called the Brush Run Church. Infant baptism and sprinkling were rejected by the group. This brought them closer to the Baptists. The Brush Run Church was admitted into the Redstone Baptist Association in 1813.

Alexander Campbell married the daughter of a well-to-do farmer who deeded to him the farm that helped to give him a considerable economic security, part of which was later donated and became Bethany College. He was a student who wanted to excel in his studies in a similar manner as a modern American young man wants to excel in football or basketball. He became a brilliant orator, writer, and scholar. In the next seventeen years, he engaged in a number of debates, traveled extensively, gave many addresses, and edited a Christian periodical called *The Christian Baptist*, which was followed by the *Millennial Harbinger*. In the former publication, Mr. Campbell attacked the authority of the clergy, the use of creeds, and "unscriptural organizations," such as synods, Bible societies, and Sunday schools. He also gave much space to outlining a primitive order of faith, practice and worship that he felt was the only one contained in the Bible. Many Baptist churches were won over to Alexander Campbell's views. Many others, however, regarded this young religious leader as a heretic.

Frontier preachers such as "Raccoon" John Smith, P. S. Fall, Jacob Creath, Sr., and Jacob Creath, Jr., added strength to the growing movement. These "reformers" were nicknamed "Campbellites"—a term to which they objected, but which, like most nicknames, could not be killed. However, the best-known leader in the movement, allied with the Campbells, was Walter Scott.

WALTER SCOTT, THE EVANGELIST

Walter Scott, originally a Presbyterian, was born in Edinburgh, Scotland, in 1796. He came to New York in 1818 and later migrated to Pittsburgh. Scott developed the famous "five-finger exercise" to outline the steps of conversion. This formula is still repeated today within the Christian Church/ Church of Christ. The simple steps to conversion were these: 1) Faith; 2) Repentance; 3) Baptism; 4) Remission of sins; 5) Gift of the Holy Spirit. Another step, confession, was added later. Scott became a flaming evangelist on the Ohio frontier, greatly increasing the membership of the movement.

In 1829, Alexander Campbell won wide attention as a member of the Virginia Constitutional Convention. In that same year, he engaged in a debate with the famous British social reformer and skeptic, Robert Owen. Previously, Campbell had debated with John Walker, a Seceder Presbyterian, in 1820, and with another Seceder

Presbyterian, William MacCalla, in 1823. Following his success in these contests, Campbell concluded that a "week's debating is worth a year's preaching."

SEPARATION FROM THE BAPTISTS

About this time, a process of separation from the Baptists was taking place. This new group differed from the Baptists on some matters of faith and practice. The Campbells and their followers stressed the New Testament as the primary source of authority for Christians. They practiced "baptism for the remission of sins." They held that the Holy Spirit operated through the Word in conversion, and rejected the Calvinistic idea held by some Baptists that Christ died only for the elect. They also rejected all creeds, held that any Christian could administer the Lord's Supper and baptism, practiced the weekly observance of the Lord's Supper, denied a special call to the ministry, and rejected the idea of voting candidates into the church. It is hard to pinpoint an exact date when those in the Campbellian movement separated from the Baptists, but 1830 is the date usually recognized when the split became final.

THE UNION OF THE CAMPBELLS AND THE FOLLOWERS OF STONE

Another far-reaching trend took place with the informal union of the followers of Barton W. Stone and those of the Campbells. Stone and Alexander Campbell first met in 1824. They had many things in common, but they also had many differences in spirit and message. Stone had begun editing a monthly newsletter called *The Christian Messenger*, in which he pleaded for the unity of all Christian people. Like Campbell, he felt the doctrinal systems were diverse. Unlike Campbell at this time, he found the primary basis of unity in Christian love at the heart of the New Testament. The point is not that Alexander Campbell rejected Christian love as a basis of unity, but he did not give it the primary emphasis Stone often gave. Campbell had developed a primitive pattern of Christianity which he interpreted from his reading of the New Testament, and he did not feel that Stone had fully grasped this system. For his part, Stone accepted the so-called primitive Gospel pattern, but he did not make it as absolute and binding as did Campbell. In *The Christian Messenger*, which began in 1824, Barton W. Stone sounded the clarion call for unity. However, in the new periodical, *The Millennial Harbinger*, begun in 1830, Campbell was willing to explore the question of unity, but he was skeptical of Stone's orthodoxy on the primitive Gospel pattern.

While Campbell called for discussion of the differences of the two groups, some of his followers were not inclined to wait to clarify the issues. Accordingly, in the State of Kentucky, growing sympathy between the two groups finally led to a meeting in Lexington, Kentucky, on January 1, 1832. While the congregations in Lexington did not unite until 1835, the impetus was provided in this meeting for informal and unofficial mergers on the congregational level in other areas. News of the meeting did not make Alexander Campbell too happy because he felt that further discussion was necessary to resolve the differences. However, the spirit of unity was too potent to be stopped at this point. The followers of Alexander Campbell and Barton W. Stone agreed to carry the message of unity to the individual churches since no convention or conference had binding authority to enforce unity between the two groups. Stone was present at the Lexington meeting, and urged the merger. His patient spirit, forbearance, and humility undoubtedly contributed greatly to the union.

Simply Speaking...

This news of "combined movements" grew rapidly. The largest gains were made among the people moving into the new frontier states of the Middle West. The movement failed to make gains in the conservative east. Today the greatest strength is in the following states: Indiana, Missouri, Illinois, Ohio, Kentucky, Texas, Oklahoma, and Kansas.

Many of the Christians, especially in New England, did not enter the merger of the followers of Stone and the Campbells. They suspected Alexander Campbell of being Calvinistic and orthodox. So far, few of our historians have recognized how hard Stone tried to bring this group and Alexander Campbell together. Stone failed in this attempt, however, but showed a great spirit of conciliation. Stone died in 1844. In spite of the fact that his movement had brought great strength to the growing body of Christians, few noted his primary contributions. One reason for this is that the ecumenical movement in America was still in its infancy during his lifetime. Another reason is that Stone died too soon to give leadership during this organizational period of the growing life of the Christians, or Disciples of Christ.

CAMPBELL'S WORK

Alexander Campbell, younger and more vigorous than Stone, made some of his finest achievements following the merger. In 1839, he published *The Christian System* that was almost a full statement of his views on many religious subjects. During 1837 when the anti-Catholic agitation in our country was strong, Campbell defended Protestantism in a debate with the Roman-Catholic Archbishop Purcell, of Cincinnati. Both men were urged to debate by the people who had heard their respective views in public lectures delivered in that city. The debate lasted eight days, marking the first time a Roman-Catholic of that high rank had taken part in such a public discussion in this country. Campbell's last notable debate was in 1843 with a Presbyterian minister, N. L. Rice, in Lexington, Kentucky. The famous Henry Clay served as moderator of the debate lasting eighteen days. This gave Campbell the chance to defend his views when he was at the zenith of his popularity. Four of the six propositions had to do with baptism and, doubtlessly, continued to center attention upon the "Christians" or "Disciples" as primarily an "immersionists" body. Campbell defended the position of baptism by immersion only for the remission or forgiveness of past sins.

THE SLAVERY ISSUE

During the 1850's the slavery issue divided both the nation and many American churches. The Methodists, Baptists and the Presbyterians split officially. The Christian Churches/ Disciples of Christ, who were nearly equal in number in both the North and the South, did not divide over the issue. All political and social questions were considered as belonging to the realm, not of necessary faith, but of opinion where people could differ without dividing the church.

Although the Christians did not divide over slavery, they did divide after the Civil War over earlier issues that were left unresolved. Two main issues split the movement: the use of organs or musical instruments in worship services, and the acceptance of missionary societies.

MAINSTREAMS AND BRANCHES

Division over Instrumental Music in Worship

Protestant opposition to instrumental music in public worship began with Zwingli and Calvin in Switzerland in the early days of the Sixteenth Century Reformation. It gave some trouble in New England churches in the Eighteenth Century. However, it seriously divided the Christian Church beginning in the 1860's.

The position against the organ was stated by J. W. McGarvey who wrote that the organ was not an aid to singing and was neither a hymnbook nor an accessory to the church building as was a stove, but was a distinctly new element in public worship. All elements of public worship must be authorized in the New Testament. Since instrumental music was not authorized, it was wrong to use it. Others felt that the New Testament did not attempt to enumerate all of the permissible elements of public worship. They believed that the New Testament did not try to outline an exact pattern of public worship. The debate over the "music" question became very bitter.

A violent storm arose over missionary societies. Tolbert Fanning in Nashville and Benjamin Franklin, editor of the *American Christian Review*, attacked the missionary societies. They sought in the New Testament a blueprint for all church procedures. Finding no such societies mentioned in the New Testament, they rejected all such societies. This was a crucial period of controversy. The arguments and mounting bitterness between the groups finally resulted in the decision of the U. S. Census Bureau, in 1906, to place the disputants into two separate groups: "The Churches of Christ" and "The Christian Church/ Disciples of Christ." The members of the conservative group are nicknamed the "antis" (because of their anti-organ and anti-missionary alliance stand). Those within the mainstream and smaller separated "antis," who oppose missionary societies and other organizations, are called the "non-progressives."

Through the influence of Isaac Errett, editor of *The Christian Standard*, a weekly paper, the tide was turned so that the larger group held to the more liberal position on the two above questions and other minor issues that helped split the "Christian Churches." This division, from today's perspective, is a major tragedy in the American religious scene. A movement that had its beginning in a desire to unify Christians by restoring the primitive church model could not agree on the details of the model. Today, in places where the three groups exist side-by-side; outsiders still confuse them and often attribute the characteristics of one to the other.

Opposition to Organized Missionary Work by the Independents

The church split yet again over the United Christian Missionary Society because some felt that the Society was not loyal to the "Old Plea" and was too "bureaucratic." The *Christian Standard*, formerly so cooperative under Isaac Errett, became the strongest critic of the new organization. "Independent" missionary societies or agendas arose. Some of these organized themselves into the "Associated Free Agencies" with the organizing center in Cincinnati, Ohio.

These free agencies founded a paper called *The Restoration Herald* that reported the work of the independent agencies and denounced the United Missionary Society and its supporters. Part of the controversy centered in whether or not missionaries in certain foreign fields were disloyal to "Our Plea" and had received Methodists and Presbyterians into church membership without immersing them. The North American Christian Convention appealed to these "independents" and the movement began to grow quickly. At the present time, the movement is the fastest growing Christian organization in the world.

We are not exempt from division within our own ranks. We have some who believe that our unity must be preserved at any cost while others feel that the maintenance of the "restoration principles" is more important than every other consideration including the unity of believers. The bitterness and energy consumed by this fight could well have been better channeled into building new and stronger churches over the nation and the world.

WHAT DO WE BELIEVE AND PRACTICE

The central beliefs and practices of the Christian Churches/ Churches of Christ are few and simple. They meet the most profound and lasting needs of the followers of Christ by stressing the lasting essentials of New Testament Christianity.

Many of the lasting concerns of Barton W. Stone, Walter Scot, and Thomas and Alexander Campbell have been partially fulfilled in a growing and common concern to return to the spirit, mind, and mission of Christ. Therefore, we no longer stress "Our Plea" so much as a religious body as we do *Christ's* plea as the Lord and Savior of mankind. We confess anew, humbly and gratefully, the slogan, "We are Christians only, not the only Christians." We do not believe that we shall save the world; rather that Christ will save those who come to him in obedience and a desire to devote themselves to His service. We further believe that He calls our independent churches to share a vital witness to the lasting and essentials of His mission and redemptive work on earth.

Our main beliefs as a movement of free and independent churches are rooted in God's Word, spoken, and still speaking through the Bible; the supremacy of Jesus Christ in His Church and all things Christian; and union and liberty of all Christians in Christ. These principles shall now be described briefly.

I. THE BIBLE ALONE AS OUR RULE AND GUIDE

We are a Bible-centered movement in Christ. As a whole, we believe that the Bible is the divinely inspired Word of God. It is our only supreme guide and authority for our faith in Jesus Christ. At our best, "We speak where the Bible speaks, and we are silent where the Bible is silent." Most of us now see the wisdom of Alexander Campbell's prophetic declaration when he stressed that the fiercest disputes among Christians were about what "the Bible does *not* say rather than about what it *does* say."

Our heritage seeks to lift the Bible above any creed and purely human traditions for the essentials of Christian faith, order, and life. Whereas some still use the Bible with legalism as though it were a static law book, the mainstream of our movement views the Bible as a book of living principles through which God speaks to the hearts of those of humble, Christ-like faith. The Bible, to us, is to be read, studied, and understood as no other book. The Bible is unlike any other book, for through it, God reveals Himself, His will, and offers us salvation—supremely and superbly. The Bible is not a weapon or a club to beat the sons of men over the head; it is God's revelation to his children to accept and share the Gospel of His Son and our Savior.

For us, the central meaning and guide to understanding the Bible as a whole is Jesus Christ. In Him, God is fully revealed and made flesh. Through Jesus

Christ, the essentials of the Gospel, the Church, and Christ-like life are founded and made known. We hold, therefore, that Jesus Christ, His living Spirit, mission, and message are the main keys to unlock and interpret the Bible as a whole. Through Him, we learn what God really requires of His followers and church in the guidance of the Holy Spirit.

II. THE SUPREMACY OF CHRIST

The central faith of the Christian Churches/Churches of Christ is in Jesus Christ as revealed in the Bible. The supreme guide to understanding the Scriptures and what is required of all Christians is rooted in the New Testament. Because of this, we often call our movement, "a New Testament people." We strongly believe in our timeless early slogan, "No creed but Christ" and the New Testament as "our only Constitution" or "rule of faith, order, and practice."

As a result, our movement rejects all non-biblical creeds and requirements as tests of church membership, belief and practice. Christ alone is our Lord and Savior, and the living and loving Church is His body of which He and He alone is the head and through which His Spirit works to guide and inspire Christian life, growth, grace, and fellowship. We have not only "no creed but Christ" but also no hierarchy of human church leaders in authority, rank, and calling. None of us is required to obey any church leaders, but we are all expected to love God, all the followers of Christ, and all human neighbors as Christ loved them. The only real difference between our ordained ministers and our laity is one of practical needs and functions within the church—not in nature, merit or status. We are all equally one in Christ Jesus, as we are all equally called to obey and serve

Christ, and to share His Gospel and extend His mission on earth.

Since the Christians of the New Testament did not vote on converts who wished to become members of the church, God alone is the Judge. Since Jesus Christ or His immediate followers did not use or require creeds, we do not. Our only traditional "confession of faith" is simple—the Biblical confession of Simon Peter that "Jesus is the Christ, the Son of the living God." This public confession meets the needs of the simplest person, or the most profound scholar. Almost all Christians can accept and understand this statement that allows freedom and permits new light to come form the past, present, and future revelation of God.

III. THE UNITY OF ALL CHRISTIANS IN CHRIST

We believe that only Christ can unify His followers. As a result, we pray, as did He, in John 17 that all who call upon His name shall, one day, be united under His name and in His body. We shall not, however, sacrifice the principles upon which the Restoration Movement was founded in an effort to "join forces" with any other group, church or other religious organization. We hold fast to the Bible as the only basis for unity.

Our movement rejects all human creeds as tests of church membership, belief, worship and practice, not only on the premise that such a stand is biblical, but also on the premise that this will work toward unity. Christ alone is our Lord and Savior, and the Church is His body of which He alone is the Head and through the Holy Spirit gives Christians life, growth and grace. All varieties of the original New Testament churches were creedless but not Christless. They had no human creed or official hierarchy of church leaders in authority, rank, or calling. All their churches and members were one in Christ. As Paul believed, we also believe in the "priesthood of all believers"—that each follower of Christ is his own high priest before God. None of us is required to obey the commands or any opinions of any church leaders, but we believe that all Christians have the equal duty to obey Christ and to love all his followers and our human neighbors as Christ loved them.

To reiterate, since the Christians of the New Testament did not vote upon admitting new members to the fellowship, neither do we. Since Jesus Christ required no creed, neither do we. Our only "confession of faith" is the timeless Biblical confession of Peter that "Jesus is the Christ, the Son of the living God to be served as our Lord and Savior."

IV. THE LIBERTY OF ALL CHRISTIANS IN CHRIST

Although the only written guide or "Constitution" of our movement is the Bible, especially the Christ-centered New Testament and the only supreme authority which we confess is Jesus Christ, we do profess that our chief watchword is the *liberty* of all believers under Christ as the Holy Spirit gives each the light to see, understand, and obey. Because of this Christ-centered freedom, we are a liberty-loving and democratic Christian movement of free churches and individuals.

Our basis of belief, worship, and membership is entirely voluntary. We are free to serve Christ, yet bound by His teachings. We believe that the New Testament is not a *blueprint* but an *imprint* of the Spirit, word, and mission of Christ for the entire Church and all His followers. The main principles and practices of the early Church were few, simple yet profoundly Christ-like enough to bind their fellowship in spite of their individual opinions and peculiar needs. The New Testament Churches had, and gave freedom among themselves. We, like them, feel that *what we have in common in Christ is more important and vital than our differences.*

Our independent congregations are free to determine the material they will use in study groups, free to determine which missionaries they will support, and free to call their own ministers. None of our churches have ministers "appointed" or selected for them by anyone else. At best, our churches are free to seek counsel and advice for needed and suitable ministers, staffs, programs, goals, and fellowship.

In the realm of freedom of choice, mind, and programs, our local congregations and individual members are as free as any in Church history. This liberty is sometimes abused, but on the whole, it has strengthened our movement. Within our membership and cooperative fellowship are almost every variety of Christian individuals and concerns. One extreme has some humanists, while the other extreme has Biblical legalists. The vast majority, however, of our mainstream movement has a high Christology and a solid Christian view of the Bible, God, man, sin, salvation, and the Church.

While we still have some demagogic individuals and churches who imply, "I am of Paul," or "I am of Apollos," and "I am of Cephas," such tendencies are forbidding to the mainstream of our brotherhood in its common love of liberty and its God-given right to make its own decisions after careful and Christ-centered considerations.

Some of our most extreme groups quibble over our main traditions and ideals as Christians, but the lasting principles and essentials of our movement have never forsaken us. Perhaps no other religious organization in history has a more sincere or thorough self-criticism of its own weaknesses, yet appreciation of its Christ-centered strength to share the Gospel.

V. THE TWO ORDINANCES OR INSTITUTIONS OF OUR LORD

In spite of our liberty in the details of practice and worship among individuals and local congregations, we all share a common heritage. As a whole, the Christian Church/ Church of Christ seek to return all believers to the original beliefs, practices, teachings, and mission of the first-century Church. We all seek to restore the common bond and fellowship of those believers. We stress and observe His only two ordinances or institutions: baptism and the weekly celebration of the Lord's Supper.

A. BAPTISM

The Christian Church/ Church of Christ seek to restore the original Scriptural meaning of the New Testament tradition of baptism. We practice and teach baptism by immersion only. At the center of this form of baptism is a very spiritual form of symbolism. Our belief is that we spiritually die and are spiritually buried and spiritually raised form the dead as Christ was literally raised from the dead. We are raised to become new creatures in Christ. We do not believe in "magic water" or "water regeneration" through baptism. There is nothing magic in the water. It is only water. It is not the act or the water that saves us; it is, rather, the Spirit of God by His grace.

No Christian Church/ Church of Christ ever practiced sprinkling or pouring as a form of baptism, nor do we accept or practice infant baptism. It is perfectly clear in the New Testament that baptism by immersion was the only baptism practiced in the early Church. In addition to death, burial and resurrection, baptism symbolizes the faith and experience of both the individual and the local congregation in the death of the old life, without Christ, the burial of former self, and rising up in newness of life, both public and private. Baptism, thus, is for the "remission of sins" and the gift of an entirely new life in Christ through faith and the power of the Holy Spirit.

Such baptism is a fulfillment of the "Great Commission." With few exceptions, all such baptized are baptized "into the name of the Father, the Son, and the Holy Spirit for the remission of sins." We further believe that there is an element of mystery in baptism as the Holy Spirit comes to live in the believer at that moment.

Actually, when the full act of baptism is understood in both its physical and spiritual aspects, few object to the time-honored method of baptism by immersion which has been practiced by the Christian Churches/ Churches of Christ. However, when it is only a physical act, it has little value for the church or the one being baptized. It is for this reason that the churches stress the baptism only of "believers" in contrast to infant baptism.

At their very best, the Christian Churches/ Churches of Christ have stated in answer to the question, "Why be baptized?" Jesus was baptized. Baptism is a symbol of a believer's willingness to submit to the example and command of Jesus. Baptism is also a symbol of beginning of a new life. Baptism symbolized the death, burial, and resurrection of Jesus Christ, our Lord. Finally, they look upon it as a rite of initiation into the Church and the worldwide fellowship of Christians.

B. THE LORD'S SUPPER: A WEEKLY OBSERVANCE

The Christian Churches/ Churches of Christ observe a second ordinance: The Lord's Supper. Many names are given to this observance, but most call it "communion." The Lord's Supper is observed weekly in our churches. Much of the spiritual strength of the Christian Churches/ Churches of Christ is found in their observance of weekly communion. Visitors have commented on the profound sense of togetherness that becomes immediately apparent at the first note of the communion hymn.

The Christian Churches/ Churches of Christ see no magic in the bread and juice. For us the bread is not His body and the juice is not His blood. They are symbols of His body and blood. We accept the Lord's Supper as containing an act of thanksgiving to God, a remembrance of Jesus Christ so that He lives again with the believer, as a memorial or reminder that He lived among men and died for them, as an act of committal to His way and His spirit, as a renewal of man's kinship with his fellow Christians all over the world, and, finally, as a foretelling of our Lord's death "until He comes again."

Here, then, is a brief sketch of the history and beliefs of the largest church that has its origins on American soil.

YOUR INVITATION

The great mainstream of our movement still bears witness to its historic mission of eliminating denominational divisions and uniting all Christians under the banner of Jesus Christ. Although in our glorious history there have been those who have not agreed, we remain dedicated to the unbroken desire to carry the Gospel of Christ to the lost. Within our family, we have had disagreements, as does any family. We can learn to agree to disagree on matters not touched upon directly by the New Testament. On such matters as are directly spoken of, however, there can be no disagreement. We are not subject to the precepts of man or the doctrines of men. Our strengths lie in the fact that we are dedicated to the renewal of the New Testament Church with all that entails.

Today, there are many denominations in America and the world, each of these professing to follow the Master, often in wasteful and disgraceful competition. In their strife, they tear the seamless robe of Jesus. If we cannot unite as Jesus prayed in John 17, how can we ever expect to win the lost for Him?

We still proclaim that we are not the *only* Christians, but Christians *only*.

Perhaps you will find that the Christian Churches/ Churches of Christ are where your spiritual needs are being met. Perhaps you have not fully committed to the Christ for whom this movement was named. Should you find a need to know more about this Christ, we invite you to come to us and allow us the opportunity to share Jesus with you. You may come to understand this great heritage and make yourself a part of the Body of Christ.

CHAPTER TWO

WHAT IS THE CHURCH OF THE NEW TESTAMENT?

INTRODUCTION: The simple answer is that it was (and is) Christ's Church. When Jesus told His disciples that He would build His Church, He was most sincere. He said this in response to Peter's reference to him as "the Christ, the Son of the Living God." After this "confession," Jesus declared His intention to build *His Church*. This occurred on Pentecost a short time later. Jesus did not leave them wondering "which" church was His. In the beginning, there was only one and it bore His name. He also told the disciples that He would not leave them alone, that He would send them the "Comforter" Who would guide them into all truth. This promise was also fulfilled on Pentecost. The assembled crowd could not help noticing the "boldness" with which these men spoke. That boldness was a direct result of the coming of the Holy Spirit. If one is seeking the New Testament Church today, one has only to look to the New Testament to find it. It exists in a similar form today as it did then.

    The Church during the first century was a simple composition with no hierarchy. It consisted of immersed believers who came together for the purpose of worship, fellowship, study, and the Lord's Supper (see Acts 2:42; 20:7). No one "ruled" over them, and they had only the authority of the apostles early on and later the authority of the New Testament writings. They demonstrated unquestioned loyalty to Christ and to Him alone. Because of the loyalty demonstrated by these believers, the Church experienced rapid growth and was spread quickly throughout the known world, so much so that by the close of the First Century, A. D., it had grown so strongly and rapidly that the Roman Empire and its emperors sought to destroy this "new religion" as they perceived it a threat to their rule.

THERE CAME A TIME OF FALLING AWAY

The apostles Paul and John envisioned a time of apostasy or falling away. Paul, in writing to Timothy, warned him of such when he wrote, "The Spirit clearly says that in the later times some will abandon the faith and follow deceiving spirits and things taught by demons. Such teachings come through hypocritical liars, whose consciences have been seared by a hot iron" (I Timothy 4:1-2 NIV). In addition, Paul makes a similar warning in II Timothy 4:3-4 (NIV), "For the time will come when men will not put up with sound doctrine. Instead, to suit their own desires, they will gather around them a great number of teachers to say what their itching ears want to hear. They will turn their ears away from the truth and turn aside to myths." These two warnings, coupled with his warning of the "Man of Lawlessness," in II Thessalonians 2:1-12 and the "anti-Christ" about whom John warned in his letters and in the Revelation, give plenty of warning that things would change. It was in less time than one might think that these prophesies were fulfilled. We are seeing similar situations

Simply Speaking...

in the Church today as people are turning from the Truth to doctrines of men.

THE DARK AGES AND THE COMING OF THE REFORMATION

The authority of Scripture was usurped by men who wanted power unto themselves; and within a few centuries, we find the power-hungry men had taken over the true Church. The people were kept in darkness and therefore, these times were called "The Dark Ages" in history. If people attempted to understand the Truth, they were persecuted and often killed for their search. It was during these "Dark Ages" that sprinkling was substituted for immersion, a professional "priesthood" was established, the teachings of "purgatory" were made known, and denominational organizations came into being.

It was at the close of this dark period of history that such men as Calvin, Luther, Huss, Zwigli, Tyndale, Knox, and others emerged. This period became known as the "Protestant Reformation." The name "Protestant" is from the root word "protest." These men, as well as others, did not accept the authority of the Roman Catholic Church and sought to reform it. The original intent was to reform the Roman Church rather than begin a separate movement. The original intention failed and others rallied around the teachings of these men. It was not long that the views of these "reformers" became the doctrines of denominations, some of which bore their names. Many of the practices began by the Roman Catholic Church, such as infant baptism, were never repudiated. While much good work came from these reformers, much that is anti-Scriptural came as well. Many human creeds were developed and became a "test of fellowship" among warring groups developed around the strong personalities of these men.

WHERE, THEN, IS THE CHURCH OF THE NEW TESTAMENT?

One does not need search too far to find the answer to that question. A movement arose on the American frontier in the late Eighteenth and early Nineteenth centuries that would seek to "restore" the New Testament Church. This movement is alive and well today and is growing with enormous speed. The Christian church/ church of Christ welcomes those who are seeking to return to the Bible and to the God Who authored it.

MORE ABOUT THE "RESTORATION MOVEMENT"

The enemies of the Movement began to call the followers of this plea as "Campbellites." This was and is a derisive term since the believers in this fellowship are not "followers" of the Campbells any more than they are followers of any man. They follow Christ and Him alone. The Campbells desired to wear the name Christian and that only and called themselves "Disciples of Christ." While the name "Disciples of Christ" currently refers to a denomination wearing the name "Christian Church, Disciples of Christ," there is a vast distinction between its doctrines and those of the "Independent Christian Churches/ Churches of Christ."

This movement became so popular that by the early 1900's the leaders felt that it was poised to "take the world for Christ." There were those who believed that by 1950 there would be over fifty million believers wearing the name of Jesus Christ only with no denominational affiliation. This was not to be, however, as Satan began to work much harder, and the movement was splintered.

Simply Speaking...

THE PERVERSION OF THE PLEA

Liberalism reared its ugly head and the unity of the movement was short lived. This liberalism was not limited to the Christian Churches/ Churches of Christ. It affected all denominations as well. Assisted by a system of thought known as "German Rationalism" (a thought that held that whatever is not reasonable is not believable), liberalism approached the Bible with a desire to cut out anything that required *faith*. For example, they removed the virgin birth of Christ because it was considered *unreasonable*. Miracles and the resurrection of Jesus were thrown out. The Christian doctrine and faith became a faith with no skeleton and a shadow of its former self. Many of the theological seminaries began to approve of this and taught it to their "preacher" students. As a result, the ministers began to espouse such to the local congregations, and a further falling away from the Truth began. "Sin" became "psychological maladjustment," and the concept of hell became "extreme nervous tension or depression." To many, we are living in the only "hell" we will ever know.

Because of this liberalism, many young men left the ministry, and many others did not enter into it. The result is a lasting shortage of men willing to study for the local ministry and a shortage of preachers today. Churches without ministers are dying all over the nation, and the "Restoration Movement" is not exempt.

When, in 1919, liberalism found its way into the Christian Churches/ Churches of Christ, a group wishing to provide for missionary support through a "central agency" developed, and it called itself "The United Christian Missionary Society." The result of this was to split the churches. When it was discovered that the "Society" was practicing "open membership" (accepting members into the church without the benefit of immersion), the more conser-

Simply Speaking...

vative group pulled away. Another problem that arose was that the more liberal group gave up the idea of unity through restoration and accepted the principle of "unity through any means."

A second perversion was that of "legalism." In like manner as those in the Restoration Movement who wanted to "give up" certain things of the New Testament to become united, there were those who wanted to "add" certain things to it. There arose those who felt it necessary to take the command of the Apostle Paul in Ephesians 5:19 "to sing and make music in your heart" (NIV), as a means to remove the musical instruments from the worship services. This view was maintained in spite of the fact that the Old Testament is filled with references to musical instruments being employed in the worship of God. Their view was that since we are a New Testament Church we should not employ any of the Old Testament practices in our worship. It is further shown that the revelation refers to "harps" in heaven (Rev. 7:8).

Today, this group, known as "The Church of Christ," has most of its followers located in the Southern States and Midwest. For the most part, they refuse to fellowship with fellow believers and have made the "keyboard" a test of fellowship. There are some, however, in the a cappella movement who are bridging the gap and are willing to worship with those who use musical instruments in worship.

What is the plea today? While there still exist millions of Christians who refuse to make the musical instrument a test of fellowship and who refuse to ignore the New Testament teachings regarding the Church and are attempting to restore New Testament Christianity, there are some within this very movement who are attempting to bring into the fellowship a "post-modern" view of "anything goes." It remains to be seen what will happen to the movement in the future. It is the strong belief of this writer that the Church of the Lord Jesus Christ will not fall and that it will endure until Jesus Christ comes again to take His Church home to heaven.

Those who are honest with themselves and others will easily find that there is much repentance to be accomplished within the fellowship on all sides. Many are not "speaking the Truth in love." As Christians, we are to love one another and bear each other's burdens. We would do well to "speak where the Bible speaks and be silent where it is silent." Since the Bible does not tell us to worship with instruments nor to worship without instruments, we are in no position to level a test of fellowship on each other either way. We must not sacrifice the Word of Truth on the alter of opinion. May we learn to agree to disagree and love our brethren as God loves us?

The Church today is built on the same confession made by Peter so long ago and the foundation which Jesus, Himself, laid. We cannot alter it nor should we try. If it were good enough for the apostles, it should be good enough for us!

CHAPTER THREE

"BUT WHICH CHURCH IS THE RIGHT CHURCH?"

INTRODUCTION: "Now that I have accepted Christ as my Savior, which 'church' is the right church? They all seem to pray to the same God and have 'basically' the same belief system! Each one of them says they are right for me, and I am so confused!"

This seems to be the cry of many. I recall witnessing to a man some years ago in the small town of Berea, Kentucky, where I ministered. As I explained the Biblical plan of salvation to him, he said to me, "How can I know what you are saying is correct? When I am confronted by so many others telling me something different?" I was unprepared to properly answer the question. As far as I know, that man never accepted Christ. Why is there so much confusion? My response would be that Satan knows that he can "divide and conquer." As Christ prayed for unity among all believers in His prayer recorded in John 17, His desire was that we all might be one as He and His Father were one. Over the centuries, the ideas of men have been brought into the church, and division has followed. While this will not be a treatise on church history, throughout the centuries the words of men have replaced the Word of God. Division comes into any organization when some think that their ideas are better than the original. The church of the New Testament was a simple organization. It was founded on Pentecost when over three thousand persons accepted Christ as recorded in Acts 2. Just a few verses after Peter told them what they should do to be saved in verse 42, Luke (the author of Acts) records, "They devoted themselves to the apostles' teaching and to the fellowship, to the breaking of bread and to prayer" (NIV). This verse speaks volumes with respect to the manner in which the early Church conducted itself. There are other references to the activities of the church that will be discussed in more detail later. There was only ONE Church in the New Testament, and they were not called by any name other than that of Christ. There was no Baptist, Episcopal, Catholic, Methodist, Presbyterian, or any other name used for these Christians. Luke records in Acts 11:26b, "the disciples were called Christians first in Antioch" (NIV). Note who were first called "Christians:" "the disciples." The word "disciple" simply means one who follows. These believers were first disciples (followers) of Jesus teachings as given by the apostles and other evangelists.

WHAT IS MEANT BY "MAIN LINE" CHURCHES?

There are two basic divisions of churches today. The "main line" churches are those that have the largest membership, most church buildings and the closest doctrines to each other. The other division would be called "cults." Cults are fringe groups of "believers in something" that have chosen a different path to find God. (This is a simplified version that in no way attempts to define the two divisions.)

Main line churches would be those of Baptist, Methodist, Catholic, Presbyterian, Episcopal, etc. There has been a movement in the last century to bring more unity between these churches and to unite under one simple belief. Among these groups, there are "liberal" and "conservative" elements and it is unlikely that there will ever be any real union.

DOES THE "NEW TESTAMENT CHURCH" EXIST TODAY?

It is the view of this writer, it is does, in fact exist, and it is alive and well! While this movement, known as "The Restoration Movement" is stronger in certain parts of the United States than in others, it is a fast growing movement. The churches are known by the name, "Christian Church" or "Church of Christ." While there are some divisions in this movement, we are united under the belief that Christ is Head of His Church, and we share a common doctrine. There is an element of the "Christian Church," known as "The Disciples of Christ" that has largely abandoned the basic doctrine of the Restoration Movement and has sought to unite with other Evangelical movements. (These divisions were discussed in greater detail in chapter one.)

Let us now turn to some of the aspects of the New Testament Church that are found in The Restoration Movement.

I. THE PURPOSE OF THE CHURCH

Jesus created a "New Society." This consisted of a tiny group of men and called "disciples" and later "apostles." To this small group of men, He entrusted His message to the world. He said to them, "All authority in heaven and on earth has been given to me. Therefore, go and make disciples of all nations, baptizing them in the name of the Father, Son and Holy Spirit, and teaching them to obey everything I have commanded you. And surely I am with you always, even to the end of the age" (Matthew 28:18-20, NIV). With these words, Jesus left those assembled on the mountain, ascended into heaven where He awaits His Father's word to return to receive those who have been faithful to Him. I would be amiss if I failed to include women. Women are prominently mentioned in the Bible by many writers and are an important part of the Church.

Luke writes a finishing word to Jesus ascension in Acts 1:9-11 (NIV), "After He said this, He was taken up before their very eyes, and a cloud hid them from their very sight. They were looking intently up into the sky as He was going, when suddenly two men dressed in white stood beside them. 'Men of Galilee,' they said, 'why do you stand here looking into the sky? This same Jesus, who has been taken from you into heaven, will come back in the same way you have seen Him go into heaven.'" With these words, we can be assured that the angels know of which they spoke and we have the assurance that Jesus will, in fact, return.

It was not long before the Feast of Pentecost, only fifty days after the Feast of the Passover, when the disciples were gathered in a room and joined together in prayer along with several women, including Jesus' mother and His brothers. It was during this time that Peter stood among the believers (numbering some 120) and proposed that they replace Judas as one of the disciples. After prayer, Mathias was chosen to replace Judas. It was only a few days later that the Holy Spirit came upon these disciples and they began to speak with authority whereupon the first Gospel sermon was preached by Simon Peter on the Day of Pentecost and the church was established. This, then, is the beginning of the "new society" or the church age that came into existence by the will of Christ.

As to the purpose of the Church, Jesus created it to bring the will and Word of God into the world. Jesus had prayed in His "Model Prayer" that the will of the Father be done and that His kingdom would come. Here, on this day, that prayer came to fruition and the kingdom came in the form of the Church.

In this kingdom (Church), all were to be brothers and sisters in Christ with Jesus as the King. Jesus was not only the "Rule Maker," King, the One with all authority, yet He was "brother" to all believers. This relationship was and is unique in any religion. To be considered on an equal with Jesus Christ, the Son of God is unheard of anywhere else in history. Those who by repentance, confession and baptism were added to the fellowship were expected to abide by the regulations that the King had given. The "regulations" were not burdensome or harsh. They were light and easy to bear and would produce joy and peace in all who followed Jesus' way. The Church was to serve as a "prep school" for all who would reach heaven.

II. A CHURCH FOR THE FORGIVEN

It is important that we note that the very first invitation of the Church was given to those who had crucified Christ! The church has been created for and is made up of sinners who have been saved by grace. Those who are looking for perfection in this body of believers will be severely disappointed. Since the invitation is for sinners to repent and come to Jesus being made a part of His body through immersion, we become "perfect" in God's view since Christ's blood has cleansed us from all sin. Peter told those Jews on Pentecost that God was willing to forgive them their sin of crucifying His Son and God makes the same statement to sinners today.

The Church remains today not as a "display for saints" but rather a hospital for the sinners and sin sick." The sinner who comes humbly following the steps to salvation can find a "cure" for the sinful world in which he/she lives. Continued forgiveness can be found by attending worship, meeting around the Lord's Table, and being faithful to the Bible. If, however, one allows this relationship to be broken through neglect of the previous mentioned things, there remains no more sacrifice for sin (see Hebrews 6:4-6). The relationship can be broken by the Christian and they can no longer claim forgiveness for sin.

III. WHAT IS OUR RESPONSIBILITY TO THE CHURCH OF THE NEW TESTAMENT?

The responsibility of every believer today is to establish the Church of the New Testament. We are to view the true Church as one that will not seek to serve man's needs and desires but God's. While the church does serve our spiritual needs because we have dedicated ourselves to His service, our primary goal to worship God and serve Him.

We should remember, however, that simply wearing a Bible name and practicing Scriptural baptism does not make a church that Christ can call His own. In order to make a Church where Christ is honored there must be a consistent effort to put Him first in all we do. We are to love God and love our fellow believers. This is much more than simple lip service. We are to show our love for God and His Church in everything we do.

There is no room for hatred, spite, envy, jealousy, or any other negative emotion that will hinder our love for either God or humankind. We must make every effort to follow the New Testament example and use the Bible as our guide.

IV. WHAT ABOUT DENOMINATIONALISM?

The Church established by Jesus on Pentecost existed long before denominations. Among the first denominations was the Roman Catholic Church. Other divisions of this church were established during a period known as "The Reformed Period" or "The Reformation." The "Protestant Movement" was simply that; a "protest" against the Roman Catholic Church. The Roman Church was not immune to a split as it divided with the division of the Roman Empire into two distinct groups: The Roman Catholic Church and The Eastern Orthodox Church (now known as the Greek Orthodox Church). There is also the Russian Orthodox Church, as well.

It can easily be seen that the Church of the New Testament was a united church which was established by Jesus Christ and was the Church He had in mind when He said, ". . . I will build my church . . ." (Matthew 16:6).

NO HUMAN NAME. The local congregations of the New Testament were called the "Church of Christ (or Christian Church) (see Romans 16:16); Church of God (I Cor. 1:2); or simply the "Church" (Acts 8:3). Nowhere do the names Presbyterian, Baptist, Lutheran, Methodist, Congregational, Wesleyan, etc. appear in the New Testament.

NO HUMAN PLAN FOR SALVATION. Sprinkling was never substituted for immersion in the New

Testament church and called "baptism." Additionally, there is no record in the New Testament where infants were received into the church by sprinkling. Those who insist on this practice not authorized by God in His Word will have to bear the consequences of such practices for the divisions they cause.

NO DENOMINATIONAL ORGANIZATIONS. The local congregations in the New Testament were free and self-governing. They were independent from outside control and responsible only to Christ. They had elders (bishops, pastors) who were responsible for the spiritual edification and welfare of the church and deacons who were responsible for the daily needs of the Church. The deacons were also responsible to assist the elders in their duties. Nowhere in the New Testament is there a place for a single "bishop" or an "arch-bishop" who would have authority over a group of congregations. There is nothing wrong with a group of congregations coming together to support a missionary, a Christian service camp, a Bible college, etc.; however, the fellowship must maintain its autonomous relationship apart from each other. Denominational headquarters, as they are today in control of many congregations, were unknown in the New Testament Church.

Conclusion: We must simply follow the New Testament Church pattern and practices to be found in favor with the Lord Jesus Christ.

Remember the chilling words of Jesus Christ when He said, "Not everyone who says to me, 'Lord, Lord,' will enter the kingdom of heaven but only he who does the will of my Father who is in heaven. Many will say to me on that day, 'Lord, Lord, did we not prophesy in your name, and in your name cast out many demons and perform many miracles?' Then will I tell them plainly, 'I never knew you. Away from me, you evildoers!'" (Matthew 7:21-23, NIV). These words speak for themselves and show that just because someone *claims* to be a Christian does not always make it so!

CHAPTER FOUR

WHAT IS THE MISSION OF THE CHURCH TODAY?

INTRODUCTION: Prior to the institution of the Church, Jesus instructed His disciples to "Go into all the world and preach the good news to all creation. Whoever believes and is baptized will be saved, but whoever does not believe will be condemned" (Mark 16:15-16 NIV). These instructions or "marching orders" were delivered just prior to Jesus' ascension into heaven. If there would ever be a time when one would want to leave instructions it would be at that time. These, then, must have been rather important to Jesus. Since God instructed the disciples to "go into all the world," one would understand that He was not only interested in "white, Anglo-Saxon, protestant" men and women for His kingdom. He intended for us to do exactly as He said. "All the world" means to people of color, Asians, Native Americans, *all peoples* of the world. We cannot pick and choose those to whom we will minister.

Following the command of Jesus, the disciples went first to Judea, then to Samaria, and finally to the entire known world today. We have the advantage of instant satellite communication and are unrestricted by use of the internet and other communication devices. We have the ability to communicate with people around the globe in an effort to reach the lost for Christ. Yet, we are employing early Twentieth Century methods, at best, to accomplish His vision of reaching the lost. The Apostle Paul became a great missionary, traveling the world and preaching Christ to the lost. Why are we not following his example?

WORLD EVANGELISM AND THE CHURCH TODAY

No Christian Church/ Church of Christ today can claim to be His should they not be interested in world evangelism. While many churches are satisfied to live with those they have and are not interested in bringing the lost to Christ, they are not following His instructions and cannot count on being called His children. Some make a feeble effort to evangelize while others do nothing at all. The growing church is an evangelizing and a missions minded church. If the church has no passion for the lost, it should not call itself Christian.

There are those churches that have the misguided idea that "missions support" is a "waste of money." Any established church should set aside a portion of its income for mission work. The missionaries who approach the local church for support should be thoroughly vetted prior to providing any support. The missionaries should be accountable to the local churches from which they draw support. God's promises of blessings to those who give are as real for churches as they are for individuals. We must have a healthy attitude toward our global mission.

One very good way for a new Christian to have a zeal for the mission is to remain focused on evangelism. There are periodicals that promote evangelism and missions that are very informative reading. In addition, one can develop and maintain a personal relationship with missionaries, both on foreign fields and at home. The best way, however, to do this is to maintain a one-on-one personal witnessing program whereby you share your relationship with Christ on a regular basis.

It is the responsibility of every Christian to share their Christian faith. We were never meant to "sit down and await the Lord's return." We are admonished to "work for the night is coming when man's work is done." Christ called some of His disciples with the words, "Follow Me and I will make you fishers of men." This implies that they were to be engaged in a life of service. This is the mission of the Church. Go, preach, teach, and baptize all nations because this is the will of Christ for His Church!

CHAPTER FIVE

WHY THE BIBLE?

INTRODUCTION: Why would an all-knowing God create such a way to reveal Himself to us? Would it not seem more plausible that He should simply make Himself known in a less complicated manner? After all, the Bible is open to so much "interpretation" that nearly anything can be proven by it. There are as many ways to "understand" the Bible as there are "churches" in the world. Nearly all of these "faiths" use the Bible as their basis of their belief, and nearly all of them have a different view of what the Bible teaches. Wouldn't it be easier had God chosen a more direct manner to reveal Himself?

All books have an "aim." They seek to teach, entertain, coerce, sell, etc. The "aim" of the Bible is simple: To reveal God to a lost humankind and to show them the way of redemption.

If we were left alone, we would invariably make more of a mess of our lives than we already do. We cannot know what is in our own best interest because we are "too close to the forest to see the trees." If left to our own devices, we would eat all the wrong foods, follow all the wrong worldly devices, and create total chaos. That is why we have a system of laws and regulations, to keep us from total and

Simply Speaking...

utter collapse. Paul, in Romans 1, shows us that we have a knowledge of God, no matter our circumstances. This means that as being "created in the image of God" we were created with a "piece" of God in all of us. Romans 1:18-19 (NIV) says, "The wrath of God is being *revealed* from heaven against all the godlessness and wickedness of men who suppress the truth by their wickedness, since what may be made known about God is plain to them, because God has made it plain to them" (emphasis mine). This simply means that God has "revealed" Himself to all humankind. Paul continues in verse 20 (NIV), "For since the creation of the world God's invisible qualities—His eternal power and divine nature—have been *clearly seen*, being understood from what has been made, so that men are without excuse" (emphasis mine). What more information do we need than this? God has shown, clearly, that He has revealed Himself in and through His creation.

Examine history and see that man, left to his own desires, will make a mess of things. Simply look at some of the events of the recent Twentieth Century. We see the advances in just the last fifty years that have made things better and, at the same time, worse. Things that can be used for peaceful purposes, such as splitting the atom, can also be used to destroy. Brilliant minds such as those in Hitler's Germany, could have been used to better all humankind, however, were used to destroy millions of people simply because of their ethnicity and religious beliefs. Humankind struggles to be "free," only to find it to be more enslaved than ever before. The Computer Age was supposed to do away with paper, yet it has produced a more paper dependent people than ever before.

God sees in humankind a wretched existence. This postmodern, secular progressive society in which we now live, people are searching diligently for answers. They seek in all the wrong places, however. Many look to politicians for the answers, while others see answers in pleasure. The real answers are found only in God's Word and being in fellowship with Him. The Word of God and the Living Word (His Son) hold the answers to all the complex questions relating to spiritual matters. God shows us the fullness of life as revealed in His Son and through the examples of Biblical characters. Some of these things show us what not to do while others show us that God has used the weakness of people to advance His kingdom. Through many of these people, we see how righteousness brought them happiness and how sin brought only misery. By seeking the truth revealed in the Bible, we can have the joy that only this truth can bring.

The "Good News" of the Gospel is that humans need not fear the wrath of God spoken of by Paul in Romans 1. We can know that we no longer need to live a life that is empty and meaningless, a life that is filled with empty promises and pleasures that only bring pain. We do not have to live a life that is filled with "sham joy." We find that God had made a new life through Jesus Christ filled with genuine happiness. The vast sorrow in the world stems from the fact that most have ignored the Word of God as revealed in the Bible and, as a result, know nothing about God or His way.

THE IMPORTANCE OF BIBLE STUDY

Many are afraid of the Bible. The reasons for such fear are many and varied. Some fear it because they feel that they will not understand it. Many fear that it will be boring, dull, and uninteresting. Some feel that it is so old that it has lost its relevance; while still others may have difficulty with the *truths* found therein and that it may have the intended effect: causing them to have a change in lifestyle. It has been said, "It's not the part of the Bible that I don't understand that bothers me; it is the part I do understand!"

The point is, however, that the Bible, like any other book, must be read to be understood. Biblical knowledge does not come from leaving it closed and lying on the table or simply by listening to what someone else has to say about its meaning. While it is true that the Bible does not offer us pretty pictures or illustrations to enjoy, it does paint the most beautiful word pictures not seen in any other work. We are admonished to make a diligent effort to master the contents of the Bible. Paul, in writing to Timothy in II Timothy 2:15 (NIV) says, "Do your best to present yourself to God as one approved, a workman who does not need to be ashamed and who correctly handles the word of truth." All Christians should make time on a daily basis to read and study God's Word in an effort to be such a person. If we read and study the Bible, praying for the wisdom and understanding that can come only by the Holy Spirit, we will be in a position to share with others the truths found only in this Book.

There are many wonderful aids to understanding the Bible. The sad fact is that many of these aids, written by men and women who do not have a true understanding of what the Scriptures have to say, have mislead many would-be believers. It is as important to "weed out" these authors and be prepared to balance what they say with the Word itself. As we search the Scriptures with an eye toward the Truth, God will assist us through His Spirit so that we can "rightly divide" His wonderful Word.

WHAT ABOUT THE CHRISTIAN AND THE NEW TESTAMENT?

I have heard many of our faith say that the Old Testament is irrelevant. Nothing could be further from the truth. In the Old Testament, we find God dealing with humans as He prepares them for His service and the initial coming of His Son. It is with this in mind that Paul tells Timothy, "All Scripture is God-breathed and is useful for teaching, rebuking, correcting, and training in righteousness, so that the man of God may be thoroughly equipped for every good work" (II Timothy 3:16 NIV). The "Scripture" to which Paul referred was the Old Testament. We need to read and understand this part of God's revelation.

The New Testament, on the other hand, is our best guide to the workings of God in our time. Whereas the Old Testament (or "will," "covenant") primarily shows God's work with the Jewish nation which God chose as the people through whom He would send His Son, the New Testament ("will," "covenant") shows God's fulfillment of the gift of His Son and the way of salvation. The first section of the New Testament is the "Four Gospels," the account by four different writers of the life and workings of Jesus as He ministered on the earth. It also gives an account of His death, burial, resurrection, and ascension. Beginning with the Book of Acts, the New Testament takes a new turn revealing Christ's Church from its infancy (Pentecost) through the travels of its most prolific preacher, the Apostle Paul. The remaining books are letters, also known as Epistles. These letters, written by inspired men, give us the tools we need to remain faithful after we have become a part of the Lord's Church. Some of these letters were written to individuals, while others were written to churches. No matter the intended recipient, the words contained in these letters are beneficial to all Christians. The final letter of the Bible is called the "Revelation." This "Revelation" was written to the "seven Churches in Asia" and contains a prophetic view of coming events, including the second coming of Jesus. This letter also gives us a glimpse of heaven. This letter is arguably the most controversial book of the Bible. More confusion regarding its contents has existed than any other writing in the history of the world. People have divided over their "interpretation" of this writing than any other. This fact, however, should not have any effect on our desire to study the Bible.

HOW DO WE STUDY THE BIBLE TO ACHEIVE BIBLICAL UNDERSTANDING?

The very first thing in understanding the Bible is to pray. This prayer should be that the Holy Spirit would guide us and prepare our hearts to understand the Word (See John 16:13-15).

Secondly, read, re-read, summarize in your mind what you have read, then re-read the passage and write your thoughts and observations in a journal.

Third, ask the following questions and write the answers in your journal:

- What is the main teaching of this passage?
- Who are the people in this passage? Who is speaking? To whom is the author speaking?
- What is the key verse in this passage?
- What does this passage teach me about Jesus?
- Does this passage point out to me any sin in my life that I need to confess and discontinue?
- Is there any command for me to obey in this passage?
- Is there any promise for me to receive in this passage?
- Is there any instruction for me to follow?

Fourth, memorize certain passages of Scripture that pertain to your personal life (Psalm 119:15-16).

Finally, respect what you have read and studied, for it is from God!

CHAPTER SIX

WHEN, WHERE, AND WHY DO I WORSHIP?

INTRODUCTION: These questions arise frequently, and the answers are varied. How can I know who is right? The Bible answers these questions, and we need not depend upon human answers.

THE LORD'S DAY

First, the question of when will be discussed. The first day of the week has been called "The Lord's Day." This is simply because the Lord was raised from the dead on that first day of the week, Sunday.

The Jews were told in the Ten Commandments to remember the "Sabbath Day" and keep it holy. This is the fourth commandment. The word "Sabbath" means "seventh" and refers to Saturday or the *last* day of the week. This was because, as God said, He created the world, etc., in six days and rested on the seventh. Jesus, as a Jew, observed the Sabbath as a day of worship. This all changed when Jesus was raised on the first day of the week. We find in our example of the early Church in the Book of Acts that

Simply Speaking...

"on the first day of the week we came together to break bread..." (Acts 20:7 NIV). In a very real sense, the "First Day of the Week" is an "Easter" celebration as we come together to observe the Lord's Supper and to celebrate the resurrection of Jesus from the dead.

WORSHIP OF THE EARLY CHURCH

The second question we will consider is "where" the early church worshipped. This is a little tricky since they did not have elaborate and modern "church houses" in which to worship. We find in our "Church history book," the Book of Acts, that in the beginning the Church worshipped *daily* in their *homes* (Acts 2:46). Later we find that they came together on the "first day of the week." Throughout the Book of Acts, we find Peter, Paul, et al., worshipping in the synagogues and in the temple courts. It is clear that the apostles went where the *people* were, and once the Jewish worship was concluded, they began to preach and teach Jesus. We are told by historians that as the persecution of the Church had begun, the Church went "underground" and worshipped where they could, in an effort, not to be found and killed. It was not until many, many years later that "places of worship" were erected. There is no requirement that the Church meet in a special building. However, it is a much more convenient place where all the facilities are in place to have a meaningful worship. I have heard people say that they can worship as well on a golf course, lake, or river. This may be; however, there should be "fellowship with those of like precious faith," an opportunity for preaching or instruction, and most importantly, gathering around the Lord's Table for the partaking of the Lord's Supper. It is true that worship can be conducted anywhere, assuming the aforementioned also take place.

Simply Speaking...

The nature of worship in the early Church included the following:

- Singing of psalms, hymns, and spiritual songs (Ephesians 5:19)
- Prayer (Acts 2:42)
- The Lord's Supper (Acts 20:7)
- An offering (I Corinthians 16:2)
- Preaching and teaching (Acts 2:47, 20:7)

These acts of worship were intended to fulfill God's plan in that they provided for spiritual renewal, which every believer must maintain an awareness of his or her purpose in keeping with following the Lord's will and keeping oneself unspotted form the world.

A second purpose was to recognize God. Worship comes from the old English word "worth-ship." In coming together in fellowship on the Lord's Day, we declare the eternal *worth* of God, Who gave His only Son for the sins of the world. God, desiring our love and praise, acknowledges our loving acts of praise and gratitude with His favor.

A third need is for fellowship. The early Christians cherished the need for fellowship so much that they met *daily* in homes, eating and praying together. It is sad that so many Christians today are willing to forego this time of fellowship and find it difficult to come together even for one hour per week. There was no sense of isolationism in the early Church. These people were bound together because of their love for one another and the binding power of Christ.

Fourth, there was an opportunity for evangelism. As discussed earlier, we see that Paul and his companions never miss an opportunity to share the Gospel of Christ wherever they went (see Acts 5:42).

Finally, the influence of the group was multiplied. One can do so much more if there is an army around. The television commercial currently running for *Verizon* shows a multitude of people known as *The Network*, implying that there are many people "behind the scenes" who are ready, willing, and able to help. This is the way it should be in the Church, though not behind the scenes. We are a people of the Light, and we should act accordingly. There is, indeed, safety and strength in numbers. When one feels alone, the usual tendency is to shrink away and begin to feel sorry for self. When we can see that we are not alone, we are refreshed and able to accomplish so much more. Since the Church is at *war* with the forces of Satan, it is imperative that there be no stragglers for him to "pick off" and carry away to hell. We can accomplish so much more together can we could ever accomplish alone.

WHAT HAPPENS WHEN I MISS WORSHIP?

As has just been discussed, it is important to fellowship. So what happens when I do not? When one does not regularly attend worship, he or she finds it easier to miss the next time and then the next, etc. With repeated non-worship experiences, we tend to lose sight of the "Prize." It is apparent to anyone who has ever served in the Armed Forces that when one is A. W. O. L. it is an abomination to a commander. Yet, we see people going Sunday after Sunday, not attending church services, and few, if any, are concerned. Despite the fact that all need the fellowship of worship experience, many would rather stay home, hunt, fish, go to ballgames, play golf, go boating, etc., than to be in the Lord's House. As a result, their influence is counted on the side of Satan rather than the Lord. Jesus said, "Whoever is not for me is against me" (Matthew 12:30). When we miss worship, we are showing that we are against

Jesus. It is impossible to "strattle the fence" when it comes to our spiritual well-being. Either we are on the Lord's side, or we are not; there is no middle ground.

Continual neglect of worship will only result in spiritual decay. In the same manner, we need physical nourishment; we need spiritual food to remain viable and alive in the Lord's kingdom. We cannot remain healthy if all we eat is junk food. The same is true of our spiritual health. Paul warned the Corinthian Church that it was in danger because they were not ready for "meat" and they were still feasting on the "milk of the Word" (I Cor. 3:2). It is important that we grow spiritually, and we cannot do so on the golf course or in the boat, etc. The unfaithful person cannot expect to receive the "crown of life" which is reserved for those who have been "faithful unto death" (see Revelation 2:10). The result of the unfaithful church member shall be spiritual death and eternal punishment.

HOW OFTEN SHOULD I BE IN WORSHIP?

While there is no Biblical precedent for Sunday night worship or mid-week worship, there is ample precedent for being in the Lord's House whenever possible. For too many, the idea of coming to "church" at all is difficult enough let alone coming to other services. The decline in Sunday night worship and the mid-week services are a testament to the climate of disregard we have for worship. If people believe that they can get "enough" "church" on Sunday morning, they are deceiving themselves. *If* we love someone, we want to be around him or her as much as possible and spend as much time with them as humanly possible. For us to devote forty or more hours per week to our secular jobs and only give the Lord *one hour* per week, even three or four, is a sacrilege. We *owe* God our very existence, and we should show our respect and love for Him with a dedication to His service. We cannot learn enough by coming to one worship service per week to grow as we should and, therefore, many are weak and sickly. It is not just a matter of "going to church." That act alone will not save us. It is a matter of worshipping the one true and living God when we are there. It is a time of respect, learning, and praise when we come into the House of God. The psalmist said, "I rejoiced with those who said to me, 'Let us go to the House of the Lord'" (Psalm 122:1 NIV).

CONCLUSION: The first day of the week is the day set aside for the Christian to worship. It is necessary and important that that day be observed and treated as no other day. It is important or four spiritual growth. This must be a way of life.

CHAPTER SEVEN

WHAT DO WE DO WITH SIN?

INTRODUCTION: Sin is taking a hit in the Post-Modern society in which we live. There are those who would be politically correct and proclaim that there is no such thing as sin. It is simply "error," or "people make *mistakes.*" There are religious scholars who have taken this view, and many denominations are following this thought to their own peril. While it may appear to be a good thing to do away with sin, it is not possible. Those who desire to bury their heads in the sand and proclaim the absence of sin shall one-day realize the folly of their thoughts and actions. Sin is a very real thing, and simply because some do not want to address it does not make it go away. Romans 3:23 says, "For all have sinned and fall short of the glory of God" (NIV). This is a most declarative statement and deserves further consideration. There exists no more definitive statement regarding sin than this one. Paul is emphatic in telling the Roman Church that *everyone* has sinned and that no one is righteous in the sight of God. Given the fact that we are all sinners, we should do everything we can to avoid the consequences of our sins. One of my pet peeves is for people to attempt to cast the *blame* for their actions on someone else. As a trained

Simply Speaking...

counselor, I have heard every excuse known to man as to why someone is not responsible for his or her actions. It frightens me to hear these excuses and for people to attempt to throw off their responsibility. We live in a society in which most people are brought up to believe that they should bear no consequences for what they do. Everything is either the result of a "bad childhood," a "bad marriage," an "abusive person" somewhere in their lives, etc. The worst thing we can do to our children is to leave them with this concept. We *must* make people understand the need to take responsibility for their actions. With this in mind, let us ask:

WHAT IS SIN?

Sin is *lawlessness*. This simply means that we are breaking the *law* of God when we sin. We cannot please God when we are in opposition to Him. John writes in I John 3:4, "Everyone who sins breaks God's law; in fact, sin is *lawlessness*" (NIV, emphasis mine). The idea that sin is "breaking the law of God" or "violating His will" is not anything new. From the beginning, God has made provision for such lawlessness.

In the Garden of Eden, where God created all things and gave man dominion over them, God made a "law" or, in other words, made it clear to Adam and Eve that they had "free reign" over the entire creation except two trees. God told them that they could eat the fruit of anything *except* the Tree of Knowledge and the Tree of Life. First, let us realize that there was no "reason" to partake of either of these two trees since there was no need for more knowledge than that which God had given them; secondly, there was no need to eat from the tree of life since there was no death! Would it be great to live in such an environment with only *two* restrictions? The two human inhabitants of Eden, however, were not content to have such a paradise and consequently broke the law. In doing so, they brought *sin* into the perfect world.

Some would say, "It does not seem *fair* that such a trivial matter as eating *fruit* would cause such a stir!" It may appear so to one who does not understand the most rudimentary nature of God. To God, sin is sin, and there is nothing trivial about it. At the very moment God pronounced His judgment on Adam and Eve, the entire creation was changed and charged with the transgression. It is obvious that when God says, "Don't do it!" we should not do it, no matter how we *feel* about it.

Sin is *rebellion*. From before the creation of the world, there was sin! The rebellion in heaven is described in Jude 6, "And the angels who did not keep their positions of authority but abandoned their own home—these He has kept in darkness, bound with everlasting chains for judgment on the great Day" (NIV). This is a reference to the "war" in heaven when Satan and his angels rebelled against God and were cast out of heaven (see Revelation 12:7-9).

There are two main types of sin. One is the sin of *omission*, that is, the failure to do the things that are right, and the other is the sin of *commission*, that is, the sin of *doing* things that are wrong in the sight of God. Let us examine each of these in turn to have a greater understanding of them.

The "sin of omission" is one that is the least understood. All of us understand "doing something" that we should not. Few fully understand the idea of *failing to do something* that we should. James makes this quite clear in his letter, "Anyone, then, who knows the good he ought to do and doesn't do it, sins" (James 4:17 NIV). This is as clear as it gets. When we *know* what we should do and do not do it, it is *sin*! Failure to do what God has commanded us to do falls into this category. Another way to sin in this fashion is to be *indifferent*. Indifference is simply "not caring." When one adopts the attitude of "Who cares?," one is saying to God that His Word is of no value and there is no need to keep His commandments.

The other manner in which one can sin is *commission*. This is when we actually *do* something that is sin. This is a *transgression against God*. There are too many ways to describe this type of sin to attempt to list them here. Suffice it to say that when we follow any path that is contrary to God's Word and will, we are committing sin. Since all are sinners (Rom. 3:23), and have failed to achieve the things that can make us "perfect" in God's sight, we need, all the more, the blood of Jesus Christ which cleanses us from all sin (see I John 1:7). When anyone does that which he knows to be wrong and does it anyway, to that person it is sin (James 4:17).

Sin has been described as "missing the mark." This analogy is that of shooting an arrow at a target and missing the "bull's eye." With all the desire in the world to do that which is right we simply fail; we fall short of the mark when we attempt to go it alone. If the ideal is "perfection" we simply "fall short" of the mark.

Sin is selfish. It seems that the world of the twenty-first century is a more self-centered world than at any other time in modern history. Once there was a time when people considered the needs of others and made efforts to help those with less than they had. While this is not totally lost, it has become more of an exception than a rule. Our society is more self-centered, and as a result, we sin more. By considering ourselves more valuable than anyone else, we place our wants ahead of God. This is to our peril, and we should come to repentance immediately. God has no place in His kingdom for those who are selfish. Love of self is important when we consider that God has made us and that we were created in His image. However, when love of self transcends love for God, we are on a slippery slope. We are told to "love God" and to "love our brothers" in that order. We might find the love of self in third place. When we put the objects of love in the proper order, there will be plenty of love left for self.

WHAT ARE THE RESULTS OR CONSEQUENCES OF SIN?

There are many consequences of sin. We will briefly examine some of the most prominent ones.

First, we see sin as something that separates us from God. This is arguably the worst result of sin. Prior to sin entering the Garden of Eden, God could come down and walk in the cool of the morning with Adam and Eve (see Genesis 3:8). This would have been a perfect relationship, a time in which God and Adam could fellowship with no obstruction. They had a time together, which was destroyed by sin. We can only imagine what that time must have been like and await heaven to experience it again. Because of the holy nature of God, He could no longer associate with Adam and Eve as He once had done. When they sinned, there was separation between God and His creation. Not only did their sin disrupt God's relationship with them, it disrupted God's relationship with *all* of His creation. Adam and Eve were driven from the Garden of Eden, and there was placed an angel at the entrance of the Garden to keep them out. For those who persist in sin and do not find the saving grace of God, there is no eternal life with God but only a fearful looking forward to judgment.

Sin destroys the peace that God offers. Isaiah made that perfectly clear when he said, "There is no peace, says the Lord, for the wicked" (Isa. 48:22 NIV). We, at Christmastime, talk about the "Peace on Earth," yet the earth cannot know peace until it comes to know the Christ who brings peace. Jesus, Himself, said it this way, "Peace I leave with you; my peace I give to you. I do not give to you as the world gives. Do not let your hearts be troubled and do not be afraid" (John 14:27 NIV). Peace in one's spirit is what we all desire. When there is turmoil in our spirits, we are most miserable. There is no peace unless there is Christ. For the world seeks peace and does not find it because they do not know Him. Paul wrote in Romans 3:17, quoting from Isaiah 59:8, "And the way of peace they do not know" (NIV). The world cannot know peace because it has abandoned God by sinning.

Suffering and death are the results of sin. Adam was told that he would surely die if he ate from the tree of knowledge of good and evil (Gen. 2:17). When Adam and Eve ate from this tree, they did not immediately drop dead; however, the curse of death was pronounced upon them and all who would follow them in this world. They were also told that they would *suffer* the consequences of their actions. Humankind has been made to suffer ever since. Death is only one result of sin; the suffering that sin brings is enormous. From the time we are born into this world until we leave it, we face the prospect of suffering. We may not all suffer in the same manner; however, we will most assuredly suffer because of our sins. It does not matter whether we are Christians or not; we will sin and suffer the consequences of our actions. These consequences are not necessarily eternal death, though that is a possibility. The suffering may well be in this life. When we sin, there are always consequences.

WHAT CAN WE DO TO AVOID THESE CONSEQUENCES?

There is little we can do to avoid the consequences of sin in this life. We can, however, do a great deal to avoid the eternal consequences of sin. When we are physically ill, we seek medical advice from a competent and qualified physician or other medical professional. When one is spiritually ill, there is no end to the places one goes to find help. We seek to find spiritual assistance in all the wrong places. Rather than seeking the source of our eternal salvation, we look to others whom we believe have the "words of wisdom" rather than the author of wisdom, God the Father.

The *cure* to all our spiritual ills is the Great Physician. When one is spiritually "sick," the only One to whom one can turn is Jesus Christ, the great Physician. Since sin has placed a barrier between God and His creation, there is only One who can destroy that barrier. The "cure" for sin is simply the blood of Jesus Christ. His sacrifice on the cross is the method that God chose to bring salvation into the fallen world. While this may seem extreme to us, God knew what He was doing. The only way to atone for sin is by the death of One who was perfect, Jesus (see I Peter 1:18-19; I John 1:7).

The only way to receive this precious blood applied to our sins, which cleanses us from all unrighteousness, is by turning to the One who died for us. We cannot *purchase* salvation nor can we *earn* it. It is a *gift* from God by means of His grace. God has chosen to provide a way of escape from the penalty of sin. This way is by the obedience to the Gospel message. On Pentecost, the people cried out, "Brothers, what shall we do?" (Acts 2:37b NIV). The answer was simple, "Repent and be baptized, every one of you, in the name of Jesus Christ for the *forgiveness of your sins*. And you will receive the gift of the Holy Spirit" (Acts 2:38 NIV, emphasis mine). The answer is so simple yet such a stumbling block to many. The *purpose* of this baptism was for the *forgiveness of sins*. The people who asked the question were guilty of murdering the Son of God! We, too, by our sins are guilty of the same crime. The only way to atone for these sins is by being immersed into the spiritual blood of Jesus Christ for the forgiveness of our sins.

The first step in redemption is hearing the Word of God; once we have heard, we believe. After believing (faith), we repent of our sins, followed by confession and then baptism into His name. These steps are so simple that they seem to be too easy. Paul said in I Corinthians 1:23-25, "But we preach Christ crucified: a stumbling block to the Jews and foolishness to Gentiles, but to those whom God has called, both Jews and Greeks, Christ the power of God and the wisdom of God is wiser than man's wisdom, and the weakness of God is stronger than man's strength" (NIV).

The only way to avoid an eternity in hell is to give yourself to God, to be blessed by Him, and remain faithful to Him in your Christian life. Remember the words of Jesus in Revelation 2:10, "Do not be afraid of what you are about to suffer. I tell you, the devil will put some of you in prison to test you, and you will suffer persecution for ten days. *Be faithful even to the point of death, and I will give you the crown of life*" (NIV, emphasis mine). The New Testament writers are constantly reminding us of the need to remain faithful (see Hebrews 6:4-6; 10:19-31).

Sin destroys both the physical and spiritual parts of anyone who will allow it to invade and take over the individual. It is imperative that we keep ourselves as pure as possible and rely on God to keep us in His grace.

CHAPTER EIGHT

"WHAT MUST I DO TO BE SAVED?"

INTRODUCTION: Of all the questions ever asked, this is the most important. No other question affects anyone as much as does this one. The answer will determine where we will spend eternity. It is critical that we get the correct answer and respond correctly. I remember when the United States was attempting to put together a manned mission into outer space. The buzz was that the calculations had to be *perfect* or else the spacecraft would lose its bearings, soar into space and be lost. The Korean Air Lines jumbo jet, flight 007, bound for Seoul, South Korea was just a few degrees off when it left California. By the time it had crossed the Pacific Ocean it had strayed into Soviet air space and was shot down, killing all on board. While it does not seem too important to err a little in one area or the other, it is crucial that we get this exactly right. I hear people say all the time, "It doesn't matter which church you attend, so long as you attend one." For far too many people the fact that one attends church is all that matters. For many others the only requirement is whether one "believes" or not; simply believing in Jesus is all that is required and salvation is applied to the believer. Still others feel that the more "works" they do for the Lord or His church the more grace they can obtain and the more "marks" they receive, the better chance they have of making it to heaven. These, and other forms of saving activities, are not what the Bible tells us at all.

MUCH CONFUSION ON THE SUBJECT

There is much confusion in modern Christianity on the subject of becoming a Christian. "Feelings" are very important to the post-modern churchgoer. It is all about how one "feels." If we think and feel that we are saved, no matter how we arrived at this thought or feeling, we are saved. We are living in a post-modern society that has all but abandoned the traditional values and teachings of the First-Century Church. These churches teach that it is okay to abandon the idea that we are saved by the *blood* of Jesus and that we should no longer discuss the words *sin* or *hell*. There are many who believe that "living a good moral life" is sufficient to save them. You have, no doubt, heard it said, "John is so good, there is no way that God would allow him to go to hell. If God is a loving God, He would not allow anyone to go to hell." Living by "The Ten Commandments" will not save anyone.

Once again, we must turn to the Bible for the answer to this most important question and to defray all the confusion. The New Testament, in the Book of Acts, records eight examples of individuals coming to know Christ as their Savior. On Pentecost, Peter preached and over 3,000 repented of their sins and were immersed into Christ "for the remission of sins" (see Acts 2). The baptism of the Ethiopian (Acts 8), the conversion of Lydia and the Philippian jailer, and his family (Acts 16), as well as others who became Christians under the direct influence of the apostles and others.

By studying the examples of these and other conversions in the Book of Acts, it is apparent that those seeking salvation were given *specific* instructions as to what they must do. Our instructions should be the same. There was a reason for these people being given the same message in each case. That reason is simple: It is God's way!

INSTRUCTIONS FOR BECOMING A CHRISTIAN

These instructions are taken directly from the New Testament and relate to everyone desiring to accept Christ as his or her Savior. There are no deviations, short cuts, or other ways to come to Christ but by these.

The first is *hearing*. Throughout the Scriptures, we find instructions for seekers of the truth to "hear." Jesus said repeatedly, "He that has ears, let him hear." He also instructed us to "hunger and thirst after righteousness." God cannot help the person who does not hear His Word. Those who are not interested enough in salvation to *listen* to what God has to say are lost by their own doing. Preaching and teaching are so vital to salvation because they furnish two essential roads by which men "hear" (cf. Matthew 28:18-20; Romans 10:10; I Corinthians 1:21). Those who allow worldly interests to obscure their hearing the Word of God cannot become Christians so long as this condition prevails.

The second section of the road to salvation is *believing*. Hearing means nothing if it is not followed by believing. God's message of salvation is of no value unless one believes what he has heard. This "belief" is far more than "mental assent." We do not simply say, "I believe that." It is a matter of putting our complete trust in what we have heard and in God. God cannot save anyone who does not place his or her entire faith and trust in Him. We read

Simply Speaking...

in Hebrews 11:6 (NIV), "And without faith it is impossible to please God, because anyone who comes to Him must believe that He exists and that He rewards those who earnestly seek Him." Faith is the foundation of our Christian experience. In the same manner as a building cannot stand without a firm foundation, neither can a Christian stand without faith. It is by faith that one desires to follow the teachings of the Bible in matters of salvation and living a Christian life.

The third part of the road to salvation is *repentance*. This may seem like an outdated theological word; however, it is an essential action toward salvation. Repentance is simply a change of heart involving sorrow for one's past sins with a sincere desire to live for Christ rather than self. It is much deeper than a simple, "I'm sorry." Just being *sorry* for something is not sufficient to *change* a life. A sinner repents when he gives-up the life of sin that has held him for so long. The one who trusts his own "goodness" to save him is clothed in "filthy rags." It is only when we put our trust completely in Jesus Christ that we can find our repentant heart. Those who repent have a change of heart and a willingness to put away the things of the world. The early church had its beginning when over 3,000 people "repented" of the sin of killing the Son of God when Peter preached to them. They realized their sin and asked, "Brothers, what shall we do?" (Acts 2:37b NIV). Repentance is not reserved only for the non-believer. It is an act that should be done on a daily basis since we all continue to sin. Peter urged Simon, the sorcerer, who had believed and was baptized, yet coveted the power of the apostles to work miracles, to "repent" (Acts 8:9-23). John advises entire churches in Revelation to "repent" (Revelation 2:5, etc.).

The fourth "mile" of the way to salvation is *confession*. Paul tells the Roman Church that confession is made

Simply Speaking...

with the mouth (Romans 10:9-10 NIV) and to Timothy in I Timothy 6:12 (NIV), "Fight the good fight of the faith. Take hold of the eternal life to which you were called when you made your *good confession* in the presence of many witnesses" (emphasis mine). Peter was the first to make this "good confession when Jesus and His disciples were on their way to Jerusalem for the final time, Jesus stopped and asked the disciples who they thought He was. He received a myriad of answers and finally Peter spoke up and said, "You are the Christ, the Son of the Living God" (Matthew 16:16 NIV). Confession, however, is not simply making such a statement before a congregation of people just prior to baptism. It is a life of "confession." It is a life of showing Christ by our actions. The person whose life has not changed after accepting Christ has a very poor confession.

The fifth part of the journey on the road to salvation is *baptism*. While many will agree with the first four, baptism becomes a stumbling block. Allow me to here state my most fervent belief that no one has the assurance of salvation by skipping this event. The assurance of salvation is not granted without baptism. This *fact* can be verified by many Scripture passages. One of the most poignant examples of this is found in Galatians 3:27 (NIV), "for all of you who were baptized into Christ have clothed yourselves with Christ." It is through baptism that a believing, confessing, repentant person is cleansed of his or her sins. Baptism, by immersion, washes away our sin (see I Peter 3:21) and frees us from its consequence. It is through baptism that the penitent believer comes into a holy relationship with Christ. Only then does one have the promise of sins being washed away (Acts 22:16). Only then does one have the promise of being accounted a son of God (John 3:5). Those who teach that baptism is not important in becoming a Christian do great harm to the Scriptures and are speaking where they have no Biblical authority to speak. Just as Christ was dead, buried, and rose from the grave, so it is in His likeness, that one becomes a Christian by dying to sin, being buried in water, and rising to walk in a new life (see Romans 6.)

There can be no argument as to the manner of baptism. The word "baptize" is a transliteration of a Greek word, baptitzo which means to "dip, plunge, and go under." Sprinkling or pouring as a means of baptism are never utilized in the New Testament and have no place in Christ's Church. These forms of "baptism" should never be recognized as acceptable practices because they are not Scriptural nor are they accepted by God. For further study of the concept of baptism, I urge you to take a careful look at the following passages of Scripture: Acts 2:38; Acts 8:36-39; Galatians 3:26-28; Titus 3:5; I Peter 3:21.

Baptism, by no means, guarantees one's salvation. After baptism, the promise of salvation can be lost through a sinful and neglectful life. John writes in the Revelation that we are to remain faithful until death in order to receive the "crown of life." Baptism is only the beginning since we are ""born again"; this means that we are babies and are instructed to grow and mature in Christ.

Among all the instructions given for salvation in the New Testament, baptism is the only one that is ever "completed." The Christian never stops "hearing," "believing," "repenting," and "confessing." Therefore, these acts are never "completed" in this life. Even in baptism, however, the symbolism of submerging oneself into the blood of Christ is never complete. It only grows stronger and more as our will becomes more in tune with the will of Christ.

THE RESULTS OF BECOMING A CHRISTIAN

The first thing that one should notice is a "change of attitude." I had the privilege of baptizing an older man into

Simply Speaking...

Christ some years ago. When he came up out of the water, his statement was, "I have never felt so clean!" Perhaps you can relate. We have never *been* so clean. As a result, we are free from the stain of sin, receive a new Father (because God cannot be the Father of one who is in sin), a new Brother, Jesus Christ, and a new *hope* for an eternity with God and our fellow saints. Our entire nature is changed, and we are no longer an alien sinner because we have been changed by the power of God.

CHAPTER NINE

WHAT'S IN IT FOR ME?

INTRODUCTION: To some, that may seem an unfair question. They would say that we should never ask God, "What do I get if I am obedient?" I believe that we have every right, and indeed a responsibility, to ask such a question. God is not harmed when we question Him. He does not become angry with us when we wonder just what we are to receive for our efforts. He does, in fact, tell us often what we can expect when we are obedient to Him.

THERE ARE *NEGATIVE* THINGS

When Jesus was asked by the mother of James and John that He would provide a special place for her sons when Jesus would come into His kingdom, His response was not what she expected to hear. The request and Jesus' response may be found in Matthew 20:20-23. Jesus said that they would have a great difficulty in following Him. He then continued with this theme by stating that they (the disciples) should be servants of all as was He (Matthew 20:24-28).

In Mark 8, just after the confession by Peter, and Jesus' rebuke of Peter because Peter attempted to assuage

Jesus from His appointed death, Jesus called the crowd to Him and said, "If anyone would come after me, he must deny himself and take up his cross and follow me..." (Mark 8:34-38 NIV). What is Jesus saying when He says, "Whoever wants to save his life will lose it, but whoever loses his life for my sake and for the gospel will save it?" He is simply telling His followers that we must be willing to not only give up our physical life for Him; rather we are to give up our own *desires* and a way of life that would be a worldly one. Jesus does not expect every Christian to *die* for Him. He is telling us to be prepared to put to death the worldly way of life. Paul tells us in Galatians 5:24-26 (NIV), "Those who belong to Christ Jesus have crucified the sinful nature with its passions and desires. Since we live by the Spirit, let us keep in step with the Spirit. Let us not become conceited, provoking each other." Since we *crucify* the "sinful nature," we have a responsibility to put on a "new nature." This may mean what the world would call *sacrifice*. In other words, we can no longer do the things that would bring us worldly pleasure. That is not to say that we must be somber, unhappy, long-faced, and never have any enjoyment in life. Those who believe and teach such are in error. Christians are to *enjoy* their walk with Christ. There are 63 references to "joy" in the New Testament according to *The New Strong's Exhaustive Concordance of the Bible (KJV)*. These references mostly refer to the Christians having joy in their hearts. We are to "Consider it pure joy, my brothers, when whenever you face trials of many kinds..." (James 1:2, NIV). The cute little song that encouraged people "Don't worry, and be happy" should be the rallying cry of every Christian. We have the joy in our hearts that can come only with and from a relationship with Jesus Christ, and there is no room for *worry*.

We are not promised that it will *be easy* to follow Christ. In fact, quite the opposite is promised. The reward, however, is tremendous.

WHAT ARE SOME OF THE REWARDS?

One of the most often discussed rewards is *eternity* in heaven. A question might arise, because we cannot really understand eternity: "How long is eternity?" Many years ago, I heard eternity described thus: "Eternity is longer than it would take a single bird to fly across the United States with *one* grain of sand from the East coast to the West coast, deposit that grain of sand and return for another until all the sand was brought from one shore to the other." That amount of time is equally unfathomable; however, it well illustrates the fact that eternity is longer than forever.

Many think that we *deserve* this heaven simply because of "who we are!" Nothing could be further from the truth. Since "all have sinned and fallen short of the glory of God" (Rom. 3:23), we are not deserving of anything from God except eternal *punishment*. Since Christ took our sins upon Himself, however, we are shown the *grace* of God and are allotted eternal salvation through His blood. We are *given* heaven as a prize for those who have remained faithful to Him. Heaven is truly a beautiful place. It is the original *paradise* and everything there is *perfect*. No matter one's *view* of what heaven will be *like*, the main thing is that we will be in the presence of God *for eternity*. Heaven is probably best described in Revelation 21. Here is John's vision and his description of what heaven will be. It is certainly a beautiful place where there will be no sorrow, crying, fear, or sin. John says in Verse 21, "I did not see a temple in the city, because the Lord God Almighty and the Lamb are its temple" (NIV). What a glorious place! Well, you might say, "That is all wonderful, but what do I do in the meantime?"

Simply Speaking...

We are to hold to that which we have received. God has placed within each of us who are Christian the Holy Spirit, Who has provided us with instructions as to how to live. The entire New Testament is a book of instruction for the Christian. I fully understand that many do not like "instruction books." Many feel that they do not need to be "told" what to do. We, especially in America, feel no need to be told how to live. We feel that we are "free and we can do as we please." While this may be the case as individuals of American citizenship, it does not apply to those who have put on Christ. We are told that we must remain faithful until the end to receive the "crown of righteousness." God expects us to be faithful to Him, and He, in turn, will provide such blessings we will not be able to hold them all. One of my father's favorite sayings was, "If it were raining five dollar bills, I would be wearing boxing gloves and be unable to pick any up." God takes away the "boxing gloves" and prepares us for heaven by sharing Himself with us here and now. God's arm is not short. If we are not living in the blessings of God, we are the ones to blame, not Him. God wants to bless each of His children, as you (if you have children) want to bless them. You want what "is best" for your children (grandchildren), and each one strives to provide for them. God, in similar manner, seeks to provide His best for those who are His.

Another question that might arise is, "How can a loving God ever condemn anyone to hell?" The simple answer is that He does not! If one goes to hell, it is by his/ her own doing. God does not *condemn* anyone to hell. We will arrive in eternity by our own actions (or inactions) and have no one to blame for our eternal fate but ourselves. Peter tells us in II Peter 3:9, ". . . He is patient with you, not willing that any should perish, but everyone should come to repentance" (NIV). It is true that God loves all His creation, as He said in John 3:16, "For God so loved the world that

Simply Speaking. . .

He gave his one and only son, that whoever believes in Him shall not perish but have eternal life" (NIV). This goes a long way in showing the love of the Father, in that He loved us enough to die for us. It is clear that He does not want anyone to be lost; however, He does not *force* His will on anyone. God has created us with a *free will*, and, as such, we have the ability to choose how and where we will spend eternity. Should we choose to serve God, we will spend eternity with Him; should we choose to rebel against God and "have it our way," we will spend eternity in a godless hell.

Another reward is *peace*. In Romans 5:1 Paul writes, "Therefore since we have been justified through faith, we have *peace* with God through our Lord Jesus Christ" (NIV, emphasis mine). Many of Paul's opening and closing remarks in his letters refer to this peace. What kind of peace is this? It is a "peace which passes understanding"; therefore, it is difficult to explain because it is so difficult to understand. Jesus said that He came to bring *peace*, and at His birth the angels announced, "Glory to God in the highest, and on earth *peace* to men on whom His favor rests" (Luke 2:14 NIV, emphasis mine). God was sending His son to bring *peace*. How could this be since He came into a world racked with war, and there have been very few years since that there has been *peace on earth*? The "peace" referred to here is not a peace that the world can recognize. Jesus said, "Peace I leave with you; my peace I give you. I do not give to you as the world gives. Do not let your hearts be troubled, and do not be afraid" (John 14:27 NIV). The peace that Christ brings is that of a *spiritual* nature. In other words, we can have peace in our *spirits*. How much better is spiritual peace than worldly peace? After all, it is our spirits that will live in eternity, not this world. We are in possession of a peace the world cannot know because it is from God, and the world does not know God. Jesus states further, "I have told you these things, so that in me you might have peace. In this world you will have trouble. But take heart! I have overcome the world" (John 16:33 NIV).

Peace is an illusive thing. It is very difficult to grasp because it means so many different things to so many. We may find it difficult to grasp because we are carnal and God is spiritual. We may never completely understand peace in this life; however, there shall come a time when we will completely understand God's peace when we shall be united with Him in His heaven.

Yet another reward is *hope*. If we have no hope, we are above all people most miserable. Paul, in I Corinthians 15:19, writes, "If only for this life we have hope in Christ, we are to be pitied more than all men" (NIV). It has been said that people held against their wills in POW camps during all wars can remain sane because they can hold on to hope. Christians, above all other people, have reason to *hope* because they have placed their eternity in Jesus.

Biblical hope has three characteristics. First, there is an attitude of *expectation*. This expectation is of something yet to come. As the writer of Hebrews put it, "Now faith is being sure of what we *hope* for and certain of what we do not see" (Hebrews 11:1, NIV, emphasis mine). Biblical hope is*knowing* that there is a certain future of being with the Lord, not of uncertainty. Secondly, this applies to our earthly hope. We can know that we shall be joyful in this life when we allow Christ to rule in our lives. Finally, hope is the knowledge that a certain future in heaven with God is assured. "What makes all this possible?" The fact is the love of God has made it possible that we can be cleansed from sin and made whole (complete) in Christ.

In the Book of Job, the word hope appears sixteen times. It would seem that a man who had lost everything would have no more reason to "hope." Yet, he was a man filled with hope. The psalmists write often of "hope." The

New Testament is filled with references to our *hope* that is in Christ. If we have no hope, we are not only miserable, we are truly lost. "How can having no hope make one lost?" Simply because Jesus came to bring hope and He gives it to all who are His. If we have no hope, we cannot claim to be God's children.

We are rewarded with *labor*. "WHAT?" you say. "How can *labor* be a reward?" Labor is a reward because we are doing it for the Lord. We labor in His kingdom to bring others to know Him, to build up those who are newer in the faith than we are, to show our love for the Father and for many other reasons. Labor has been viewed as a "task" or "drudgery." In the service of Christ, labor has no such connotation. We should rejoice in our labor for Christ and view it as a privilege. In I Corinthians 15:58 we see, "Therefore, my dear brothers, stand firm. Let nothing move you. Always give yourselves fully to the work of the Lord, because you know that your labor is not in vain" (NIV). Our labor for the Lord will be rewarded in multiple ways.

All Christians have been called to a life of *service*. We are to serve the risen Lord and one another. One of Jesus' final acts prior to His arrest was to wash the feet of His disciples. How can Christ, the Son of God, humble Himself to the point of taking a basin of water and a cloth and literally wash the feet of *His* disciples, those who had pledged to *serve* Him? It is only when we come to understand that He came to serve rather than be served that we can understand the nature of Christ. Being a Christian is being a *servant*.

From the time of the patriarchs, Abraham, Isaac and Jacob, and even prior to that time, God calls people to a life of service. The reason for the existence of Israel was to serve the purpose of God—bringing His Son into the world. The purpose for Israel was to prepare the world for the coming of the Messiah. It took hundreds of years, and

Simply Speaking...

God's relationship with Israel was a stormy one. However, in the end the mission was accomplished; Christ came and accomplished His mission. The idea of serving the Living God has not diminished since the first coming of Christ. We are to continue to serve Him "with gladness" until He returns or until we are called to "go home" to Paradise. While Israel was to prepare the way of the coming of the Lord, we are to proclaim His coming until He comes again.

John the Baptizer was a man whose *service* was to preach repentance and preparation for the imminent coming of the Christ. He came "baptizing in the desert region and preaching a baptism of repentance for the forgiveness of sins" (Mark 1:4 NIV). His service was unique and necessary to "prepare the way of the Lord" (see Mark 1:2-3). Our service may not be as unique as was his; however, there are many people within our "circle" of family, friends, and co-workers who need to hear about the coming of Jesus, and we can prepare the way of the Lord for them. Our service in the kingdom is to be a "presenter of the Gospel" to a lost and dying world. You may well say, "I am no preacher!" You may not be in the sense that the statement is made; however, we are all called to *witness* to others, and we can do that by our life of example and by our speaking with others. If you feel that you will not know what to say, pray for the guidance of the Holy Spirit and wait for Him to prepare you. You will be amazed what He can and will do for and through you. Step out on faith and allow God's service to be accomplished through you. God will bless you in a mighty way.

Newness of life is a promise related to becoming a Christian. When we are immersed, we "rise to walk in newness of life." What does that mean? It simply means that we are a "new creation." We have put to death the old self in a spiritual sense, and we are raised, as in a resurrection from the dead, to be a new being. The former has given way to the new in much the same way that a caterpillar, after entering the cocoon, emerges as a butterfly. We do not undergo such a metamorphosis as that; however, we do have a total change in our spiritual life. Before, we were dead in our sins; after, we are alive in Christ. This new existence is one that enables us to be at peace with God because we become His children. We now have a truly loving family, a family that cares about our spiritual welfare and not our physical welfare only. We are to grow in the grace and knowledge of Jesus Christ and prepare ourselves to serve the risen Lord. Since we are not born "fully matured," neither are we *born again* fully matured. As a child, we undergo certain physiological changes as we mature. Some (mostly boys) experience "growing pains." These pains, usually in the night, are severe and cause a great discomfort in the legs. As Christians, we may well undergo certain "growing pains." Never are we promised that this "new life" will be an easy one. We grow and develop as Christians in much the same manner as we did when we were children. Paul used the human analogy when he referred to the Christians at Corinth. He said in I Corinthians 3:1-2, "Brothers, I could not address you as spiritual but as worldly—mere infants in Christ. I gave you milk, not solid food, for you were not yet ready for it. Indeed, you are still not ready" (NIV). In Hebrews 5:12-13 we read, "In fact, though by this time you should be teachers, you need someone to teach you the elementary truths of God's Word all over again. You need milk, not solid food! Anyone who lives on milk, being still an infant, is not acquainted with the teachings about righteousness" (NIV). The analogy is clear. Many who claim the prize of salvation have not grown past the age of infancy in Christ and cannot truly know His righteousness.

    This is not an exhaustive list of the blessings that come from a life of service to the Lord Jesus Christ. These are listed only as a beginning point of service. May each of you find your place of service and blessing so that you may be closer to the fellowship of Christians and to the Lord.

WHAT HAPPENS IF I "MESS UP" REALLY BADLY?

As we have seen, there may come a time when a baptized believer can fall from grace. When this occurs, there can be no more sacrifice for the sins of that person. There is, however, hope for anyone who is still alive and wishes to *return* to the Lord. A very good example of such a return is shown in Acts 8. The situation occurred when one Simon, known as Simon the Sorcerer, believed and was baptized. He heard the Word preached by Philip and followed the plan of salvation. As to whether he was a Christian or not is not in dispute; he was. The "problem" arose when Peter and John came from Jerusalem to give Spiritual gifts to some believers. Upon doing so, Simon saw what they had and wanted to *purchase* these gifts. Peter severely rebuked Simon for his request and told him that his "heart is not right before God" (Acts 8:21 NIV). Peter further advised Simon that he should *repent* and *pray* to the Lord. Peter, in this response, does not tell Simon that he should be re-baptized for his actions, rather to repent and pray with the idea that God perhaps would forgive Simon. Peter told Simon, "I see that your heart is full of bitterness and captive to sin" (Acts 8:23 NIV). This exchange comes at a crucial time in the infancy of the Church. It was very important that the apostles stop such thoughts and show that God's gifts are not for sale. Peter viewed this request as a grievous sin and was intent on stopping it in its tracks. This shows the divine way to *return* to the Lord through repentance and prayer. As long as one is able to recognize his/her sins, repent of them, and pray for the Lord's

Simply Speaking. . .

---

forgiveness, one has "crossed the line" into an eternity with God.

When we "mess up really badly," we can still find forgiveness with God by following the plan as set forth in Acts 8. Paul, in his letter to the Corinthian Church, tells them that have "messed up very badly." He shows them the "error of their ways" while not losing his love for them or telling them that they have no place in God's kingdom. He disciplined them in the "spirit of grace" while advising them as to just what they needed to do to return to a right relationship with God.

The letter to the Hebrews is written to a group of Jewish Christians who were concerned that they had made a "mistake" in following Christ and becoming Christians. They were seriously considering abandoning their new faith and returning to Judaism. The author carefully and completely explains the consequences of such a decision to them. Were they Christians? Yes, indeed, they were! The warning is to all Christians who *leave their first love*. In fact, all the letters of the New Testament serve as reminders of the need to remain faithful.

Paul told Timothy in I Timothy 4:15-16, "Be diligent in these matters; give yourself wholly to them, so that everyone may see your progress. Watch your life and doctrine closely. Persevere in them, because if you do, you will save both yourself and your hearers" (NIV). Can you see the importance of remaining faithful, not only in your service, but also in your "life and doctrine?" There are so many who begin the journey of faith only to be carried away by other *doctrines*.

In writing to the Church at Ephesus, Paul wrote, "Then we will no longer be infants, tossed back and forth by the waves, and blown here and there by every wind of teaching (doctrine) and by the cunning and craftiness of men in their deceitful scheming" (Ephesians 4:14 NIV). Here is yet another reference to *infants*. Paul is telling all his readers that we must be very careful in understanding the *truth of God's Word* so that we will not be carried off by doctrines that are not the Truth. It is a terrible thing for those who have come to know the Truth of God's Word only to reject it when it does not suit their purposes and move to a doctrine that does. There are too many who have heard the Word only to choose to reject it and move to denominationalism because it fits their "needs" or "desires." When one loses touch with the Truth of the Word, one loses more than his or her church fellowship; one is in danger of losing eternity with God. I urge all to think carefully when "something happens" that "upsets" you, not to "quit" and go elsewhere if the doctrines espoused by that church are not that of the Bible.

"I TRY REALLY HARD BUT I CAN NEVER BE SURE!"

Such an attitude is counterproductive to being a Christian. To be certain, we reject the *Doctrine of Once in Grace, Always in Grace*; however, this does not mean that we cannot have certainty regarding our salvation. We can *know* that we are saved by the presence of the Holy Spirit and the assurances of the Bible. God promised that by our being obedient in following the TOTAL "plan of salvation" we have the assurance we need of salvation. As previously stated, however, we must remain faithful unto death to receive the reward of heaven. Those who are not certain of their salvation are depending upon "being good enough" to be saved. This is a "works" based salvation and is rejected in the Scripture. Because we are saved by *grace* not *works*, we must reject the idea that we can "be good enough" to inherit salvation. Our faithfulness is the key factor in our salvation; therefore, our salvation can be assured when we are faithful. The *always trying, never sure* crowd is as incorrect as the *once in grace, always in grace* crowd, and, as such, we must realize that we are simply *forgiven*, not *perfect*. We will never achieve perfection, as we understand perfection, this side of heaven. By the blood of Jesus Christ, we are 100% forgiven and completely free from the condemnation of sin. Paul, in Romans 8:1-2 makes this perfectly clear when he writes, "Therefore, there is now no condemnation for those who are in Christ Jesus, because through Christ Jesus the law of the Spirit set me free from the law of sin and death" (NIV). Since we are *free* and under no condemnation, we should rejoice and be extremely happy as Christians. No one wants to be enslaved to anything, yet we often allow ourselves to return to the very sins that had enslaved us prior to our accepting Christ.

Another reason to be *sure* is the fact that God has *sealed* His children. We read in II Corinthians 1:21-22, "Now it is God who makes both us and you stand firm in Christ." He anointed us, set His seal of ownership on us, and put His Spirit in our hearts as a deposit, guaranteeing what is to come" (NIV). Also in Ephesians 4:30, Paul admonished his readers, "And do not grieve the Holy Spirit of God, with whom you were *sealed* for the day of redemption" (NIV; emphasis mine). We have the assurance that we have been sealed by the Spirit of God and, therefore, can know that He is in us and working through us.

"What if I don't feel it?" If we do not feel the presence of the Holy Spirit, there is a breakdown in our relationship with the Lord. We discussed earlier that "feelings" can be and are often dangerous. They can change in an instant. The "feeling" of the Holy Spirit, however, is a different matter. We should *know* that He exists in us as He works with our spirit to bring the peace of the Lord to us. Should we not have this feeling and assurance we need to re-establish our relational lines of communication with the Lord. This is accomplished by fervent prayer and repentance of our sins. The lack of prayer in the life of a Christian is a breakdown of communications with the Father and may result in tragic consequences. Restore that prayer life and be restored to the Holy Spirit.

CONCLUSION: As you can easily see, there is a lot "in it for me!" We have only touched on a few of the blessings offered by a benevolent Father whose desire is to bless us greatly. He has promised to do so, and the failure in receiving the blessings is totally ours. When we think about blaming God for not blessing us, we need to look no further than ourselves to see that we are the cause of this failure.

CHAPTER TEN

HOW CAN I *KNOW* I AM SAVED?

INTRODUCTION: This is an intriguing question. Peter writes in II Peter 1:10-11, "Therefore, my brothers, be all the more eager to make your calling and election sure. For if you do these things, you will never fall, and you will receive a rich welcome into the eternal kingdom of our Lord and Savior Jesus Christ" (NIV). "That is great," you say, "but how can I be *certain*?" Would it not be nice were there some "magic pill" that we could take and never need to question our salvation? For those who believe in the D*octrine of Eternal Security* (Once in Grace, Always in Grace) this is less of a problem. There is, however, no Biblical basis for such a doctrine. While there are some Scriptures that *seem* to teach such, so many more refute this doctrine. (More on that later.)

Perhaps we should, at this point, define *salvation*: "Being saved from our sins and the *eternal* consequences of those sins. It is a generic term used in the Bible to describe deliverance by God, especially of a spiritual redemption from sin." This salvation is a direct result of the redemptive power of Jesus Christ as accomplished by His atoning death on the cross and results in one's being prepared, in this life, for an eternity with God. While we are being saved from the "eternal consequences" of our sins, we have no such assurance of the earthly consequences of our sins. Salvation is a beginning point for the Christian to come to an understanding of the heaven God has awaiting their faithful obedience to Him. It is begun by God's grace and continued by the Holy Spirit's arrival at baptism. It is completed when we hear the words of Jesus, "Well done, good and faithful servant! You have been faithful with a few things; I will put you in charge of many things. Come and share your master's happiness!" (Matthew 25:21 NIV). How, then, can I get to the point where I can truly sing, "Blessed assurance Jesus is mine . . .?"

WE HAVE GOD'S *WORD*!

God said it; therefore, it is true. The more time one spends questioning their salvation the less time they have to "work it out." Paul admonished the Philippian Church to, "Therefore, my dear friends, as you have always obeyed—not only in my presence, but now much more in my absence—continue to work out your salvation with fear and trembling. . ." (Philippians 2:12 NIV). In verse 5 of Philippians 2, Paul writes, "Your attitude should be the same as that of Christ Jesus." It makes sense that *if* we have the same attitude as Christ, we will be His.

Paul, in writing to the Church at Rome, had a lot to say on the subject. The entire eighth chapter of Romans is a treatise on living with the Holy Spirit in the Christian. (It would be good for the reader to, at this moment, read Romans 8). In Romans 8:9, Paul wrote, "You, however, are controlled not by the sinful nature but by the Spirit, if the Spirit of God lives in you. And if anyone does not have the Spirit of Christ, he does not belong to Christ" (NIV). We are "more than conquers through Him who loves us" Rom. 8:37 NIV). The words of Paul here are most encouraging and should be studied in depth by every Christian.

One of my favorite "Christian songs" is "Jesus Loves Me." I know that that is a children's song, yet it says so much about our relationship with our Savior. "Jesus loves me, this I know, for the Bible tells me so!" How much more information do I need to know than is found in the *fact* that Jesus loves me? We find assurance in the fact that we are loved by our Heavenly Father and our Brother, Jesus Christ. The Bible is full of references to the fact that we are loved by God and are assured of our salvation *if* we are living in Him and following His will. The key here is *being in Him*. While it is true that God loves the "sinner" and He has made His love known in many ways, it is equally true that God has no place in His eternity for those who have refused to be washed in the blood of Jesus Christ. He has made this quite clear; yet there are many who incorrectly believe that a loving God would not allow any to be "lost." While God does *desire* that any should be lost, He does not force His love on anyone. He wants all to come to Him by repenting of their sins and accepting His love offering of His Son.

John writes in I John 5:13, "I write these things to you who believe in the name of the Son of God so that you *may know* that you have eternal life" (NIV; emphasis mine). John writes we may have a certain knowledge that we are assured of eternal life *because* God has given us that assurance. If we are not certain of our salvation, we will spend the bulk of our time wondering what we must *do* or *believe* to have that assurance. God wants us to be a people of joy and peace. We cannot achieve these qualities if we are concerned over our salvation. If we are motivated by fear of being lost, we cannot live the kind of life Jesus would have us to live.

WE HAVE GOD'S BLESSINGS

Another way that we can *know* that we are saved is by the blessings we receive. These blessings may seem aloof, in that we take them for granted. We can sometimes believe that we are not blessed by God because we have come to feel that God *owes* us all these things. It is especially difficult when we are having difficult times in our lives and we wonder, "Where is God?" The poem "Footprints" tells it all. When we think that God has abandoned us, we find that it was then that He carried us. We have all suffered loss in our lives and most have wondered why God would allow these things to happen to us. We must learn that God does not seek out those whom He can *hurt*. God has put certain "natural laws" in place, and when one breaks these laws, one suffers the consequences. For example, if you put your hand in a fire, you will be burned. It is equally true that one of the "consequences" of Adam's sin was to bring death to all creatures. The only way to avoid death is for the Lord to return. While it is tragic for a family member to die, especially a child, we must remember that God does not "cause" this tragedy and that He is not simply waiting for us to "mess up" so that He can "whack" us.

Blessings can come in many forms. Sometimes when we think that something is a tragedy, in the end it is a blessing. Just allow God's blessings to flow over your life and accept them as a wonderful gift from a loving God. The closer we walk with God, the more He will bless us.

WE HAVE THE POWER OF THE HOLY SPIRIT

I will address the Holy Spirit in more detail in a later chapter in this book; however, at this time I would like to examine His role in our assurance of salvation.

Simply Speaking...

On Pentecost, when Peter preached to the assembled crowd, the Holy Spirit was most prominent. It was through the power of the Holy Spirit that Peter and the others spoke. Luke records, "When the day of Pentecost came, they were all together in one place. Suddenly the sound like the blowing of a violent wind came from heaven and filled the whole house where they were sitting. They saw what seemed to be tongues of fire that separated and came to rest on each of them. All of them were filled with the Holy Spirit and began to speak in other tongues as the Spirit enabled them" (Acts 2:1-4 NIV). The *power* of the Holy Spirit came upon them, and as a result, the disciples were emboldened, and it was seen that they were speaking with the authority of God.

You might say, at this point, "These men were different. They were the 'apostles.'" Yes, you would be correct. They were the "apostles." However, the power of the Holy Spirit was not limited to these men. The Book of Acts is replete with examples of the Apostles giving "Spiritual gifts" to others.

In an attempt to understand this power and how it affects the Christian today, we must understand that God gives His Spirit to all who have obeyed Him in Christian baptism. As we continue to read in the second chapter of Acts, on the same day and at the end of Peter's sermon, when some three thousand people responded to the plea, Peter said, "repent and be baptized, every one of you, in the name of Jesus Christ for the forgiveness of your sins. And you will receive the *gift* of the Holy Spirit" (Acts 2:38 NIV; emphasis mine). That *gift* is the indwelling of the Holy Spirit. He comes to take up residence in the Christian and to work "alongside" the spirit in each one of us. We can *know* that we are being saved by the indwelling of the Holy Spirit. He makes God's Word a living part of the Christian's daily life. If you do not know that the Holy

Spirit is alive and well in you, you need to re-examine your relationship with your Savior. The fervent "fire" of the Holy Spirit can be quenched by the actions of the Christian. In I Thessalonians 5:19, Paul writes, "Do not put out the Spirit's fire." This commandment was directed to all Christians. It is especially important that new Christians be mindful of this command. It is too often seen that people come to Christ and they are "on fire" for the Lord. It is not long before they become less and less enthused; often the "fire" is extinguished, and they are "pew fillers" with no zeal to serve the Lord. They have placed themselves in the place where those who have gone before them are awaiting "church to be over." What a shame and a disgrace! One of the great needs for Christ's Church is a Spiritual *revival* where the fire is rekindled and the fervor of those who have all but forgotten what it means to "be on fire for the Lord" can be brought back. Often those who have quenched the fire of the Holy Spirit drop out altogether and are never seen in the Lord's House again. This is even a greater tragedy because it is most difficult to re-kindle the fire once it has been extinguished.

WHAT ABOUT *FEELINGS?*

"Feelings" are not reliable. It made the title of a great song in the 1970's, and the word "feelings" became a counselor's watchword during that same period; however, feelings can lead one astray. Satan has a way with feelings. Some believe that salvation comes from a "certain feeling." Some would call it "conviction." They would have us believe that the Holy Spirit "convicts" us of our sins by a "feeling" that we get at a certain event or time in our lives. We must examine these "feelings" closely as they can be something that can bring us false "hope." While I am not saying that the Holy Spirit does NOT convict of sins because He certainly does, I am saying that relying on a "feeling" that one gets at an emotional time does not mean that the Holy Spirit is at work in one's life. The real meaning is that too many believe that once they have had this feeling they are "saved." I know women who have experienced "false pregnancy." They *believe* that they are pregnant, and no one can convince them otherwise. Others have "false labor pains" and believe that they are about to deliver a baby, only to be sent home to await the "real thing." Satan is the master manipulator. He can put "feelings" in people and cause them to believe that they are saved because of this feeling. I want to caution all who believe that they are "saved" because of a "feeling" to re-examine your relationship with the Holy Spirit. You will find that much more is involved in salvation than feelings.

Feelings not only cause a false sense of security but also can cause people to commit all manner of sins. If we were to rely solely on our feelings, we could make any sinful situation into a Christian experience. For example, there are those who blindly follow a person (persons) who have demonstrated an ability to make one "feel good." These "false teachers" have demonstrated a natural ability to make people feel good about themselves, and they have shown that they are good leaders. Since many are "seeking" to follow something (someone) who can make them "feel good," they are easily led astray. The Bible repeatedly warns us against such. Paul, in his writings to individuals and churches, repeatedly advises them to avoid those who would lead the saints astray. It is so easy to "feel" secure and to "feel" that we have made all the provisions we need to make to be "saved." We must avoid such feelings since salvation is a continuing process, not a "once and done" feeling!

Simply Speaking...

Knowing that our salvation is sure is as simple as knowing that Jesus died for our sins, knowing that we have obeyed His commands for salvation, and *trusting* Him for the rest. We must continue to rely on God's Spirit and the assurance He provides us. We must "work out our salvation with fear and trembling, for it is God Who works in you to will and act according to His good purpose" (Philippians 2:12-13 NIV). Paul did not say that our salvation was already assured, rather, that it is an ongoing experience and must be "worked out."

If we were to rely on *feelings* alone, what, then, do we do with those "bad feelings" that often accompany our lives? We may have a great feeling one moment and be in the pit of despair the next. There may be a tragedy in our lives that makes us feel terrible, and we wonder why a loving God would allow such, and then conclude that God simply does not care.

Another question regarding feelings that arises is, "How do I interpret my feelings?" Since subjective feelings are subjected to a myriad of interpretations, how can one ever know which is the correct interpretation? Nowhere in the Bible are we told that subjective feelings are an assurance of our salvation. Since this is true, we should *never* rely upon our "feelings!"

WHAT ABOUT *GOOD WORKS*?

How sad it is for anyone to link salvation with good works. For many, there seems to be an endless procession of "good deeds" which they feel will bring salvation to their eternal spirits. This is no more true than trusting in one's feelings. As we have already seen, we are saved through the blood sacrifice of Jesus Christ and through the grace of God. There is nothing we can do to "earn" our salvation. I have heard so many say that this person or that person must be in heaven because of the things he or she did on earth. Jesus makes this abundantly clear when He said, "Not everyone who says to me, 'Lord, Lord' will enter the kingdom of heaven, but only he who does the will of my Father Who is in heaven. Many will say to me on that day, 'Lord, Lord, did we not prophesy in your name, and in your name drive out demons, and perform many miracles?' Then I will tell them plainly, 'I never knew you. Away from me, you evildoer'" (Matthew 7:21-23 NIV).

While this may *seem* to refer to "works" since Jesus said that we must *do* the will of His Father Who is in heaven, it is not referring to the "good deeds" many believe will save them as Jesus so perfectly explains in the balance of the reference. We are to "work" and follow the commands of the Father. Those who believe and teach that works are not important have never read the Epistle of James. James makes it most clear that one's faith is void and dead if not accompanied by works (see James 2:14-26). Paul said that if a man was unwilling to *work* he should not eat and we know from Proverbs that work is a noble thing. The types of *works* that show our faith are the types God will reward. We have only to review the Bible and see that God has always rewarded His faithful who continue to "produce" in His "vineyard."

Since we are "saved by grace" and "justified by faith," how can anyone rely upon one's own "goodness" to bring salvation (see Romans 3:28)? The grace of God was poured out to us while we were still in our sins God loved us enough to send His Son to die for us. Where in that does one feel "good enough" to *earn* salvation?

WHAT ABOUT *EXPERIENCE?*

Along with the concept of "feelings" and "works" we find that of "experience." While some base their salvation on feelings or works, others base theirs on *experiences.* Experiences are simply feelings put into actions. As with feelings, experiences may vary and often do. For one to say that we should all have the same *experience* as they had in order to be saved is absolutely nonsense. To some it may be that "warm, fuzzy feeling" they experienced while in prayer; others will find that they were given certain "gifts" and claim that the Holy Spirit has chosen them to prophesy, speak in tongues, interpret tongues, etc. They claim that if you have not had such an "experience" or "encounter" you are not saved. This leaves many with the "feeling" of being "left out" of God's salvation because they were not privileged to have such an experience. I recall that at an early age I was called to preach. My dearest friend, a member of a different church, was interested in my "experience" with Christ, my "vision" in which Christ "called me to preach." I was left wondering if, in fact, I had been "called to preach" because I did not have such an "experience" with Christ. I now realize that that was simply the "belief" of his church, and that is not how God calls His servants. We have an "encounter" or "experience" with the Holy Spirit when He "convicts" us of our sins, and we have another encounter with all three of the Godhead when we are immersed into their names. It is not necessary to have a "vision," "experience," or "encounter" with God, other than the ones previously mentioned, to experience salvation.

CONCLUSION: Since God has promised us eternal salvation should we be faithful to Him unto death, there should be no other consideration. Jesus said in Revelation 2:10, "Do not be afraid of what you are about to suffer. I tell you, the devil will put some of you in prison to test you, and you will suffer persecution for ten days. Be faithful, even to the point of death, and I will give you the crown of life" (NIV). This is an oft-quoted verse of Scripture because it gives us the assurance that, *if* we remain faithful even to being put to death for our faith, Jesus has a "crown of life" for us. What great assurance this is, to know that when we are faithful that He has *promised* to be faithful.

CHAPTER ELEVEN

WHAT IS THIS "LORD'S SUPPER" ANYWAY?

INTRODUCTION: The "Lord's Supper" or "Communion," as it is often called is simply a memorial "meal." It consists of a wafer made from unleavened bread (meaning that the wafer has no yeast in it) and a small amount of grape juice (a small number use wine). This memorial is to the suffering Savior as He gave His life for us on the cross.

It is a means of communing and fellowshipping with Christ and His fellow believers. Some mistakenly believe that the wafer and juice literally become the body and blood of Jesus Christ. This is incorrect as they are simply spiritual representatives of such. Should this be true we would be cannibals, as we would be feasting on the body and blood of a real human being. Others have the understanding that Christ literally appears at the "table" at this time. This is also incorrect as Christ is with us always, and though this is a very important part of worship, Christ does not "appear," visibly or invisibly, at this time any more than He does at any other time.

Simply Speaking. . .

The Lord's Supper is a time of re-dedication. We re-dedicate ourselves on a weekly basis, asking for forgiveness of our sins and spiritually using these representations to find peace in our hearts as we realize that we are being forgiven if we truly repent. We renew our covenant with Christ as we partake (see Luke 22:20).

Paul said in I Corinthians 11:26, "For whenever you eat this bread and drink this cup, you proclaim the Lord's death until he comes." This speaks volumes to all who observe this meal. We are saying to the world that we are being faithful to Christ's words when He said that we should do this in His memory. We remember His sacrifice *for us*! An additional aspect of this observance is that we show that we believe that He lives. If Jesus were not raised from the dead, there would be no need for such an observance.

WHEN DID THIS BEGIN?

On Thursday night before Christ died on the cross on Friday, He met with the twelve disciples in a room where they observed the Passover Feast. This was a very important feast for the Jews as it was a remembrance of the time when the first-born of Egypt died and the Israelites who had the blood of a lamb spread on the doorposts and headers were spared. The next day Moses was called before Pharaoh, and the Israelites were released from Egyptian bondage and set free. This feast was to be observed as a memorial of that event. The Gospel writers tell us that "after supper" Jesus took bread, broke it, and gave it to the disciples, telling them to eat it, that it was a representative of His body. In a similar manner, He took the cup, blessed it, gave it to them, and told them to drink it as a representation of His blood. Hence, the "Lord's Supper" was instituted. For 2,000 years, Christians have observed this greatest of all feasts and shall continue until the Lord returns.

HOW OFTEN SHOULD THE LORD'S SUPPER BE OBSERVED?

Once again, using the Book of Acts as our guide, we see that the observance was weekly. When the Apostle Paul met with the Church at Troas, Luke records the event: "On the first day of the week we came together to break bread. . ." (Acts 20:7a NIV). It is perfectly clear that the main purpose of meeting on the first day of the week was to "break bread." The fact that Paul was "in town" was secondary to any other purpose for coming together to worship.

We also see in Acts 2:42 (NIV) that the disciples "devoted themselves to the apostles' teaching, to the breaking of bread, and to prayer." This "devotion" was not quarterly, monthly, semi-annually, or annually. The Lord's Supper was observed as often as the listening to the apostles' teaching and public prayer.

Paul admonished the church at Corinth in I Corinthians 11:17-ff, that they were not properly remembering the Lord in the observance of the Lord's Supper. Paul re-emphasized the need to treat the event with the reverence that it deserved. He admonished them to "examine" themselves and properly partake lest they were condemning themselves.

Another factor in weekly observance is that Church historians all agree that the Lord's Supper was observed weekly by the early Church. This fact should be enough evidence for us to partake on a weekly basis.

WHO CAN PARTAKE?

Many denominations limit those who can partake of the Lord's Supper to their own members. These have to be "in good standing" in the church as a further requirement. This custom is totally un-Scriptural and should be abandoned immediately. There is no precedent in the New Testament for such a practice. No one has the right to deny any Christian the right of partaking in the Lord's Supper. All who have accepted Christ as their Savior have the right to meet around this table and partake. The *only* restriction is set by Paul in I Corinthians 11: 28 where he admonishes the believers to partake "examining themselves." It is for all believers who have sinned as a renewal of the sacrifice of Jesus. Those who have strayed are in need all the more.

The question might arise, "What about a non-Christian who might take the bread and juice as it is passed? Will it harm them?" My response would be no! To them it is nothing but a wafer and a small amount of juice. There is nothing magic in these emblems. The "magic," if you will, is in the spiritual renewal of the Christian. It should be no cause for alarm. I have often been asked by anxious parents who have said that their children partake as the emblems are passed. There is absolutely no harm done. There is no reason for panic as this is not a sin.

HOW SHOULD ONE OBSERVE THE LORD'S SUPPER?

Since this is a "memorial" feast to the risen Lord, it should be observed thoughtfully, reverently, and prayerfully. There should be no thoughts of anything other than the death of Christ on the cross. We must turn our attention to His death, burial, and resurrection. This sacrifice of Jesus on the cross at Calvary is the only reason we have for hope in an eternal state with God. This is no time for thinking about the afternoon's activities, the week ahead, or anything else that might enter our minds.

Observing the Lord's Supper in such a manner that does not glorify Christ will result in doing so in an "unworthy manner." Again looking at Paul's admonition in I Corinthians 11:27 (NIV), "Whoever eats the bread and drinks the cup of the Lord in an unworthy manner will be guilty of sinning against the body and blood of the Lord," we see that it is crucial that we partake in a manner that would be considered worthy. It is better not to partake if we cannot properly prepare our spirits than to partake unworthily. We are guilty of "murdering the Son of God" should we not be in a proper frame of mind.

In many Christian Churches / Churches of Christ, the elders preside at the table, and the deacons pass the wafers and cups. There is no Biblical precedent for this practice. There are no requirements for anyone to serve. This has simply become a traditional practice. While there is nothing wrong with this practice, the "wrong" would be for those who believe that this is the "way the apostles did it." Though there are no Biblical precedents for the handling of the emblems, this should be done by godly people who represent well the One who was crucified.

HOW IMPORTANT IS THE LORD'S SUPPER?

The simple fact that this is the final instruction given by Jesus to His followers prior to His crucifixion and that He considered it important enough to tell them to "do this in remembrance of Me," speaks to the importance of the event. Each Christian should be in the Lord's House to partake of this feast on a weekly basis. To neglect this practice is to forsake the sacrifice of Jesus. The observance of the Lord's Supper is the single most important thing that the Christian does on a weekly basis. It is imperative that those who have been washed in the blood of Jesus to remember His sacrifice on a weekly basis.

CHAPTER TWELVE

HOW CAN I *KNOW* THE WILL OF GOD?

INTRODUCTION: Have you ever prayed that God would reveal His will to you in order that you would be in a position to *do* His will? Have you ever *believed* that you were acting within the will of God only later to come to the understanding that you were *not* acting in His will? If you answered "yes" to any of the above questions, this is for you!

The question is: "How can I *know* the will of God?" Would it not be great if God operated today as He has in the past? He could "talk" to us directly and "write" His will on tablets of stone or something like that. Would it not be great if God would use that "still small voice" as He did with Elijah? Why, do you suppose, God has changed His way of communicating with His creation, mankind? It seems that with each answer a new question arises which we must answer. Okay, let's get started.

REVELATION

Perhaps it would be good to understand the term *revelation*. REVELATION, as defined in *Webster's Dictionary*, as: 1. "An act of revealing;" 2. "Something revealed;" 3. "An enlightening or astonishing disclosure." Still confused? No wonder. REVELATION as defined in *The Dictionary of the Bible,* edited by James Hastings, is as follows: "The English word which comes from the Latin implies the drawing back of a veil, the unveiling of something hidden. It is the almost exact equivalent of the New Testament word *apocalypse* or 'uncovering' (see Revelation 1)." For our purpose as used in this writing we shall see REVELATION as it is specifically applied to the Word of God, the "unveiling" of the unseen God to the mind and heart of mankind.

How has God shown Himself? This is answered in several ways: first, through nature, as it impacts the wisdom, power, and purpose in the material world around us (see Romans 1). Secondly, the revelation of God in man as it applies to the traces of God in mankind's conscience with its sense of obligation, in his or her emotional nature with its desire and capacity for fellowship, and in his or her personality, which demands personality for its satisfaction. Thirdly, the revelation of God in history, meaning the marks of an over-ruling providence and purpose in the affairs of mankind, of a Divinity that has shaped mankind's ends, and the traces of a progress and onward sweep in history. (All these aspects of revelation are usually summed up in the term "natural religion," and do not touch the meaning of revelation which is associated with Christianity.) Fourth, the revelation of God as found in Judaism and Christianity. By revelation applied in this fashion, I mean a special, historical, supernatural communication from God to mankind. This is not merely information *about* God, but a revelation—a disclosure of God Himself in His character and relation to mankind. In addition to revelation through nature, conscience, and reason, Christianity implies a special revelation in the Person of Jesus Christ.

This revelation is the final revelation God has made. While many believe that "God speaks to them personally," I would strongly disagree with that view. God has, indeed, spoken to each of us "personally" through His Word and through His Holy Spirit. He has not, however, given anyone a "special revelation" since the completion of the Bible. The writer of Hebrews began his work by saying, "In the past God spoke to our forefathers through the prophets at many times and in various ways, but in these last days He has spoken to us by His Son, whom He has appointed Heir of all things, and through whom He made the universe" (Hebrews 1:1 NIV). The significance of this statement is simple: God intended that His Son would have the *final* say! Those who believe that God reveals Himself in "special revelations" unique to them are simply wrong or misunderstand the true nature of God.

There are many reasons why God does not choose to operate in this fashion any longer. The main reason is that He has told us everything we need to know in His Word. The Bible is complete and perfect and, as a result, has no need of a special revelation. This is one area where the Church of Jesus Christ of Latter Day Saints (the Mormons) is in error. They contend that Jesus Christ gave their "prophet," Joseph Smith, a special revelation and thus began a new sect. This is simply against God's other revealed testament and cannot stand against this scrutiny. Since God has revealed His will and Himself through His Son and in His Word, there need be no other revelation. Paul told Timothy in II Timothy 3:16, "All Scripture is God breathed and is useful for teaching, rebuking, correcting, and training in righteousness" (NIV). Taking this as our model, there need be no other revelation.

The need for revelation is simple: We could not have *fully* known God as He desires had He not made this special revelation. We could have never known of our need for salvation had God not given the Law, and we could have never known the *way* of salvation had God not revealed Himself in His Son. Amid the sins and sorrows, the fears and trials, the difficulties and perplexities of life, we need such a Divine revelation that will assure us of salvation, holiness, and immortality. Our deepest instincts cry out against the thought that sin is final or permanent, yet it is equally clear that nothing but an interposition from above can deal with it.

The fact that revelation is credible is seen in several ways: First, *speculatively*. We may argue that the universe points to idealism, and idealism to theism (a belief in and understanding of God), and theism to a revelation. Second, *historically*. From a historical perspective we have many witnesses in miracles, prophesy fulfilled, and spiritual adaptation to human nature. Behind all these are the *presuppositions of natural religion* as seen in nature, man, and history. The ultimate credibility of Christianity as a revelation rests on *the Person of its founder*, and all evidences converge toward and center in Him. Christ is Christianity, and Christians believe primarily and fundamentally in the *fact* and trustworthiness of Christ. Herein lies the final *proof* of the credibility of Christianity as a Divine revelation.

Therefore, the essential purpose of revelation is *life*: the gift of the life of God to the life of mankind. Its practical character is stamped on every part. The "chief end of revelation" is not philosophy, though it has a philosophy profound and worthy. It is not a doctrine, though it has a very satisfying doctrine worthy which is inspiring, as well. It is not enjoyment, though it has lasting and precious experiences. It is not even morality, though it has a powerful and unique ethic. Christianity *has* all these, but *is* far more than them all. It is the religion of redemption, including salvation from sin, equipment for holiness, and provision for life lived in fellowship with God and for His glory. The "chief end" of revelation is the union of God and mankind, and in that union the fulfillment of all God's purposes for the world. The elements of sonship, stewardship, worship, fellowship, heirship, practically sum up the purpose of Divine revelation as it concerns mankind's life—a life in which we receive God's grace, *realize God's will*, reproduce God's character, render God's service, and rejoice in God's presence in the Kingdom of grace below and the Kingdom of glory above.

Now that we have a clear understanding of the "Divine revelation" we can move to an understanding of God's will.

THE WILL OF GOD

One of the best known times when the "will of God" is mentioned is in "The Model Prayer." Jesus said, "Thy *will* be done" (Matt. 6:10b, KJV, emphasis mine). To pray with power, Jesus teaches us we must first get God in our minds and recognize His sovereignty. As we pray, "Thy will be done," right there is where many hesitate, lose their nerve, and turn away from God. I think I know why.

When I was studying psychology in college, I worked out a number of word tests I would use on colleagues and friends. For example, take the word "Christmas" and ask someone for the first word that comes into his or her mind. I would get such answers as, Santa Claus, decorations, snow, gifts, etc. Rarely would Christ be mentioned. As a result, I would conclude we had commercialized and paganized the Lord's birthday. I think the test was valid, with some limitations.

Simply Speaking...

Let us try it on ourselves. I will name a phrase and check your first thought. "Will of God." What does that bring to your mind? Does the death of a loved one, some great disaster, severe suffering from some incurable disease, or some hard sacrifice bring this into focus? Most people will think of some dark picture in relation to the will of God.

Perhaps one cause is Jesus' prayer in Gethsemane, "Nevertheless not my will, but Thine be done" (Luke 22:42, KJV). From His surrender to God's will we see Christ walking up Calvary and being nailed to a cross. God's will and crosses come to be synonymous terms for us.

However, we can go back much further as we examine Job's situation. He lost his wealth, his children were killed, he suffered in body, and his wife deserted him. Job associated all those disasters with God, so he said, "The Lord gave, and the Lord hath taken away; blessed be the name of the Lord" (Job 1:21, KJV). When our hearts are broken we say it is "the Lord's will." Naturally, we shrink from such a will.

It seems to be a general belief that the will of God is to make things distasteful for us, like taking bad tasting medicine when we are sick, or going to the dentist. We think we would be much happier if we disregarded God's will. We never say, "No, I forever turn my back on God's will." But we do say, "For the time being, I will back my own judgment and follow my own will."

Someone needs to tell us that sunrise is also God's will. There is the time for harvest, the harvest which will provide food and clothing for us, without which life could not be sustained on earth. God ordered the seasons; they are His will. In fact, the good things in life far outweigh the bad. There are more sunrises than tornadoes.

Simply Speaking...

Jesus said, "Thy will be done in earth, as it is in heaven." "As in heaven," He said. What do you think of when the word "heaven" comes to your mind? You think of peace, perfect joy, plenty, and the absence of pain, suffering, and tears. John saw it all and recorded his vision in Revelation 21. That is exactly what we want here and now in our lives. John says that is *God's will for us*.

Before we can pray, "Thy will be done," (Matthew 6:10b, KJV) we must believe that it is the best way. All too often we surrender to the immediate, while God considers life as a whole. A good example of this is Joseph, the darling of his father Jacob's heart. Home for him was a place of great joy. He was not required to work as did his brothers, and they became jealous. This jealousy welled up in his brothers, and they determined to kill him. They decided, instead, to sell him into slavery, and Joseph was taken to Egypt where he was purchased as a household slave. Quite a difference from his "home life." It was only a few years when those same brothers stood before Joseph and were begging him for food. Joseph said to them, "And now, do not be distressed and do not be angry with yourselves for selling me here, because it was *to save lives that God sent me ahead of you*" (Genesis 45:5, NIV, emphasis mine).

Surely Joseph's way was one of hardship, but he kept his faith, never giving up, and at the end he could look back and see, as we read in *Hamlet*, "There is a divinity that shapes our ends." Out of the surrender of our Lord in Gethsemane came cross, but beyond the cross lies an empty tomb and a redeemed world.

We would do well to remember that sometimes it is not God who leads us through deep valleys and dark waters. It may be our own ignorance and folly. Even then we can feel his presence, for out of our mistakes God can make something beautiful. God did *not* bring Job's tragedies, but because of Job's faith God could use those tragedies for Job's final good. It's wonderful what God can do with a broken heart when we give Him all the pieces.

Not only is God's way the best and happiest, it is also *within our reach*. Many shrink from God's will because of a fear that God will ask them to do more than they can do. There was the man with one talent who buried his money in the earth. In explaining his failure, his not even trying, he said to his master: "Lord, I knew that you are a hard man, harvesting where you have not sown and gathering where you have not scattered seed. So I was afraid and went out and hid your talent in the ground. See, here is what belongs to you" (Matthew 25:24-25, NIV).

He was afraid of unreasonable demands by his master. He felt that even his best could not please his master. There are some things we cannot do. Not many of us can be great artists. Conspicuous leadership is beyond the reach of most. We could list thousands of things we cannot do.

Of one thing, however, we can be certain: we *can* do the will of God. Moses thought he could not. When God told him to lead the children of Israel out of bondage, he made excuses. He sincerely felt it was beyond his abilities. But he did it! With complete faith and confidence, we can pray, "Thy will be done" because God is a loving Father who knows His children better than they know themselves. He wants our best, but he expects no more.

God's will is on earth. It is operating in your very life. For example, we did not decide in what century we would be born; we were not privileged to choose our parents, the color of our skin, our sex, or our physical appearances. All of these were decided by a higher will, God's will.

Simply Speaking...

HOW CAN I KNOW THE WILL OF GOD FOR MY LIFE?

Many will never know, because God does not reveal His will to triflers. No one can walk into His holy presence on hurrying feet. If we merely pray, "Lord, this is my will, I hope you will approve," you are wasting your breath. Only those who sincerely want God's will, and have faith enough in Him to dedicate themselves to His will, can ever know it. To pray, "Lord, show me Your will. If I like it, I will accept it," is a futile prayer. We must *accept* it before we *know* it. Whether or not we can do that depends on what opinion we have of God.

To the sincere, God reveals His will in many ways. We often learn through the process we call *insight*. A psychologist friend once said to me, "Either a person has insight or he hasn't. It isn't something that can be learned." I tell you; however, it is something that God can *give*.

I have counseled with people who have baffling problems. Perhaps they have tossed and turned many hours at night as they attempted to sleep, but could not do so because of a problem. In the quietness of my office, we have discussed God and His love and concern for us. After a prayer, we discussed the problem. Often I have seen a "light" in their faces; as suddenly the answer came, a solution came to mind. I believe God gave them insight. Some call it "the inner light." I do not care what you choose to call it; I believe it to be an "insight" as they came to understand the will of God.

God may choose to reveal His will through the advice of others, through circumstances, through the experiences of others, through the experiences of history, through the discovery of His laws by scientific investigation, through the voice of His Church, or in many other ways. There is no "set-certain" manner in which we can learn God's will for us. The one thing that we must keep in mind in attempting to ascertain the will of God is that we must be *living in His will* before He can reveal His will to us. The closer we are to Him, the easier it is to understand what His will is. One of the best places to see His will is in His Word and in the life and teachings of Jesus Christ.

The assurance that we are within the will of God does more to eliminate the fears and worries of life than any other one thing. I quote Dante: "In His will is our peace." Surrender to His will takes the dread out of tomorrow. We know, absolutely we know, that if we do His will today, tomorrow will be according to His will. I am no fatalist; instead, I can say with the psalmist, "I was young and now I am old, yet I have not seen the righteous forsaken or their children begging bread" (Psalm 37:25, NIV). Obedience to his will today means that God assumes the responsibility for tomorrow.

If we look at the prophets of God, we see that they were in the will of God, yet they suffered. They were preaching in the name of the Lord, yet they were persecuted. This persecution came from both within the people to whom they prophesied as well as those outside the Jewish faith. We can find encouragement from these prophets of God by realizing that God cares for us when we encounter suffering for Him and when we are in the will of God. Satan would have us believe that we are suffering only because we are *outside* the will of God due to our own sin. While this may be true on some occasions, it is not true in every case. We need only look at the Prophet Elijah. Elijah was a righteous man and a great prophet of God, yet he suffered at the hands of the wicked Queen Jezebel. He also suffered as a result of the three and one-half years of drought in the land. Other examples of prophets who suffered while in the will of God were Daniel, Ezekiel, and Jeremiah, to name a few.

Even those who died while serving God were not left out of God's grace. He promised to care for our spiritual needs and when Jesus returns He will bring His rewards with Him. A question may arise, "Why it that those who speak in the name of the Lord often endure great trials and hardships?" The answer: It is because their lives back up their messages! People do not want to hear that they are sinners and, as a result, they cannot stand against the messenger of God who is "walking the walk, while talking the talk." The impact of a faithful, godly life has a great amount of power. The prophets are all dead and gone, yet we remember their messages and respect their work.

It is important to know that, as has been said, "The will of God will never lead you where the grace of God cannot follow!" This is one of the most profound statements I have ever read. I find this statement so important if we are to understand the "will of God." We can go into the will of God with the assurance that God's grace shall be there and with us.

Being in the will of God never ends. We are instructed to "remain faithful until death" if we want to receive the "crown of life." There is no provision for those who want to begin the race then drop out and expect that they are spiritually okay. We are required to serve Him with a sense of urgency and desire in love for Him.

CONCLUSION: God has shown His will in His Word and has made no new revelation since the completion of the Bible. We are to search the Scriptures and learn from the Holy Spirit if we truly want to know the will of God. He has a will and a purpose for each of us if we would only seek it. When we pray, "Your will be done," we are praying for a mighty thing. He will work His will with or without us; however, it is far better to be in His will than out of it. We should work to remain in His will in all that we do. God's blessings come to us only when we are in His will. The blessings of God come only *after* we have endured. We cannot persevere unless we have had trials in our lives. There can be no victories unless we have had battles. We cannot appreciate the mountain peaks unless we have gone through the valleys. If we want the blessings, we must be prepared to carry the burden and fight the battle. God balances blessings with burdens, and privileges with responsibilities, else we would become spoiled children and never fully understand the will of God.

God will never *force* His will upon us. He does, however, use our mistakes to accomplish His will. We must learn from our mistakes and seek His will in our daily lives.

CHAPTER THIRTEEN

WHAT IS THE POINT AND PURPOSE OF BAPTISM?

INTRODUCTION: There are many volumes on the subject of baptism. There are those who believe that baptism is essential for salvation and those who do not. There are those who feel that "sprinkling" or "pouring" are acceptable forms of baptism, while others believe that "immersion" is the only acceptable form of baptism. This one word has been the cause of so much division in all of Christendom for centuries. What anyone "believes" is irrelevant, in the grand scheme of things, since God has spoken definitively on the matter. There should be no real discussion or question regarding baptism since the Bible not only tells us the reason for the practice, it tells us the manner by which we should perform it.

This is not intended to be a treatise or a definitive word on the subject of baptism. The intent of this chapter is to simply expand upon the section in the chapter entitled "What Must I Do To Be Saved?" We will explore baptism in a little more detail simply because there is so much controversy surrounding the practice.

Simply Speaking...

BY WHAT MANNER SHOULD BAPTISM BE PERFORMED?

Since this is the simplest question, I shall consider it first. The Bible is clear on the subject of manner since the word "baptize," itself, is not an English word. It is rather a Greek word that was transliterated into the English language. This simply means that it was brought into the English language directly from the ancient Greek and refers to the following: "To plunge, go under, to immerse." The original word, *baptizo* (meaning "I immerse") then applies to those who were "immersed" in water. The Greek word, *baptizma* means "immersion." There exists nowhere in the New Testament the practice of "sprinkling" or "pouring" and should not be confused with the practice of immersion as a form of baptism. This is crystal clear, and only the "blindness of men" can cause any change in this practice.

WHO SHOULD BE BAPTIZED?

There is an equally simple answer to this question, and it is a Biblical one. Those persons who should be immersed are those who have realized that they are sinners in the sight of God; possess faith that Jesus is the Christ, the Son of the Living God; are willing to confess Him before men; and confess their sins to Him and have repented of those sins. It is at that point that one is ready to complete the salvation act of being immersed *into* the names of the Father, the Son, and the Holy Spirit.

A sub-question arises: "At what age should one be baptized?" This is a somewhat difficult question to address in that there is no prescribed *age* in the Bible. It is usually considered that when one reaches the *age of accountability* they should make this decision. The question that would arise from this response then is, "When does one reach such an age?" The answer varies from person to person. Most often, we answer this question by saying, "When a person *knows* "right from wrong." This is tricky because there is evidence that we learn that at a very young age. I would answer the question by saying, "When a person expresses an interest in knowing the Lord and understanding what sin and salvation are about. When a person can explain what it means to him or her to become a Christian." There may be other criteria that are as simple; however, this is the criteria that I use. Suffice it to say, there is no "magic age."

There are many compelling reasons for baptism. These are clearly seen in the New Testament. Each reference to those who became Christians were concluded by a reference to their baptism (see Acts 2: 38; Acts 8:36-39; 9:18 and 10:47-48). These are but a few of the references to baptism in the Book of Acts.

Peter, in his first letter, makes it clear that baptism is an instrument of salvation. He said, ". . . and this water symbolizes baptism that now saves you also. . ." Peter makes it perfectly clear that baptism is a part of God's saving action and that it is essential for salvation.

Since we have seen that baptism is an integral part of salvation, as written by the Apostle Peter, let us look at some other reasons why this is true. Paul writes often regarding the matter. Perhaps the most poignant is found in Romans 6:3-5: "Or do you not know that all of us who were baptized into Christ Jesus were baptized into His death? We were therefore buried with Him through baptism into death in order that, just as Christ was raised from the dead through the glory of the Father, we too may live a new life. If we have been united with Him like this in His death, we will certainly also be united with Him in His resurrection" (NIV). If, having been baptized *into* Christ, we were *united* with Him in both His death and resurrection, we are now in a *saved* state. Just as union in marriage is a binding arrangement as instituted by God, we are "united" in a binding relationship with Christ. Thus, He could call the Church His "bride." Paul makes it perfectly clear that we are "dead to sin and alive to Christ." This means that since we are "united" with Christ in His death and resurrection we are no longer to live in a state of sin, but rather to live in a state of righteousness. This is what it means to "repent." When one repents and puts his or her old life behind, one is a candidate for baptism by which all sins are washed away.

We use Jesus' examples of things He did as evidence of many things we should also do. Why then should we not use His example of baptism? He was baptized by John prior to beginning His ministry. If it were good enough for Jesus, it should be good enough for us.

There are many other Scripture references by the Apostle Paul with respect to baptism. Please allow this to be a beginning point of your study of the Bible on this subject.

SHOULD WE BAPTIZE INFANTS?

The simple answer is NO! Although there is no precedent in the Scripture for such a practice, many denominations practice infant baptism. Some of those who baptize infants for the purpose of salvation are the Roman Catholics and Lutherans. They believe that babies inherit the sin of Adam and Eve and are *guilty* of sin at birth. Others, such as the Presbyterians and Methodists practice infant baptism because they believe that babies are automatically members of the church. They also equate the practice of baptism with the covenant of circumcision of the Old Testament. The "baptism" is simply an outward act showing that these infants are members of the church.

There are many very good reasons for *not* practicing infant baptism. Chief among them is that it is not Scriptural.

Simply Speaking...

The concept of "Original Sin" is not found anywhere in the Bible. Babies are *not* born with sin attached to them because of Adam's sin. Since baptism was and is for the remission of sin (one's own sin), it is something that should be reserved for a time when that person knows what sin is. These babies are born into a sinful world; however, they are not responsible for it. They are innocent of sin at birth. Christ's death on the cross has already atoned for the sins of Adam, and no one is responsible for his sin anymore.

A second reason for refraining from infant baptism is found in the fact that we are under a "New Covenant." Membership into the family of Abraham was by circumcision. Those who believe that by baptizing these infants they become a "member" of the New Covenant do not correctly understand the purpose of baptism or the manner in which one becomes a "member" of the family of God. Since the Old Covenant was totally fulfilled by the redeeming death and resurrection of Jesus Christ, there is no longer a need for such a practice (see Luke 22:20).

A child born to Jewish parents was a member of the family (Old Covenant) by birth in the same manner as we are members of our families by birth; however, there is no "spiritual" birth here. Remember the words of Jesus to Nicodemus, "I tell you the truth, no one can see the kingdom of God unless he is born again" (John 3:3 NIV). This more than implies a "re-birth," and that does not come as a physical infant. One's spiritual birth is something that occurs when one is ready to become a child of God, and that does not occur until that person is "spiritually prepared." Jesus continues His explanation to Nicodemus by saying, "Flesh gives birth to flesh, but the Spirit gives birth to spirit" (John 3:6 NIV).

Since New Testament baptism is preceded by other actions, such as hearing the Word of God, believing in Him and His Son, repentance, and confession, there is no way that an infant can perform these actions. It is an abomination to believe that infants are subject to sin "at birth" and that they are responsible for the actions of others.

There are other reasons for not practicing infant baptism. These reasons are listed as an opportunity to understand that the practice is simply not Scriptural.

CONCLUSION: Being immersed into Christ for the remission of sins is only the beginning. As it was when we were born into an earthly family, we are born into the family of God. We were infants then, and we are infants at our re-birth. It is our responsibility, and that of the Church, to grow in "grace and knowledge." We cannot simply sit down and quit. If we never mature, we will never know the blessing God has in store for us. We will simply die, and all the efforts we have made to this point will be in vain.

CHAPTER FOURTEEN

WHY IS THE *ONCE IN GRACE, ALWAYS IN GRACE* DOCTRINE WRONG?

INTRODUCTION: The Doctrine of Eternal Security or "Once in Grace, Always in Grace" is a false doctrine that has deceived millions over several centuries. The doctrine had its origins in the teachings of John Calvin. Calvin was born in Noyon, France on 10 July 1509. He was born into a strict Roman Catholic family and was destined, by his father, to become a priest. He was educated in Paris and befriended a group of individuals who were reform-minded. It is suspected that in 1533 Calvin experienced "the sudden and unexpected conversion" about which he writes in his foreword to his commentary on the Psalms. Calvin became one of the most ardent supporters of the "Reformation Movement" and is credited with a number of theological doctrines, not limited to *Eternal Security*. Our focus here is on the *Doctrine of Eternal Security*. Calvin wrote, "If God has ordained salvation and you once go through the motions of it, you cannot be lost, regardless of what you do."

Many in the denominational world have been greatly influenced by Calvin's teachings including the "Doctrine of Pre-Destination." It is so sad to see so many who believe that they cannot "fall away" from the grace of God. The prevailing view is that they can do anything and never be lost.

SOME SCRIPTURES THAT *SEEM* TO TEACH THIS

Those who believe in this doctrine cite many passages of Scripture as "proof texts" for their belief. We will not attempt to cite all of them here; however, we will cite a few.

The first Scripture that would tend to agree with this doctrine is I John 3:6. John writes, "No one who lives in Him keeps on sinning. No one who continues to sin has either seen Him or knows Him" (NIV), (c.f. Romans 6:1).

A second passage is also found in I John. I John 3:9 says, "No one who is born of God will continue to sin, because God's seed remains in him; he cannot go on sinning because he has been born of God" (NIV).

A third reference from I John 5:18 where John writes, "We know that anyone born of God does not continue to sin; the one that was born of God keeps him safe, and the evil one cannot harm him" (NIV).

You can also see I John 1:8-11; 2:1-2 and John 5:24. As previously stated, this is only a taste of the Scripture references that, those who believe in Eternal Security, have brought to the argument. Time and space do not permit us to account for all of them. Suffice it to say here that anything can be proven by the Scriptures. We shall attempt to "prove" that statement as follows: "Then he (Judas) went away and hanged himself" (Matthew 27:5); "Go and do likewise" (Luke 10:37b); "Whatever you are about to do, do quickly" (John 13:27b). (All above taken from the NIV). What does this prove? Only that if anything is taken out of context, one can "prove" anything by the Bible. According to the above quoted Scripture, one could conclude that one is to hang himself or herself and to do it quickly. Simply put, the person who seeks to "prove" a theory by the Bible can do it if they are willing to distort the true meaning of the Word. Those who believe that the "Doctrine of Eternal Security" is true have badly misappropriated the Scriptures.

THE TEACHINGS OF JESUS AND THE APOSTLES WARN AGAINST FALLING AWAY

Jesus warned that a person should count the cost of becoming a Christian, lest he make a start and not be willing to go the distance (Luke 17:27-30). In illustrating the dangers of apostasy, Jesus warned, "Remember Lot's wife" (Luke 17:32). Jesus also said in Luke 9:62, "No one who puts his hand to the plow and looks back is fit for service in the kingdom of heaven" (NIV). In Matthew 10:22, Jesus said, "All men will hate you because of Me, but he who stands firm to the end will be saved" (NIV).

Paul, in writing to the Church at Corinth says in I Corinthians 9:27, "No, I beat my body and make it my slave so that after I have preached to others, I myself might not be disqualified for the prize" (NIV).

Peter tells us that not only is it possible for us to fall from grace, but that when we do so that his last state is worse than the first (II Peter 2:20-22). He also warns against our falling from our own steadfastness (II Peter 3:17).

Again Paul tells us that those who are in the greatest danger are those who are standing strong in the Lord (I Corinthians 10:12). The writer of Hebrews makes it perfectly clear in Hebrews 6:4-6 and in 10:26-27 that should one fall away, there remains no more sacrifice for sins and that it is impossible to restore such a one to the faith since he or she is crucifying the Son of God afresh. Many other Scriptures indicate the same as previously mentioned. We hope that this is sufficient to bring about the true teaching of the Bible on this subject.

The Bible not only speaks of the falling away as a *possibility* but as a fact that there will be those who will and have done so. In Revelation 2:4, we read that the Church at Ephesus had "left its first love." In the parable of the sower, Jesus said that some would receive the word with joy, yet, in time of temptation, would fall away (Luke 8:13). Paul said that the Galatians had deserted the Gospel, "in favor of a different gospel" (Galatians 1:6). It is as though Paul knew just how this doctrine would be distorted; therefore, he made it very clear that the Galatians had, in fact, fallen away from grace. He said in Galatians 5:4, "You who have been trying to be justified by law have been alienated from Christ; *you have fallen away from grace*" (NIV, emphasis mine). Were it not possible to do so, why would he have thus spoken? *If* they had fallen, then it is possible to do so!

In Paul's letter to the Colossians, chapter one, Paul writes that we have hope only *if* we continue in the faith (Colossians 1:21-23). We can all be happy in the security of knowing that we are being saved only as long as we remain faithful to His Word. Unfortunately, many are casting aside the faith they once held in favor of something that looks *good* and *new*. There is a general falling away occurring at this very moment. More and more are being carried away by false doctrines that *seem* to be right. All who are reading this are familiar with someone who once professed to be a disciple of Christ, including many leaders, pastors, and ministers who have left the faith and are seeking to find the answers in "all the wrong places."

The Book of Hebrews tells us not to harden our hearts. We are warned in Hebrews 3:13-14, "But encourage one another daily, as long as it is called today, so that none of you may be hardened by sin's deceitfulness, we have come to share in Christ if we hold firmly till the end the confidence we had at first" (NIV).

WHAT HAPPENED TO *CHOICE*?

The main thing separating humankind from animals is the ability to *choose*. Since humankind was given this ability, we were told to exercise it. While it is true that nothing can separate us from the love of God in Christ, as stated in Romans 8:37-39, we must know that God will *never* violate our ability to choose. We can will ourselves out of the love of God by *choosing* to do so. This choice may be conscious or through our sub-consciousness. God shall never force anyone to accept Him or His Son's sacrifice. This idea goes against the very nature of God. If we *choose* to come to Christ, we can certainly *choose* to leave Him. For those who believe in the "Doctrine of Eternal Security" to say "those who go back into the world were never saved in the first place," violate the very Word of God since it is quite possible to fall from grace. The epistles were written *to* Christians, *for* Christians and repeatedly warn against the coming "apostasy" or falling away!

CONCLUSION: If it were true that one could not fall away and be lost, then all these warnings from Jesus and the apostles would have no meaning and be worthless.

This "Doctrine of Eternal Security" is a very dangerous one because it provides a false sense of security among many. Remember the words of Jesus in Matthew 24:12-13, "Because of the increase of wickedness, the love of most will grow cold, but *he who stands firm to the end will be saved*" (NIV, emphasis mine).

CHAPTER FIFTEEN

WHY PRAY?

INTRODUCTION: The real question should be, "Why not pray?" If one truly loves God, as we should when accepting His Son as our personal Savior, we should have a burning desire in our hearts to communicate with our Father. There should be nothing more natural than the "lifeline" offered to us by our heavenly Father through prayer. Prayer should be the most natural thing we do. It should be as easy as breathing. Paul admonished us to "pray continually" (I Thess. 5:17 NIV). "But," you say, "what if I do not know how to pray?" or "I simply do not have *time* to pray." Each of these is simply an excuse. If you can form thought, you can pray. The mistaken idea that praying is using some special language or forming words in a certain way is a trick of the devil. God wants, as much as anything, to hear from us! He patiently awaits our daily conversation with Him. As far as time is concerned, we do not have time *not* to pray. We must set aside a certain amount of time daily to pray and share with our heavenly Father. Let us look at some aspects of our prayer life, as it should be as a Christian.

PRAYER IS A NATURAL RESPONSE

Jesus refers to God most often as "Father." It is a natural thing to speak to our fathers. I know that for some this is simply not true since the earthly father has abandoned the family or is simply not in the "picture." It is difficult for many to relate to the term "father." While this may be the case in some, it is still the "natural" thing to do. As children of God, we should have a desire to talk with Him on a regular basis. We need not be "afraid" of God. This is such a terrible way to view God. The Bible tells us to "fear" God. This does not mean that we are to "be afraid of Him." It simply means that we are to hold Him in reverence and respect. We should never be afraid of the One we love and the One who loves us. We "talk" with God and He communicates with us through His Spirit and His Word. While it is not a typical conversation, we can maintain a "conversational" tone with God. Jesus, in the "Model Prayer" (Lord's Prayer) gave us an outline as to how we should pray. That outline is simple, it tells us that we should address God as "Our Father," then simply acknowledge His greatness and holiness. Following that, we pray for His kingdom (the Church) and His will to be done. The next part of our prayer is for ourselves, that He would bless us and forgive us in like manner, as we forgive others. We then pray for His guidance for our thoughts and actions finally to show that we recognize His great sovereign nature for evermore. If we follow this basic outline in our prayer time, we can never go wrong. This prayer was never intended to be repeated as Jesus prayed it; rather it was intended to be a "model" to teach us *how* to pray. Prayer should be as natural as breathing, sleeping, and eating.

By studying the life of Jesus, we see the need for a prayer life. Jesus, though the Son of God, never missed an opportunity to pray. At the beginning of His ministry, after His baptism, Jesus went into the wilderness to pray and fast. Prior to His choosing the "Twelve," He prayed all night (Luke 6:12). We see Him rising early in the morning to pray, and other times He prayed all night. In the Garden of Gethsemane, prior to his arrest, trial, and crucifixion, Jesus prayed *for hours*. As He was dying on the cross, His last words were in the form of a prayer. If the *perfect*, sinless Son of God needed to pray, how much more do we, as sinners, need to pray?

The early Church was a praying Church. One of the things mentioned in Acts 2:42 that they continued was *prayer*. The apostles were in prayer when the Holy Spirit came upon them prior to the birth of the Church. If we look at the lives of the apostles as recorded in the Book of Acts, we see a continuance of prayer. The Church was praying after Peter and John were released by the Sanhedrin (Acts 4:23-31). Stephen, while being stoned to death, prayed, and God gave him a vision of heaven (Acts 7:59-60). There are many other examples of prayer in Acts and the epistles that follow.

History is filled with men and women of God who prayed and were responsible for changing the world. Is it any wonder that President Abraham Lincoln, during the darkest days of the Civil War, was often seen in prayer; generals, admirals, and presidents throughout our nation's history, have been seen in prayer at times of greatest need. Can anyone forget the days after 9/11/01 how the nation came together in a time of prayer. Prayer is powerful and world events can be influenced by its great power. It is a natural act and should be viewed as such.

WHAT HAPPENS TO ME WHEN I PRAY?

As we think of prayer wondering what it does for me, we must, first, realize that prayer is worthless if we are not in submission to the will of God. God is *not* a heavenly Santa Claus Who grants us our every wish. He is not poised upon a throne with a bag full of "goodies" just waiting for us to ask for them. "What's in it for me?" is a life of spiritual blessings, the likes of which we will not be able to receive. God wants to *spiritually* bless us in ways we never imagined. Remember the old adage, "Be careful what you ask for, you just might get it!" This is ever so true with God. If we ask for spiritual blessings, we just might receive them, and they just might change our lives. When we are in the will of God and are seeking to serve Him, He will never leave us without. I cannot guarantee that you will get what you want, as God never promised us our wants. He has, however, promised us our "needs," and He is ready and willing to deliver on that promise and provide for us. Our service and attitude toward Him is the key. Far too many pray for *things*; when they are not rewarded with the things for which they ask, they are too quick to say, "See, I told you God does not answer prayer!" The real answer is that He *does* always answer prayer. It just may not be the answer we want!

 In answering our prayers with a "yes," "no," or "wait," God is in total control. We live in an "instant" society. We want, and even demand, that everything be done instantly. The internet was not *fast* enough; therefore, someone developed *high-speed* internet service. This is just one of many illustrations we could give. Suffice it to say that we are never satisfied with the word *wait*. "Patience" has become a dirty word to many in our society. It may take years to get an answer; however, remember that God knows what He is doing, and we must "wait upon the Lord." God is never wrong.

WHEN AND WHERE SHOULD I PRAY?

There is no such place as the "proper place" to pray and there is no time like the present to begin. We can pray anytime and anywhere. Since God is everywhere at once (omnipresent), He is all-powerful (omnipotent), and He knows everything (Omniscient), it matters not where we are and when we pray. God hears our every prayer! It should be said, however, that since we are creatures of habit, we should set aside time each day for prayer. If we do not do so, we tend to neglect this awesome tool God has placed at our disposal. We should have a time of personal devotion, Bible reading, and prayer. The more time we devote to these things, the more spiritual we will become. Whenever you follow these steps, make certain that you make allowances for interruptions. Do not let time get away without spending time with your heavenly Father.

WHAT ARE SOME THINGS THAT KEEP ME FROM PRAYING?

It is an easy thing to allow our minds to "wander." This can be and often is discouraging. Many find it difficult to keep "on message." This is a naturally occurring phenomenon and should not be discouraging. It is a human trait not to concentrate on something for a long period. Should you find yourself in this predicament, simply come back to your thoughts and continue. It might work best for you to pray "out loud."

Other times it may seem that your prayer is "dull" or "dry." Should this happen to you, try changing your own model. God will hear your prayer. Remember what Paul said in Romans 8:26-27, "In the same way, the Spirit helps our weakness. We do not know what we ought to pray for, but the Spirit Himself intercedes for us with groans that

Simply Speaking...

words cannot express. And He who searches our hearts knows the mind of the Spirit, because the Spirit intercedes for the saints in accordance with God's will" (NIV). This should lift the spirits of every Christian: to know that we have One who is able to take our prayers to God and "intercede" on our behalf since we do not know for what we ought to pray.

If you are not used to praying, five minutes may seem like an eternity. However, do not become discouraged. Time will become less and less a factor as your prayer life grows and as you become more comfortable in it. Remember, a new pair of shoes usually hurt your feet at first until they are "broken-in." Do not give up! God will assist you in your daily talk with Him. Remember that He loves you and longs for these "little chats."

CHAPTER SIXTEEN

WHAT DO WE DO WITH THE HOLY SPIRIT?

INTRODUCTION: A study of the work and presence of the Holy Spirit would require more than we can devote to it in this chapter. Our desire here is to simply introduce you to the Holy Spirit and leave you with a desire to learn more. There are many insightful books on this subject, and we would highly recommend your reading some of them. One of the best books on the subject is *Power From On High*, written by Dr. Jack Cottrell and published by College Press, Joplin, Mo.

The work of the Holy Spirit is most evident in the New Testament writings. He is also seen from the beginning of the Bible where in Genesis 1:2 we read, "Now the earth was formless and empty, darkness was over the face of the deep, and the *Spirit of God* was hovering over the waters" (NIV, emphasis mine). We, therefore, see that from the very beginning, before there was creation, the Holy Spirit was active.

From the Greek we see that the Spirit is closely associated with "breath." The idea of wind or breath is often used to denote the Holy Spirit. On Pentecost, the Spirit was seen as a "sound like the blowing of a violent *wind* came from heaven and filled the whole house where they were sitting" (Acts 2:2 NIV, emphasis mine). Paul wrote to Timothy, "All Scripture is *God-breathed* and is useful for teaching, rebuking, correcting and training in righteousness" (II Timothy 3:16 NIV, emphasis mine). The "God-breathed" Scripture is the work of the Holy Spirit.

WHAT IS HE DOING TODAY?

The Holy Spirit is as active, if not more so, today than at any other time in history. He has been active throughout time and became more prominent after Pentecost. We, as Christians, are baptized *into* His name, and we are promised "the gift of the Holy Spirit." That "gift" is the indwelling of the Spirit when we are immersed into Christ for the forgiveness of our sins.

Jesus promised His disciples that He would not leave them alone; rather, He would send the Holy Spirit who would guide them into all truth. In John 14:16, we read, "And I will ask the Father and He will give you another *Counselor* to be with you forever" (NIV, emphasis mine). This "Counselor" is the Holy Spirit, and He is, indeed, with us. He is the One who provides comfort and peace; He convicts us of our sins and points the way to repentance. He is the One who leads us into "all truth." It is by the Holy Spirit that we can read and understand the Word of God that He wrote. Is it not wonderful that we can have the "author" of the greatest Book ever written as our guide to understanding it? When we pray for and properly seek the Spirit's guidance, we can unlock the wisdom of God and know how to reach Him. This is the most powerful "tool" at our disposal and is so often ignored.

Since the King James Version of the Bible translates the word for "Holy Spirit" as "Holy Ghost," there has been much confusion regarding Him. The word "ghost" is a completely incorrect translation. The Holy Spirit is *not* a ghost. The word "ghost" as defined by Webster is as follows: "The spirit of a dead person which is believed to appear to or haunt living persons." Does any of that represent the Holy Spirit? Is He a "spirit of a *dead* person?" Should this be true, we would have to believe that God is *dead* or that Jesus was never raised from the dead! No, this is not a true representation of the Holy Spirit. He is alive, well, and living in every Christian. We need have no fear of Him as He takes up residence in us because He is there as a guide and as One who assists us in our Christian walk. Do not fear His presence. Accept it as a blessing and a loving gift from a loving Father, since that is exactly what He is to all Christians.

The Holy Spirit is active in conversion since it is He Who convicts us of sin. In John 16:8 we read, "When He (the Holy Spirit) comes, He will convict the world of guilt in regard to sin and righteousness and judgment" (NIV). (It would be good to read the entire context here, beginning with John 16:5-16. The Holy Spirit's coming is explained in great detail in this passage of Scripture.

The question might arise, "How does the Holy Spirit *convict* one of sin?" The answer is "through the Word!" Paul encouraged the church at Ephesus to "Take the helmet of salvation and the sword of the Spirit which is the Word of God" (Ephesians 6:17 NIV). James, in James 1:18 said, "He chose to give us birth through the Word of Truth, that we might be a kind of first-fruits of all He created" (NIV). Paul, in Romans 10, refers to the need to hear the Word. He told the Roman Church that it was necessary to *hear* the Word before one could "call upon the name of the Lord," and he questioned how this might happen without those who preach that Word (see Romans 10:14-15). In his writing to the Church at Corinth, Paul re-emphasized the importance of preaching when he said, "For since in the wisdom of God the world through its wisdom did not know Him, God was pleased through the foolishness of what was preached to save those who believe" (I Cor. 1:21 NIV).

The Holy Spirit uses the Word of God to convict people of their sins. As alluded to earlier in the chapter entitled "How Can I *Know* I Am Saved?" the Holy Spirit is most active through the Word and this is the manner in which He convicts of sin. It is not by some "feeling" that He uses to accomplish this feat.

The Holy Spirit is *active* in believers. We must understand that in order for the Holy Spirit to be *active* in us, we must be *active* in Him. The inactive Christian is not likely to use the power of the Holy Spirit in his or her everyday life. In Acts 5:32, the apostles were witnessing regarding Christ and said, "We are witnesses of these things, and so is the Holy Spirit, *whom God has given to those who obey Him*" (NIV, emphasis mine). In Galatians 4:6 Paul writes, "Because you are sons, God sent the Spirit of His Son into our hearts, the Spirit Who calls out, *Abba*, Father" (NIV). Paul wrote to the Roman Church in Romans 8:9, "You, however, are controlled not by the sinful nature, but by the Spirit, *if* the Spirit of God lives in you" (NIV, emphasis mine). We can see by these passages, and others (see Acts 2:38; I Corinthians 3:16; and 6:19-20) that the Holy Spirit is active in those who are active in Him.

Another purpose of the Spirit is to assist us in producing fruit. In Galatians 5:22-23, Paul lists the *Fruits of the Spirit*. In Ephesians 3:14-19, Paul prayed for the church that it might receive strength with "power through the Spirit." When we allow the Spirit to work within us, we can produce fruit to glorify God and grow His Church.

Looking still further in the purpose of the Holy Spirit, we see that He *sanctifies* the Christian. This word simply means "to make holy." We are to be "holy" because God is holy. It is important that as Christians we are sanctified or "set apart" for the service to which we have been called. The writer of Hebrews said in Hebrews 12:14, "Make every effort to live in peace with all men and to be holy; without holiness no one will see God" (NIV). In making the Christian "holy," the Spirit also provides intercession for us. He is the One who takes our prayers before the Most High God and speaks on our behalf. In Romans 8:26-27, Paul wrote, "In the same way, the Spirit helps us in our weakness. We do not know what we ought to pray for, but the Spirit, Himself, intercedes for us with groans that words cannot express. And He who searches our hearts knows the mind of the Spirit, because the Spirit intercedes for the saints in accordance with God's will" (NIV). This is a wonderful blessing since we are totally dependant on God's forgiveness.

WHAT ABOUT *SPIRITUAL GIFTS?*

We can define "Spiritual Gifts" as gifts given by the Holy Spirit that enabled Christians to do extraordinary things. These would be speaking in tongues (languages) not known by the speaker, the gift of interpreting that tongue (language), the gift of prophesy, the gifts of healing, wisdom, knowledge, extraordinary faith and others (see I Corinthians 12:1-11).

These gifts were given *after* baptism. In other words, there were *no* spiritual gifts given to anyone who was not a Christian (see Acts 19:1-7). There existed at the time of the First Century church a lapping over of John's baptism and that of the risen Christ. The baptism of John was insufficient to make one a Christian; therefore, there was a need to provide baptism "in the name of the Lord Jesus." Point being, these gifts were not given until after Christian baptism.

Simply Speaking. . .

The Spiritual gifts accompanied the "baptism of the Holy Spirit" (see Acts 2:4; 10:47-18—48). This was a special baptism given only at the beginning of the Church age and has not been repeated since. There is no need for such a baptism at this time because we have the written Word of God. This baptism occurred only twice in the New Testament, on Pentecost and at the household of Cornelius.

The question might arise as "to whom" and "by whom" were these gifts given? They were given *to* the apostles first and then *by* the apostles to those whom they deemed would use them wisely. In Acts 8:14-17, we read that these gifts were distributed in Samaria when Peter and John went there and "laid hands on them, and they received the Holy Spirit." Paul, in Romans 1:11 wrote, "I long to see you so that I may impart some Spiritual gift to make you strong. . ." Acts 8:18 clearly states that the gifts were given by "the apostles laying on of the apostles' hands." This shows that these gifts were given by the apostles and no other.

To answer the question of "purpose," we turn again to the Bible. One purpose was the revelation of the *Truth* (see I Corinthians 14:26-33). Another purpose is found in I Corinthians 12:7, "Now to each one the manifestation of the Spirit is given for the *common good*" (NIV, emphasis mine).

Still further, we read in Hebrews 2:1-4 the importance of remaining in the faith. In verse 4, the writer says, "God also testified to it by signs, wonders and various miracles, and *gifts of the Holy Spirit* distributed according to His will" (NIV, emphasis mine). After Jesus ascended into heaven, the final verse of Mark's Gospel account says, "Then the disciples went out and preached everywhere and the Lord worked with them and *confirmed His Word* by signs that accompanied them" (NIV, emphasis mine). Is there any doubt that the Lord used these Spiritual gifts to spread and confirm the Word that was being preached?

A final purpose for these gifts was to guide and edify the new Church (see I Corinthians 14:1-31 and Romans 1:11). In the infancy of the Church, as in the infancy of a human, there is much nurturing and education to be accomplished. This is reflected in the need and use of Spiritual gifts. They were to aid the Church to grow and establish itself. Since the Church is well established in this time, there exists no more need for such "gifts."

WHAT HAPPENED TO THE SPIRITUAL GIFTS?

The short answer is: they ceased! While this is true, there are reasons for their cessation. If one would carefully examine I Corinthians 12-14, one could easily see the demise of Spiritual gifts. In particular, one should view I Corinthians 13:8-12 as the most definitive statement regarding the fate of Spiritual gifts.

There are those today who would have us believe that these gifts are still available and that the Holy Spirit imparts them to those whom He has chosen. There is no evidence in the Scripture that these, or any other such gifts, would continue after the end of the "Apostolic Age."

Many who have claimed the "gift of healing" have been shown to be charlatans, while *others who have claimed the gift of "prophesy" have also been proven false.* There are those who may be able to perform miracles. Indeed, we were told that there would come false prophets and those who could perform many signs and wonders who were not of God. Remember the words of Jesus in Matthew 7:21-23. Jesus was referring to those who would attempt to "sneak" into the kingdom. He told them to depart from Him, "I never knew you!" There are those who have been empowered by Satan and can do many seemingly good things. These are done to confuse Christians, deceive them, and to lead them astray. It, unfortunately, works with many.

Just because someone does things in the Lord's name does not mean that they are of the Lord. We are to maintain vigilance that we will not be led astray. The proof is in the "continuing" to do the will of the Father. Are these "miracles" done for the glory of God or for the glory and profit of the "miracle worker?"

We simply need to understand that Spiritual gifts are no longer needed because we have the written Word of God and that, along with the guidance of the Holy Spirit, is sufficient.

IS THERE SUCH A THING AS AN *UNPARDONABLE SIN*?

In a word, "YES!" There can come a time when one can "grieve" the Holy Spirit to the point that He will leave and make no more effort to work within the spirit of that person. As to just *when* that time comes is variable. There is no set time or a particular "sin" that is so grievous that it cannot be forgiven. Take for example, those who crucified Christ; He asked that God would forgive them because they did not realize what they were doing. The "unpardonable sin" may be described as a "collection of sins" that makes one so unrepentant that they no longer desire to ask for forgiveness. It is a time in one's life when that person *chooses* to leave the Comforter and go out on his or her own without any restraint from the Spirit. When people get to the point that they no longer care about their relationship with the Lord through the Holy Spirit, then the Holy Spirit has no choice in the matter. The "leaving" was done by the individual more so than by the Holy Spirit.

The writer of Hebrews makes it quite clear that one can willfully sin to a point that there remains no more sacrifice for sin. In chapter ten, the author refers to the need to come together on the Lord's Day. He indicates that should we forsake the meeting around His table we are guilty of re-crucifying the Son of God and that "no sacrifice is left." There is no doubt that the author is referring to Christians and to no one else.

In the sixth chapter of Hebrews we read, "It is impossible for those who have been once enlightened, who have tasted the heavenly gift, who have shared in the *Holy Spirit*, who have tasted the goodness of the Word of God, and the powers of the coming age, *if they fall away*, to be brought back to repentance, because to their loss they are crucifying the Son of God all over again and subjecting Him to public disgrace" (Hebrews 6:4-6, NIV, emphasis mine). One can easily see here that the author is referring, again, to Christians who have fallen away. Note the first words of the reference, "*It is impossible.*" There comes a time when even the Holy Spirit is powerless. It is, however, not a hopeless situation. As long as people *return* in true repentance, realizing their sin and seeking forgiveness, they may be restored. It is only when there is no such repentance and *desire* to be restored that those who are in such a state will face an eternity without God.

Do not be afraid of such a state because this is reserved for those who have rejected the workings of the Holy Spirit, both in the un-believer and in the Christian.

CONCLUSION: The Holy Spirit is not an entity to fear or shun. He is a part of God and is given to those who are obedient to Him in baptism as a free gift. The Holy Spirit is someone to aid the believer in understanding the deep things of God and is important in our relationship with our Father. We should cherish this gift and allow Him to lead us in our walk with the Savior.

CHAPTER SEVENTEEN

WHAT ABOUT SPIRITUAL GIFTS?

INTRODUCTION: Spiritual gifts have been the source of much confusion among those who wear the Christian name. There are those within the Restoration Movement who believe that they still exist today despite overwhelming evidence to the contrary. Those who believe that spiritual gifts still exist in the Church today have not properly understood Paul's writing in I Corinthians 11, 12, and 13. Here Paul puts an end to the idea of spiritual gifts. It is in these three chapters that Paul reminds the Corinthian Church of the fact that these "gifts" were given for a specific reason and "when perfection comes, the imperfect disappears" (I Cor. 13:10 NIV). We shall begin our chapter on spiritual gifts with the following question:

WHAT WERE SPIRITUAL GIFTS?

Simply put, spiritual gifts were gifts from the Holy Spirit used by the first century Church for the purpose of edifying the Church. In other words, the "gifts" were employed to assist the Church in Spiritual growth. Those who received these gifts were to use them for a specific purpose and that was: to glorify God while building up the faith of those believers who might be struggling with their faith.

The most complete list of spiritual gifts is found in I Corinthians 12:8-11. It is in this listing that Paul reminds his readers that although these gifts were given to various people they were all from the same Spirit. There was no room for anyone to elevate himself or herself over another who had a different gift.

Any attempt to explain these gifts will meet with resistance because there is no definitive description given in the New Testament as to their nature. The following will be a brief explanation of those "gifts" listed in I Corinthians 12.

The message of wisdom. This first gift listed is not ordinary wisdom that may be gleaned from books or sitting at the feet of a learned person. It is an extraordinary gift that places *miraculous* wisdom in someone. The recipients would have not been able, on their own, to have gained this wisdom. It was a *special* wisdom that came directly from the Holy Spirit and given for specific events. James says in his letter that wisdom is available from God and all one needs do is ask (James 1:5). This is not the same "wisdom" as the miraculous wisdom of this gift. It does, however, tell all Christians that wisdom is available from Gods if we would simply ask for it. The overall purpose for such a miraculous wisdom is unclear, however, there may have arisen certain situations in the churches whereby someone (or more than one) may have had need to be able to make difficult decisions regarding spiritual matters. This "wisdom" would have been used to make the difficult decision facing the congregation. Jesus promised His followers, "For I will give you words and wisdom that none of your adversaries will be able to resist or contradict" (Luke 21:15 NIV). To see where this was accomplished see Acts 4:8-

14; 6:10. These references show clearly that the Spirit gave these men *words* and *wisdom* that they would not ordinarily possess.

The message of knowledge. This knowledge, as in the case of wisdom, is not gained by study or lecture; it is a *special knowledge* that came directly from the Holy Spirit. This knowledge was given to certain persons who could take the message of the Gospel to others without taking the time to *learn* it from being taught. Since in the infancy of the Church time was of the essence, it would have been a great gift to be able to spread the Word quickly and make disciples of many.

Faith. This gift was not "saving faith." This "faith" is the faith spoken of by Jesus in Matthew 17:20 when He said, "Because you have so little faith. I tell you the truth, if you have faith as small as mustard seed, you can say to this mountain, 'Move from here to there and it will move. Nothing will be impossible to you'" (NIV). Many read that verse and wonder why they cannot possess that kind of faith. They think that they are lacking in something because they cannot seem to have a faith that is that *strong*. Allow me to assure you that that "kind" of faith was given as a spiritual gift, was used to strengthen the Church, and exists no more. Paul refers to this same faith in I Corinthians 13:2 and equates it with the gifts of tongues, prophesy, and discernment, saying, ". . . and if I have a faith that can move mountains, but have not love, I am nothing" (NIV). This faith was given by the Holy Spirit and was not expected to be repeated in the modern age.

Gifts of healing. This "gift" is in the plural, *gifts*. The indication is that this is for the purpose of healing the various diseases that existed. It can easily be understood by examining the current medical professionals. Nearly every physician is a "specialist" in one part of the body or a specific disease. Though we will never (in this life) know for sure the reason there were "gifts" for healing, we can see examples of this in Acts 3:1-10; 9:32-35; and 28:7-10.

The gift of miraculous powers. This gift of "miraculous powers" or "working of miracles" was for extraordinary powers such as casting out demons (Acts 16:16-18), raising someone from the dead (Acts 9:36-42), the striking of one, Elymas, blind for his opposition to the Gospel (Acts 13:6-12), as well as other miracles recorded in the New Testament. This miraculous power would have included the "gift of healing" as well.

The gift of prophesy. When we think of prophesy, we normally think of someone who can foretell the future. While this is an act of a prophet, it is not the only thing a prophet does. The Old Testament prophets were able to reveal God's future developments as to the nations of Israel and Judah; however, they had an additional reason to prophesy. This second use of prophesy was *preaching* or presenting God's message to the people with the aid of the Holy Spirit. The prophets did more preaching than foretelling the future. There are various references in the Book of Acts as to people having the "gift of prophesy," (Acts 11:28; 15:32 and 21:9-10). Paul, in I Corinthians 14:5, 18-19 and 23-25, refers to this very gift as being greater than speaking in tongues.

The gift of distinguishing between spirits. The purpose of this gift was for one to be able to distinguish between false and true teachers/preachers. If there is any "gift" the Church could use today, it would be this gift. Unfortunately, we have come to the point whereby we desperately need, such a gift. With all the false doctrines being put forth today, it would be a wonderful tool to have someone in each congregation who could make the teachers and preachers *tell the Truth*! The person(s) with this gift would be in a position to tell the congregation when someone was teaching something false. Paul, Peter, and

John warn against such false prophets and teachers among the Christians at the time of their writings; how much more exists false teachers/ preachers today than then? Peter, in II Peter 2:1, gives this warning, "But there were also false prophets among the people, just as there will be false teachers among you" (NIV). Peter is advising his readers that this is no new phenomenon; since there were false prophets among the Jews, there will also be false teachers in the Church. With this gift, those who had it could warn the Christians as to who were and who were not teaching the Truth.

The gift of tongues. This reference is to being able to speak *languages* previously unknown to the speaker. This is first observed at Pentecost when the apostles were enabled by the Holy Spirit to speak in other *languages* and other *dialects* that were totally unknown to them. The necessity is seen in the fact that there were many gathered at Jerusalem who did not speak Aramaic (the language spoken by the apostles). In viewing Acts 2:4 and 7-8, it is clear that the "gift of tongues" was truly languages, not some foreign tongue known to no one. This gift accompanied the "baptism of the Holy Spirit" which occurred only twice in the New Testament, Acts 2 and Acts 10:44-ff. There are no other references to this "baptism." There are, however, other references to "speaking in tongues," and each of these references has to do with languages. We will examine this gift in more detail later since most of the controversy regarding spiritual gifts revolves around this one.

The gift of interpretation of tongues. Imagine that you were in another country where your native language was not spoken. You attend a church service and can understand everything being said in your native language because there is someone who does not know your language who is able to interpret it for you. This is what is meant by this gift. It is simply the ability to speak the language of the hearer even though the interpreter has no such *learned* or *natural* ability.

HOW WERE THESE GIFTS GIVEN?

There were only two ways to receive these gifts. One, as already mentioned, was directly by the Holy Spirit though the "baptism of the Holy Spirit." The other was by "prayer and the laying on of hands by the *apostles*." This latter means was a direct result of their being able to impart such spiritual gifts as the Spirit gave them the ability to do so. It is important to note that when the apostles died, there was no other way to receive these gifts. This being true, there is no manner in which to receive these gifts today!

In the Book of Acts we see this brought out very clearly. In Acts 8:14-17, we read, "When the apostles in Jerusalem heard that Samaria had accepted the Word of God, they sent Peter and John to them. When they arrived, they *prayed* for them that they might receive the Holy Spirit because the Holy Spirit had not yet come upon any of them; they had simply been baptized into the name of the Lord Jesus. Then Peter and John *placed their hands on them*, and they received the Holy Spirit" (NIV, emphasis mine). It is clear that Phillip, an evangelist, could not give these gifts, even though he most likely possessed one or more of them. Had he been able to do so, there would have been no need for Peter and John to make the journey. This is not to be confused with "receiving the gift of the Holy Spirit," which is the indwelling of the Spirit given at baptism (Acts 2:38).

Secondly, the Apostle Paul, in Acts 19:1-6, is in Ephesus and found disciples of John the Baptizer who had not received the Holy Spirit because they had not received the baptism of the Church. They had not even heard of the Holy Spirit (Acts 19:2). Paul, after teaching them about Jesus, baptized them into Christ, laid hands upon them, and they were able to speak in tongues and prophesy (Acts 19:6).

While these are the only examples of the manner in which these gifts were given, it is sufficient to see that it required the apostles to impart these gifts.

TO WHOM WERE THESE GIFTS GIVEN?

It is important to note here that the recipients of these gifts were *Christians*. In Acts 8 we learn that a certain person named Simon and referred to as a sorcerer, wanted to *purchase* these gifts. Simon was a Christian, yet rebuked by Peter because of his desire to purchase these spiritual gifts with money. Peter said to Simon, "May your money perish with you, because you thought you could buy the gift of God with money! You have no part or share in this ministry, because your heart is not right before God. Repent of this wickedness and pray to the Lord. *Perhaps* He will forgive you for having such a thought in your heart. For I see that you are full of bitterness and captive to sin" (Acts 8:20-23, NIV, emphasis mine). This not only shows that the gifts of the Spirit are not for sale, it also shows that one who has believed and has been baptized can fall away. Peter uses the word "perhaps" God will forgive him, not stating that because he was a Christian, forgiveness was *automatic*.

It is a stretch to believe that Timothy could have received a spiritual gift by the laying on of hands by the elders. Paul writes in I Timothy 4:14, "Do not neglect your gift, which was given you though a prophetic message when the body of elders laid their hands on you" (NIV). This reference is most likely to the time when Timothy was ordained to the ministry. Though Paul is not clear here, it most likely has to do with a reference to Timothy's "gift" of preaching.

There is no evidence that *every* Christian was given a "gift." The Spirit apparently chose those to whom the gifts were to be given and there is no evidence that the apostles, in imparting these gifts, were able to determine which gift(s) a recipient was to receive. This is evidenced in Paul's statement in I Corinthians 14:1-5 in which he says that he would have all of them speak in tongues, but more to the point he would rather they have the gift of prophesy. It would appear that Paul had no control over the particular gift given by the Spirit. There was no promise that anyone would have a particular gift, if any at all. No one was to seek out a particular gift since the Spirit gave to those whom He wanted to have them.

FOR WHAT PURPOSE WERE THESE GIFTS GIVEN?

The primary purpose for these gifts was to strengthen the Church. Paul, in I Corinthians 12:7, said, "Now to each one the manifestation of the Spirit is given for the common good" (NIV). This is simply stating that the *purpose* of these gifts was for the common good of the *entire* assembly. Those who possessed these gifts were to use them to edify or build up the congregation and not for their own purposes. In I Corinthians 14:26 Paul writes, "What shall we say, brothers? When you come together, everyone has a hymn, or a word of instruction, a revelation, a tongue, or an interpretation. *All* of these must be done for the strengthening of the church" (NIV, emphasis mine).

"How were these gifts used to strengthen the church?" you might ask. Paul gave the answer in I Corinthians 14:26. Just as he said that through bringing a hymn (singing), a word of instruction (teaching), a revelation (revealing the Truth of God as it has been revealed to this person), a tongue or an interpretation (one who could speak a language foreign to him or the one who interpreted that language to others), all of these were to be used in strengthening the church. The need for these gifts was great in the early days of the Church since the New Testament was not yet completed.

Another purpose of these gifts was to protect the Church from false teachers. As earlier stated there were many false prophets in the early Church. The goal of Satan (through these false teachers) was to destroy the Church in its infancy. I John 4:1 says, "Dear friends, do not believe every spirit, but test the spirits to see if they are from God, because many false prophets have gone out into the world" (NIV). It was important that the discerning of spirits be accomplished to protect the believers from these false teachers. We do not have such a gift today because we have the completed New Testament. The sad fact is that the false teachers today are using the same Bible to "prove" their points.

A second part of this protection was in the "gift of prophesy." This gift is well seen when a prophet named Agabus had a vision that there would be a severe famine in the entire Roman world. Having had this vision and advising the Church at Antioch, they decided to assist the Christians in Judea and sent their offerings to the elders by Barnabas and Saul (Paul), (Acts 11:27-30).

A third purpose of these gifts was the confirmation of the Word. Since the New Testament was not complete at this time, it was important and necessary that there be some confirmation as to what was being taught was being confirmed by God. Another reason we no longer need these gifts is found in the Gospel of John as he closes his Gospel account. John 20:31 says, "But these are written that you may believe that Jesus is the Christ, the Son of God, and that by believing you may have life in His Name" (NIV). With this in mind, we can easily see that the New

Testament was written for this purpose, to make believers. The New Testament not only testifies about the Lord, it *confirms itself*. The miracles, etc., that accompanied the early disciples, teachers, and evangelists were necessary to "get the point across." The Holy Spirit uses a different tactic today since the written Word is available.

HOW LONG DID THESE GIFTS LAST?

From the inception of these gifts there was no intent that they should be permanent. I Corinthians 13 makes this fact quite clear. Many see this chapter as the "love" chapter. While it does consider the importance of love in the life of the Christian, it is easily seen, when taken in context, that it is referring to the demise of spiritual gifts. In verses 8-10 Paul makes it quite clear that "love never fails." On the other hand, prophesies shall cease, tongues will be stilled, and knowledge shall pass away. This is an indication that there would come a time when these gifts, as a whole, would cease. There are two schools of thought on the time when the end would come. One of these says that these gifts shall cease when the end of time comes. These believers conclude that the references in I Corinthians 13 refer to the time when the church will be taken up into heaven at the end of the world. The "perfection" referred to here is the "perfect redemption" when Christ returns. The other school of thought holds that the term "perfect" refers to the completion of the New Testament and the distribution of it. This would be the "perfection" of the revelation of God and at the time of the death of the last person, who was granted these gifts at the hands of the apostles, marked the end of the gifts.

There are some compelling reasons for believing the later view. Some of those reasons follow:

First reason is that these gifts belonged to a time when the church was young. I Corinthians 13:11 Paul writes, "When I was a child, I talked like a child, I reasoned like a child. When I became a man, I put childish ways behind me" (NIV). The thought here is that Paul is referring to the infancy of the Church and that it needed these gifts to grow. These gifts served as a "tool" to assist in the building of the Church. When the Church reached maturity, these "tools" were no longer needed. For those who would long for the return of these gifts, we can only ask them, "Why would you desire to return to your infancy?"

A second reason for the demise of the spiritual gifts is found in the fact that there is no one left who can impart these gifts. Since the gifts were given through "prayer and the laying on of hands" by the *apostles* (who are all deceased), there is no one left who can deliver these gifts. If one might say, "The Holy Spirit can do as He pleases and deliver these gifts in any manner He chooses," I would totally agree. However, the Holy Spirit *chose* to deliver the gifts by the apostles and no other means stated in the New Testament. Since this is the case, I see no reason to believe that He has had a change of mind in this century or at any other time.

A third reason for the cessation of gifts may be found in the fact that they are no longer needed. The reason for the gifts in the first place, as previously stated, was to strengthen the body of believers and provide "proof" as to the validity of those bringing the Word of God. The full revelation of God now exists in the completed Bible; therefore, there no longer exists a need for these gifts.

All the evidence in the New Testament points to the fact that these gifts were used for a specific purpose and that the need for them has ceased. Since God is not one to be redundant, it can easily be seen that the spiritual gifts have done what they were intended to do and that they are from another era in the rich history of the Church.

A FURTHER LOOK AT THE "GIFT OF TONGUES"

There are but three examples in the Book of Acts where "speaking in tongues" are mentioned. They are Acts 2:14; 10:44-46, and 19:1-6. In the first two, they accompanied the only reference to the "Baptism of the Holy Spirit," and in the third, the reference is to a time when Paul bestowed the gift upon twelve men in Ephesus. Surprisingly these are the *only* references to the gift of speaking in tongues in The Book of Acts. With the first two, the sign was given as a herald of the coming of the Holy Spirit on someone(s). As on Pentecost, the sign was that the Holy Spirit had come upon the apostles, and in the second, the Holy Spirit had come upon the household of Cornelius to show Peter that God had ordained the preaching of the Gospel to the Gentiles. In the case of the third, Paul encountered believers in Ephesus who had not been baptized into the name of Jesus, rather only the baptism of John the Baptizer. After Paul baptized them into the name of Jesus, he gave them the gift of speaking in tongues and the gift of prophesy. It is likely that this was done to glorify God and edify the Church at Ephesus. The same Greek word, *glossa*, is used in all the above cases. This word means *language* and refers to their being able to speak *languages* with which they were not familiar.

The only other mention of "speaking in tongues" occurs in Paul's first letter to the Corinthian Church. In chapters 12-14, he refers to them as the lowest of all gifts. Those who believe that the use of tongues as indicated in chapter 14 as unknown sounds or "the language of mystery" is found in verse 2, "For anyone who speaks in a tongue does not speak to men but to God. Indeed, no one understands him; he utters mysteries with his spirit" (NIV). The argument is:

1) The speech is addressed to God, not to man (Vs. 2, 28).
2) The person doing the speaking does so in "mystery" (v. 2).
3) The person speaking does so for his own edification and for no one else (4).
4) The speaker's "mind is unfruitful as he speaks in his 'spirit'" (v. 14).
5) The question arises, "How can those who do not understand say 'amen' when he does not understand?" (v. 16).
6) Those who do not understand will think the speaker is "out of his mind!" (v. 23).

While those who do not accept the idea of speaking in tongues in the Church today will accept the aforementioned arguments as factual, it can be said that these arguments also apply to *languages*. If the speaker were speaking in a language foreign to him, then it would make sense that he may well not understand what he is saying. The speaker is relying on the Holy Spirit to say what he should be saying. This, then, would be a "mystery" to him. Were it true that no one understood what he was saying (including himself), where would be the edification of the church? It is no wonder that anyone coming in from outside the faith would likely think that the speaker had, indeed, lost his mind. Paul makes it quite clear that he could out-speak all of them in tongues, but that he would "rather speak five intelligible words to instruct others than ten thousand words in a tongue" (NIV), the point being that when these "tongues" were used, they were used to edify (build up) the faithful, not to glorify oneself.

The original language does not include the word *unknown*. Those who have added this word have created a meaning not originally intended by Paul. When anyone attempts to *add* to or *take away* from the Word of God, those people are creating something not intended by the Holy Spirit and are dealing with a dangerous situation. It is best to allow the writers of the Bible who spoke with the aid of the Holy Spirit to have the final say and not attempt to create something else entirely.

CONCLUSION: While it is clear that much more can and has been said on the subject of spiritual gifts, and especially the gift of speaking in tongues, my hope is that I have piqued your interest to the point that you will learn more on this subject.

CHAPTER EIGHTEEN

WHAT CAN I DO TO SERVE?

INTRODUCTION: "Now that I am a Christian how can I be of service?" Far too many Christians want to "sit out" the service aspect of Christianity. They like the fact that they can attend a large church in which they can "get lost" and not be asked to serve. They want to attend church services when they have nothing else to do and feel good about their Christianity. A life of service is an experience that brings us untold blessings and prepares us for heaven. We need only look at the life of Christ to see that service was His passion. Let us examine some of His sayings about service. Matthew 20:28 (NIV) says, "just as the Son of Man did not come to be served, but to serve, and give His life a ransom for many." A short time later Matthew records these words of Jesus in 23:11, "The greatest among you will be your servant." Luke 22:27 (NIV) says, "For who is greater, the one who is at he table or the one who serves? Is it not the one who is at the table? But I am among you as one who serves." Jesus did not come to be served by others even though He was King of kings. Rather, He came to be the servant of all. Consider Jesus actions just prior to His arrest when He washed the feet of His disciples. Jesus was a most humble servant. His greatest service was His giving

His life for us. His life is our most supreme example of service.

WHAT KIND OF SERVICE WILL GLORIFY GOD?

I grew up on a farm and one of my "chores" was to gather the eggs from the henhouse. I never saw a human sitting in a henhouse expecting to lay an egg. The same is true of 'Christians. We cannot expect to sit on a church pew weekly and consider that service. The kind of service that will glorify and please God is one of sacrificial service. There are those who will come to "church" regularly and think that they have served because they have sat through a "church service." James tells us to be *doers* of the Word. In James 1:22 (NIV) we are told, "Do not merely listen to the Word, and so deceive yourselves. Do what it says." It is simply not enough to hear the Word of God; we must *practice* it. God has called His people to a lifetime commitment of service. This involves action. We must serve His Church in any way that will glorify Him. If this means working in the nursery, Children's Church, youth groups, cleaning, painting, showing up for certain "clean-up" days, sharing the Gospel by visiting un-believers; whatever needs to be done. It has been said that 100% of the work of the church is done by 20% of the people. This is sad because the other 80% of the Christians are missing blessings from God. Christianity can be as worthless as the faith of the Pharisees unless the Christians are people of action. We must have a positive role in the Lord's service to please Him.

WHO CAN SERVE?

There are those in the Church who are of the opinion that God has given certain "talents" to certain ones and they are the only ones who are "called" to serve. Nothing could be farther from the truth. God has called *everyone* who wears His name to serve Him. It may be as simple as a phone call or a handwritten note or card. There are no exceptions or exemptions. As long as we are able to do anything, we are called to serve. Jesus spoke of those who could only give a cup of water as His servants.

Others are of the mindset that they are "exempt" from service because they are "too busy" doing other things. When we accept Christ as our Savior, we are taking on an entirely new way of life. That is the meaning of "rising to walk in newness of life." Life is filled with "decisions." We make decisions daily and often do not even realize that we are making them. We must *decide* to serve the Lord. See the decision made by Joshua recorded in Joshua 24:15. The setting is at Scechem and the subject is "Covent Renewal." Joshua challenges Israel to remember the covenant relationship between themselves and God. In this verse, he says, "But if serving the Lord seems undesirable to you, then choose for yourselves this day whom you will serve, whether the gods of your forefathers beyond the River, or the gods of the Amorites, in whose land you are living. But as for me and my household, we will serve the Lord." Joshua was making it personal and giving the people a choice; but requiring them to *choose* whom they would serve. The point is that we will serve something. Whether we serve the God Who has redeemed us, ourselves, or other gods. It is true that we become like that which we revere. Should we choose to serve an entity other than God we will become like unto it. God was not kidding when He said, "You shall have no other gods before me" (Exodus 20:2b NIV). He must be *first* and take priority in all our decisions.

WHAT ARE SOME WAYS I CAN SERVE?

One way is in the life we live. In other words, then Christian life to which we have been called. We should live the kind of life that will glorify our Heavenly Father. When people see us, they will know Whom we serve by our actions and the example we set will be Christlike. The language we employ, the attitude we present, and our honesty are but a few things that show the new life we have in Christ. We should all be walking sermons.

A second way of service is through prayer. All of us are capable of praying and prayer aids us in our own spiritual life. We should not only pray for ourselves, but also for our church, its leaders, our families, the sick (both spiritually and physically), missionaries and many others with whom we come in contact. Remember that all prayer is answered (see chapter on prayer).

A third manner in which service can be rendered is by being active in worship services. Attending worship services and actively participating in them is an important manner of service. It is not to simply sit in the pew and "watch" what happens. While not everyone can be active at the same time, this would cause chaos, there are always things one can find to do that will enhance the worship services. Your attendance at the worship service and other services of the Church are very important. It may be by your example that others will come to know Christ by your devotion to being in worship services. Far too many Christians seek and find every excuse to "stay home" on the Lord's Day and at other times when they should be in the church building worshipping God. When you are in a worship service, it is incumbent upon you to "pay attention." The attentiveness you display will assist others in doing the same. None of us can learn and properly worship when we allow our minds to wander. Should you be bored or otherwise inattentive, you are allowing Satan to exercise his control over your life. Open you heart, mind and spirit so that the Holy Spirit can communicate with you and you can grow in knowledge. It is the hearers' responsibility to *listen* to what is being taught or preached.

A fourth way to serve is to participate in the song service. In this day of controversy over the "style" of worship, we can all find a place where we can feel comfortable. Should you be a "traditionalist" and want to use the piano and organ as accompaniment for the old hymns, you can find churches still worshipping in this style. Should you be more comfortable with "contemporary" music, a more upbeat style, there are places that can meet those needs as well. Some churches offer "blended" styles in which they offer some of each, while other churches offer two or more, services where both styles are offered separately. Still others adhere to strictly one or the other. Whatever style suites your fancy, it is available somewhere and there is no excuse for not attending. Many in our "Restoration" heritage choose no instruments at all. We must recognize their right to worship with an a cappella style should that be their desire. Making a "test of fellowship" over any worship style is against God's desire for unity among His children.

Many can serve by "calling." While the practice of "knocking on doors" is, in many areas, outdated, we can still call upon those who have expressed an interest in knowing more about the Lord and His Church. Many people within "our circle" do not know the Lord. We should make an effort to reach them for Christ and share the Gospel with them. There are also many "shut-ins" who would love a call from a fellow Christian as many of them are alone and lonely.

Perhaps you have the "gift of teaching." There is a need for those who can teach the Bible in our churches today. While there is a definite shortage of preachers, there is an equal shortage of competent and qualified teachers of the Word. The "Children's Ministry" is a great place for many.

While the above is simply a short list of ways to serve, it gives a beginning. There are many others ministries in which you can serve. Seek and find the ministry that best suits your abilities. There is no real Christianity without service.

CHAPTER NINETEEN

DO I HAVE TO GIVE MY MONEY?

INTRODUCTION: Now comes the *hard* part. "You preachers are all alike! All you are interested in is my money!" I have heard variations of this theme many times. Why, do you suppose, it is so difficult for people to learn to be "cheerful givers?" We live in the most charitable nation ever in the history of the world. Up to this point, you may have been in agreement with what you have read. Let there be a need in the community, and people will "dig deep" in their wallets to give to it and feel good about having helped. When the Church has financial needs, however, it is the same old song, "What do they need more money for now? They seem only to waste what they have!" I must admit that this is a difficult area for me to discuss. It is not that I do not give, because I give with joy; it is because there seems to be reluctance in me to ask others to do so. I know that the Lord expects His followers to give with a cheerful heart and not give grudgingly; however, it is still difficult for me to preach on giving. Perhaps it is because many feel uncomfortable hearing sermons on this subject.

Simply Speaking. . .

The old adage, "You can't take it with you" is so true. Some, however, act as though they are not going to "go," still others believe that they have worked so hard for what is *rightfully theirs* and they feel no need to share anything with God.

In this chapter we will explore the manner in which giving effects each Christian, both positively and negatively.

WHAT IS MY RESPONSIBILITY TO GOD?

Jesus, in Matthew 22:21, said, "Give to Caesar what is Caesar's and to God what is God's" (NIV). This was in response to a question on the subject of paying taxes. No one enjoys paying taxes, yet Jesus said that we should do so, and, furthermore we should give to God what is rightfully His. This is to say that in the same manner in which earthly governments have needs, so does God's spiritual kingdom.

Never consider God as being *needy*. God *owns* all things and is not in "need" of our financial aid. His kingdom, however, has certain needs that must be met. Paul, in speaking to the Greeks on Mars Hill said, "The God who made the world and everything in it is the Lord of heaven and earth and does not live in temples built by hands. And He is not served by human hands, as if He needed anything, because He Himself gives all men life and breath and everything else" (Acts 17:24-25 NIV). Our offerings do not "support" God; however, giving is the manner in which God ordained that the Gospel be spread around the world. We have a very real obligation to give, and we should consider it an honor to share our financial gain to advance the kingdom of God.

Giving is a form of worship. Worship is far more than simply coming to a church service on Sunday morning.

Worship has many aspects, and one of them is *giving* our money. In I Chronicles 16:29 we read, "Ascribe to the Lord the glory due His name. *Bring an offering* and come before Him; worship the Lord in the splendor of His holiness" (NIV, emphasis mine). The inference here is that we should "bring an offering" when we present ourselves before God in worship. This is as much a part of worship as is singing, fellowship, the Lord's Supper or anything else!

DO I HAVE TO "TITHE?"

The "tithe" was a requirement of God for the Children of Israel to bring one-tenth of *everything* they had to God and present it to Him as an offering. The practice actually predates the giving of the law when Abraham gave a "tithe" to Melchisedec, king of Salem and a high priest. This was not just one-tenth of their money; rather it was one-tenth of all they possessed. The practice continued through the time of Malachi where Malachi wrote in 3:10 (NIV), "Bring the whole tithe into the storehouse, that there may be food in my house. Test me in this, says the Lord almighty, and see if I will not throw open the floodgates of heaven and pour out so much blessing that you will not have room enough for it." When we speak of a "tithe" today, we usually mean one-tenth of our *net* income. This income is that which is "left over" after taxes and other deductions. If we were going to tithe, we would be *required* not only to give one-tenth of our *gross* income (that received before deductions), but one-tenth of everything else we have. There is much controversy as to just how much and on what basis we should give.

Tithing is not limited to the Old Testament. Jesus commended the Pharisees for their devotion to the tithe (see Matthew 23:23). While the Pharisees were negligent in many areas of their personal lives, they were, at least, faithful in their giving.

We see in Acts, chapter four, that the early Church was a giving Church. When a food crisis arose among them, they sold their possessions in order to provide for those in need. Paul advised the Corinthian church to give. He says in II Corinthians 8:7 (NIV), "But just as you excel in everything—in faith, in speech, in knowledge, in complete earnestness, and in your love for us—see that you also excel in this *grace of giving*" (emphasis mine). Paul continues this theme throughout this chapter and through chapter nine. It is in chapter nine, verse seven, that Paul writes, "Each man should give what he has decided in his heart to give, not reluctantly or under compulsion, for God loves a cheerful giver." Paul earlier, in I Corinthians 16:2 (NIV), giving instruction as to when to give, writes, "On the first day of every week, each one of you should set aside a sum of money in keeping with his income, saving it up, so that when I come, no collections will have to be made." Can there be any doubt as to when and whether we should give?

The principle of the tithe, far from being abolished, is given a loftier place in the concept of giving in the New Testament. Since we, as Christians, are under grace and not the law, should have a greater desire to give more than the Jews were *required* to do. Since Calvary was more than Sinai, the Christian, who has been far more blessed by God than the Jew, should feel a stronger desire to give as God has prospered him. This should mean that giving one-tenth of one's income should be a starting point and proceed from there.

We must realize that all things are owned by God. Since He created all things, He owns all things. We read in Genesis 1:1, "In the beginning *God created* the heavens and the earth" NIV, emphasis mine). It was God who created

Simply Speaking. . .

everything, including humankind. Since He created everything, He owns everything. Moses wrote in Deuteronomy 10:14, "To the Lord your God belong the heavens, the earth and *everything in it*" (NIV, emphasis mine). In Psalm 24:1-2, David addressed the question of ownership by writing, "The earth is the Lord's, *and everything in it, the world and all who live in it;* for He founded it upon the seas and established it upon the waters" (NIV, emphasis mine). We see here that not only all things belong to God, but all people as well.

This being true, we should understand that we are but *stewards* of the things on earth, including our own bodies. Since we *own* nothing, we are left to realize that we are simply caretakers of that with which God has blessed us. It is unfortunate that many Christians believe that they give to the church because they *must*. This is an incorrect attitude and should be corrected immediately.

If we were to view the things God has *given* to us when we deserved nothing, we would change our attitudes about giving. Let us examine, briefly, some of the gifts from God:

- HIS SON. God, under no compulsion, gave His "only begotten Son" to bring salvation to a people who had all but rejected Him (see John 3:16).
- SALVATION FROM OUR SINS. The reason God gave His Son was to provide this great salvation to us. It is a *gift*. It means that no one can purchase salvation; it is by the grace of God that we are saved. There is nothing we can *do* to earn it; we simply receive it by faith and obedience to God.
- ETERNAL LIFE. The result of this salvation is eternal life with God in heaven. The end result of it all is that we are permitted to spend eternity with Him and not in hell.

Simply Speaking...

There are many other "gifts" from God in this life too numerous to mention here. Since we are so blessed, we should have a strong desire to give to the work of God here in this world.

To answer the question posed at the beginning of this section, "Do I have to tithe?" The answer is not a simple one. There is no repeat of the commandment of tithing in the New Testament. We are asked to give as "God has prospered us," however. The tithe is a great place to begin, and we should give more than this amount.

Because God is a generous and loving God, He will bless each of us who give and will withhold His blessings from those who do not give. This is the *negative* aspect of not giving. God will withhold His blessings. I do not know of anyone who does not want God's continued blessings, and one way to keep them coming is to continue to give.

WHAT CONSTITUTES LIBERAL GIVING?

"Liberal giving" means different things to different people. Some will make reference to the "widow" referred to by Jesus in Luke 21:1-3. Jesus said of her, "This poor widow has put in more than all the others" (NIV). The fact is that she put in only "two very small copper coins." How could this be more than all the others? The answer is, simply because she gave "out of her poverty." This poor woman had very little, and she was willing to give possibly the last she had to the temple, while the others gave only a small portion of what they had. Liberal giving is conditional on what we have.

Those who have much and give only a small amount of that wealth, even though it may be a lot of money, are not giving liberally. You may have heard the old saying, "Give until it hurts; then give until it feels good!" This may be a good idea. Some think they are giving a lot, when, in reality, they are giving very little.

In the Book of Acts, it is said of the early Church that they sold all that they had and pooled their resources so that no one had a need. There is even an account of a husband and wife who lied and said that they had brought *all the proceeds* of their sale to the Church. Peter told each of them, in turn, that they had "lied to the Holy Spirit" and they each fell dead and were carried out and buried (See Acts 5:1-11).

If we give "as the Lord has prospered us" we will give generously and liberally with no malice and without hesitation.

OTHER REASONS TO GIVE

We should give to advance the kingdom of God. Our monetary gifts are to provide for those who are bringing the message of God to the world, both at home and abroad. There exists in this time a "paid ministry." Whether this is a New Testament office is subject to debate and not a subject that shall be addressed here. The fact remains that these ministers, who give up their opportunities in the secular world to devote themselves to the preaching and teaching in the Church, must be compensated. The precedent for this is seen when God established the Nation of Israel. He gave to each of the twelve tribes a plot of land except the Tribe of Levi. To them, God gave the priesthood and told the other eleven tribes to care for them and give one-tenth to their support. It is, then, up to those of the local congregation to provide for their welfare. Many, however, are of the mindset, "Lord, You keep him humble; we will keep him poor!" This is unfortunate for many reasons. While the minister(s) should not "be in it for the money," they are "worthy of their hire" and should be compensated in accor-

Simply Speaking...

dance with the work they are called upon to do. There are many other "needs" of a local church. There are ongoing commitments with respect to the utility bills, literature, programs, etc., which must be met. Many churches operate under a budget, which is an intelligent manner in which to operate. It allows the congregation to know the weekly needs of said budget.

Another important reason to give is to provide for those who are giving themselves in missions around the country and world. Many have given their lives; some literally, in bring the Word of God to the world. They rely upon the support of local congregations to provide for their daily needs. It is not easy to give up the "comforts of home" to serve the Lord in other lands.

One very important reason to give is because we will stand before the judgment bar of God and "receive an account of the deeds done in the flesh." This will include giving, or lack thereof. During the "Sermon on the Mount," Jesus said, "Do not store up for yourselves treasures on earth, where moths and rust destroy, and where thieves break in and steal. But store up for yourselves treasures in heaven, where moth and rust do not destroy, and where thieves do not break in and steal. *For where your treasure is, there your heart will be also*" (Matthew 6:19-21 NIV, emphasis mine). It is quite clear from this passage of Scripture that our hearts are where our treasure is. If our money is our "treasure," then we will burn up with it; if our money is used for the advancement of the kingdom, we will be blessed as will many others.

Jesus also gave us another reason to consider our worldly wealth when He said, "I tell you the truth, it is hard for a rich man to enter the kingdom of heaven. Again I tell you, it is easier for a camel to go through the eye of a needle than for a rich man to enter the kingdom of God" (Matthew 19:23-24 NIV). This was in response to the rich young man who came to Jesus and asked what he needed to do to get eternal life. Jesus told him to go and sell all that he had and give to the poor and come and follow Him (Jesus). The young man refused because he was quite wealthy. The point of this is not that rich people cannot be saved. It is simply that when the money comes between the holder and the service of Christ, the money is of greater import than that service. When we refuse to give as we have been prospered, we are like this young man in that our money is more important than our worship through giving.

CHAPTER TWENTY

WHAT PLACE DOES LOVE HAVE IN THE CHRISTIAN LIFE?

INTRODUCTION: Millions of books and millions of songs have been written about the idea of love. When one is asked to describe or define *love*, we see just how elusive a description or definition can be. Love is the "glue" that binds us together. An experiment was conducted some years ago in an orphanage in a European country where babies were separated into two control groups. The babies in one of these groups received everything they needed. They were well fed, diapers changed, cared for in every aspect *except* one: they received no love. They were never held or nurtured in any loving way. It would have been as though machines did for them. The other group received the exact same care with the addition of love. Not surprisingly, the babies in the first group did not fare very well, and many of them died, while the babies in the second group thrived. The only difference was that the second group was *loved*. The power of love is enormous. When people do not feel loved, they are more likely to be criminals, sociopaths, and other negatives aspects of society. A marriage cannot survive where no love is shown. We could go on and on with examples of negative things in society where there is a lack of love. We shall, however, turn our attention to Christian love.

SOME DEFINITIONS OF LOVE

Since the New Testament was written in Greek, it is difficult to completely understand Christian love without some knowledge of the original language. The Greek language has four words for love. They are: *eros, philia, storge,* and *agape.* It is not my intention to delve deeply into the meanings of each of these words or to take up much time in explaining them; however, it is important that we know a little about each one.

Eros is a word used primarily to describe a love between man and woman. It speaks to a sexual type of love or a physical love. Although this word does not appear in the New Testament, it is a strong Greek word for love.

Phila is a word used to describe an intimacy or a warm personal affection one has for others. It would include the word *like*, as in "I *like* you." This word was used most often in the context of a personal relationship and may even include a physical relationship. This word is used in John 5:20 where Jesus is speaking of the love the Father has for the Son, ""For the Father *loves* (phila) the Son and shows Him all He does. Yes, to your amazement He will show Him even greater things than these" (NIV, emphasis mine). It is also used to describe a type of God's feelings for His children (see John 16:27).

The third Greek word, also not found in the New Testament, is *storge*. This word is most often found in Greek writings and relates to a familial type of love. This would be a love between parents, children and siblings.

Simply Speaking...

The final Greek word for love is *agape*. This is the most often used word for love in the New Testament. This word is most powerful and relates the love for God to His children, the love for Christians to God, and the love for each other. There exists no more powerful and forceful word on the planet. When one refers to *agape* (love), one is making it an act of will. This is not some mere feeling or emotion; it is something that we have a very strong *desire to do*. It is because of this that Jesus was able to say, "A new command I give you: *Love* one another. As I have *loved* you, so you must *love* one another. By this all men will know that you are my disciples, if you *love* one another" (John 13:34-35 NIV, emphasis mine). It is important that we see that Jesus used the word *agape* four times in these two verses, and the meaning is clear. No one can "command" emotion. We cannot be commanded to love someone emotionally. Parents make efforts to *command* their children to "love" each other to no avail. This type of sibling love comes with time. The kind of love that Jesus "commands" us to have is an act of responsibility and a desire to do so. It is with this in mind that we understand Jesus' words when asked, "Which is the greatest commandment?" Jesus replied, "The most important one, answered Jesus, is this: 'Hear, O Israel, the Lord your God is one. Love the Lord your God with all your heart and with all your soul and with all your mind and with all your strength.' The second is this: 'Love your neighbor as yourself. There is no commandment greater than these'" (Mark 12:30-31 NIV). Since all the commandments are "rolled-up" in these two, it would stand to reason that loving God and loving our neighbor are the greatest things we can do. Our entire eternal future is predicated on the manner in which we keep these commandments.

WHAT DOES ALL THIS MEAN TO ME?

When we consider the depths of this type of love that conquers all ill will and malice in the one who loves in this fashion, we cannot help being amazed. The love that is willing to give up all for the one loved is something to be considered. Jesus said, "As the Father has loved me, so I have loved you. If you obey my commands, you will remain in my love, just as I have obeyed my Father's commands and remain in His love. I have told you this so that my joy may be in you and that your joy may be complete. My command is this: love each other as I have loved you. *Greater love has no one than this, that he lay down his life for his friends.* You are my friends if you do what I command" (John 15:9-14 NIV, emphasis mine). We can easily see that Jesus is referring to His own death here, yet He does make it clear that He expects His followers to do the same as He is willing to do. Should it come to pass that we would be required to die for the cause of Christ, would we have that kind of *love*? The short answer should be an emphatic *YES*!

We also see in this passage the word "command." Jesus does not *ask* His followers to love one another; He *commands* it. Jesus uses the strongest possible terms to tell His followers to love one another. We have no choice in the matter if we desire to please God. John refers to this idea when he says, "This is the message you heard form the beginning: We should love one another" (I John 3:11 NIV). This is nothing new; the concept that we should love each other in Christ is as old as the Gospel and as fresh as the sunrise. John continues the theme previously mentioned in the quote from the Gospel account by John when he wrote in I John 3:16-18, "This is how we know what love is: Jesus Christ laid down His life for us. And we ought to lay down our lives for our brothers. If anyone has material possessions and sees his brother in need but has no pity on him, how can the love of God be in him? Dear children, let us not love with words or tongue but with actions and in truth" (NIV). What more needs to be said for us to grasp the concept that we are to love one another? This is not an *attitude* but an *action*!

WHAT ARE THE PARTS OF THIS LOVE?

In the great "Love Chapter" of the Bible, I Corinthians 13, Paul breaks down this type of love into its component parts. Let us examine these parts and see how *agape* affects us.

The first characteristic is *patience*. This is an elusive quality that seems to be less and less evident in the world today. Take, for example, "road rage." We have become a society of impatient people. We can hardly wait for anything. Fast food is not fast enough; computers were too slow, so now we have faster and faster models; the list is endless. Paul, when he referred to love as being "patient" was referring to being "longsuffering." He had people in mind versus situations. Paul, in Romans 15:1, 4-5, wrote that patience (endurance) is the manner in which we are to deal with one another. The same is found in Ephesians 4:1-2. Patience with our brothers and sisters in Christ must be a given in that God has been *patient* with us. How often have we failed Him, yet His love is unwavering for us. God is patient, and we must be also.

Love is *kind*. Kindness is another of those characteristics that seems to be lacking in so many Christians today. Our post-modern world has all but done away with kindness. We seem to equate kindness with weakness. If one is kind to another, the immediate response is, "What do you want?" When we show kindness, however, we show the spirit of Christ. His ministry was marked with loving-kindness, and He demonstrated the fact that His followers were to be kind as well. When we love (agape), we are kind.

It *does not envy.* Envy is the equivalent of jealousy. We all know what a jealous spirit can do to us. There are many examples of envy or jealousy in the Old Testament. We need look no further than the account of Joseph being sold into slavery by his brothers, King Saul's jealousy of David, Israel's envy of their neighbors in worshipping false gods, just to name a few. In the New Testament, we see the envy of Jesus' enemies that caused them to seek to kill Him. Envy is a very dangerous condition and must never be a part of the life of the Christian. Where there is love, there can be no room for envy.

It does not boast. Boasting is for those who feel they need to make themselves look good to others. Arrogance and boasting go together. Those who are proud of themselves and their accomplishments are those who are most likely to boast of their feats. There is no room in love for the boastful and the braggart.

It is not proud. Pride can lead to so many distractions and sins that we cannot begin to enumerate them at this point. Pride is selfishness; it leads us to believe that it is all about our desires and needs. When pride enters one's life, the results are often disastrous. When one is proud, they are less likely to see the needs of others and act upon them. They put themselves ahead of their service to God. If anyone had reason to be proud, it would have been Jesus. Remember the incident just before His betrayal? As He was in Bethany, He washed the feet of His disciples. Humility is a strong Christian characteristic and one to be sought. One of the most often quoted proverbs is found in Proverbs 16:18, "Pride goes before destruction, a haughty spirit before a fall" (NIV). Love is never proud as it seeks to build up not destroy the spirits of those who are the objects of this *agape.*

It is not rude. Wow! There is one we all need more in the world today. Does it not seem that rudeness is the order of the day? Whatever happened to "customer service?" Rude behavior is almost in vogue, and the more rude behavior one exhibits the better. Love demonstrates no rude behavior. Where there is love, rudeness cannot exist.

It is not self-seeking. Those who love do not insist that their own interests be met *first*. Another aspect of our current society is a "me-first" attitude. "Once *my* needs and desire are satisfied I *might* think about helping you with yours" is the attitude of many. For those who believe that "life *owes* me everything," life is going to be very difficult. Self-seeking people are bound to be disappointed because life will deal them severe blows, and many are unable to cope with these.

It is not easily angered. Note the words "not easily." Paul does not say that there can be no anger because there are times when "righteous anger" is necessary. We must be very careful to distinguish the difference between "righteous" anger and unrighteous anger. The type of anger envisioned by Paul here is a lack of self-control. It is so easy to "loose one's cool" at something or someone. Usually we cannot control or change the situation over which we have become angry, and we should learn not to be so sensitive and control our emotions. The apostles, including Paul, were constantly abused in many ways. There is no record of their becoming angry and treating those who had abused them with anger. Jesus spoke of this attitude often, and He became angry, yet did not sin. Paul told the Church at Ephesus, "In your anger, do not sin. Do not let the sun go down while you are still angry, and do not give the devil a foothold" (Ephesians 5:26-27 NIV).

It keeps no record of wrongs. This simply means, "Do not hold a grudge." Those who hold a grudge against anyone are only harming themselves. It is unusual for people against whom the grudge is held even to know of the grudge. The "wrong" you feel has been committed against you is often forgotten by the offender. By carrying a grudge, the carrier is not able to love as he or she should. Jesus repeatedly advised His followers to forgive those who had wronged them. It is impossible to love someone and carry a grudge against them at the same time. We must learn to *let it go!* If we were to attempt to remember and "keep records" of all the wrongs or slights done to us in a lifetime, we would have no time for anything else.

HOW CAN I GET THIS LOVE?

There is no "magic potion" or some incantation by which one receives this *agape*. The Bible is quite clear as to just how to achieve this type of love. It is made available to those who have given themselves to God. This love comes *from* God and is given to the Christian via the Holy Spirit. This is another of the ways in which the Holy Spirit distributes His gift to the Christian. The love that we receive from God is "recycled" into the lives of those with whom we come in contact.

In I John 4:19 John wrote, "We love because He first loved us" (NIV). John continues with a reference to our need to love our brothers/sisters as he wrote, "If anyone says, 'I love God' yet hates his brother, he is a liar. For anyone who does not love his brother, whom he has seen, cannot love God whom he has not seen. And He has given us this command: Whoever loves God must love his brother" (I John 4:20-21 NIV). Love comes from God to us and through us to our brothers/sisters. The reason we are able to love is that He first loved us.

Paul, writing to the Church at Galatia wrote regarding the "fruit of the Spirit" and *love* is the first fruit mentioned.

Without this *agape*, the other "fruits" would die on the vine.

HOW IS THIS LOVE MANIFESTED?

There are many ways in which this *agape* is shown. We will seek to show only the main one at this time. One is that we are moved to *do something*. Our motivation to get-up and take action is only realized when we see the love that God has for us and the love that He wants to distribute to all around us. God is not a *passive* being rather He is *active*. Since "God so loved the world that He *gave* His one and only Son" (John 3:16 NIV, emphasis mine) to die on a cross for *the world* we see God as a God of action. God seeks those who are willing to *work* in His kingdom. It is not sufficient for Christians to simply "sit-down" once they have been brought into a saving knowledge of Jesus Christ. We must be doing something for Him. When we experience the *agape* of God, we have a strong desire to work for Him. The desire to be active in the kingdom will spur us onward toward the other manifestations of love, such as continued obedience, showing a concerned attitude toward the needy, assisting in teaching the newer Christians the continual responsibility toward God and each other, etc.

Paul, again in I Corinthians 13, shows the fact that "love never fails" (V. 8). He refers to all the spiritual gifts that were a part of the life of the churches at the time of his writing and explains that they will fail, yet love shall always exist. In verse 7 he says, "It (love) *always* protects, *always* trusts, *always* hopes, *always* perseveres" (NIV, emphasis mine). The fact that he uses the word "always" here is an indication that there is no end to love, that it is eternal.

Love is something that will identify the Christian. John, in The Gospel of John, chapter 13, wrote of Jesus saying,

"By this [love] all men will know that you are my disciples, if you love one another" (v. 35 NIV). Love is the thing that separates the believer from the non-believer. In I John 3:14, John wrote, "We know that we have passed from death to life, because we love our brothers. Anyone who does not love remains in death" (NIV). This simply shows that we are newly born. In Christian baptism, we *die* to sin and are *made alive* through the blood of Jesus Christ. In so doing, we are given the gift of new life and receive the love of God that changes us completely. This *agape* is that which identifies us as belonging to Christ; it is the *mark of the Savior* that is placed upon us at our new birth.

DO I HAVE ANY CHOICE IN THE MATTER?

Of course, the choice is always there for the Christian and the non-Christian alike. We can choose to accept or reject the love of God, and should we reject it, we will find ourselves in a lost condition. If we accept this love, however, it will mean a life of doing His will. There are strings attached to accepting the *agape* of God. James gives the best definition of "religion" in James 1:27, "Religion that God our Father accepts as pure and faultless is this: to look after orphans and widows in their distress and to keep oneself from being polluted by the world" (NIV). What other motivation than *agape* can there be to keep these two commandments? We can only truly assist those less fortunate than ourselves if we have love. While there may be those who give of their money to charity that assists these people, to do so on a religious basis that is acceptable to God there must be a genuine love.

CONCLUSION: It is not an easy task to love, as God would have us love, and to do the things that the new found love requires. Should we truly desire to be His children,

Simply Speaking. . .

however, we must do everything to keep it and to show it to the lost world. When we fail to show the love of God within us toward Him and toward our fellow Christians, we are simply not His!

CHAPTER TEWNTY-ONE

WHAT ABOUT SUFFERING AND THE CHRISTIAN?

INTRODUCTION: Suffering and Christianity go hand in hand. It seems that since the inception of God's dealing with man after the fall, suffering has played an important role. God told Adam and Eve that they would suffer because of their sins. Adam was told that it would be very difficult to grow the food they would need to sustain themselves, and Eve was told that childbirth would be brought about with suffering. The Old and New Testaments give ample examples of God's people suffering, and the idea of a "Suffering Savior" is foreign to the world. Those who do not understand the need for Christ to suffer and die on a cross make up most of the world.

In this chapter, we will explain the basis of suffering and the Christian's response to it.

"WHY SHOULD I SUFFER WHEN OTHERS DO NOT?"

That is a very good question. Suffering is not limited to one "group" or "class" of people. As a Christian counselor, I have seen many people over the years who have asked that very question. They cannot understand that since they were "good people" and that they were "trying" to do what was "right" and live a Christian life, why were they suffering when those who were "bad people" and "not trying" to be good and not interested in living a Christian life should prosper! The answers to these questions are complicated ones.

Let us begin with the concept that we are *good*. Jesus said in Matthew 19:17, "Why do you ask me about what is *good*? There is only One who is *good*. If you want to enter life, obey the commandments" (NIV, emphasis mine). The King James Version has a little different take on this verse, "And He said unto him, 'Why callest thou me good? There is none good but one, that is, God: but if you wilt enter into life, keep the commandments.'" This rendition of the same verse makes it clear that *goodness* belongs to God, the Father. Although God looked upon His creation and pronounced it *"good,"* this was before sin entered the creation. After sin entered, the *goodness* was no more. While we may think of ourselves as "good," we must realize that we are fallen creatures as well. The manner in which we use the term "good" is limited and must be used correctly to be understood from a spiritual perspective. Being morally *good* is to be commended, and we should all strive to be so; however, our "goodness" will not save us nor prevent us from suffering.

Suffering and pain are unavoidable. Even the so-called "bad people" are not immune. The question as to why some suffer more than others is equally unavoidable since we are human and we feel that it is not "fair" that some should suffer when others seem not to suffer. Fairness has nothing to do with it either. When suffering comes to the Christian, it often seems that God has abandoned us. This, of course, is not true. God never abandons

His own. The suffering may be due to a particular sin or sins, it may be due to the actions of others, it may be due to something totally unavoidable. Suffering is something we shall all experience. The dividing mark is *how we handle it*. When we suffer, we are told to "rejoice." Are you surprised that we are commanded to rejoice when we suffer? This is certainly foreign to the world, yet is a very real presence for the Christian. Near the close of his life, the Apostle Paul reminded the Philippian Church to rejoice. In Philippians 4:4, he says it TWICE! "Rejoice in the Lord always. I will say it again: Rejoice!" (NIV). The entire Book of Philippians is a letter to be joyful. About what did they have to be joyful? Simply put: their relationship with Jesus Christ. When we are in Him, we can rejoice even in suffering. Paul's life was a constant reminder of the suffering for the cause of Christ. He even listed some of the things he had suffered. In II Corinthians 11:16-ff, he is speaking of his sufferings. In verses 24-28 he wrote, "Five times I received from the Jews the forty lashes minus one. Three times I was beaten with rods, once I was stoned, three times I was shipwrecked, I spent a night and a day in the open sea, I have been constantly on the move. I have been in danger from rivers, in danger from bandits, in danger from my own countrymen, in danger from Gentiles; in danger in the city, in danger in the country, in danger at sea; and in danger from false brothers. I have labored and toiled and have often gone without sleep; I have known hunger and thirst and have often gone without food; I have been cold and naked. Besides everything else, I face daily the pressure of my concern for all the churches" (NIV). Can any of us match that list of sufferings? I rather doubt it. In addition, we can add to the list that he was imprisoned and later beheaded all for the cause of Christ. To add "insult to injury," Paul refers to his "thorn in my flesh." Since this "thorn" is not revealed by him, we can only speculate as to what it may have been. We do know that Paul prayed three times that this "thorn" be removed; it was not, and he was advised by Jesus, "My grace is sufficient for you, for my power is made perfect in weakness" (II Cor. 12:9b NIV). There are none of us who have even come close to the sufferings of Paul and many other Christians. While we understand this fact, it is also true that viewing the sufferings of others does not really relieve our sufferings or make them less painful. What can make my sufferings go away? There is no simple answer to that question. Perhaps there is *nothing* that can relieve your suffering. Should that be the case, understand, as did Paul, that Christ's power may well be made perfect in our weakness. I understand that it is often very difficult "simply to pray" or to "grin and bear it." Others say these things to us when we are suffering and they are always options when the pain is too great. We must, if we are to be Christian, understand that God has a reason for allowing our suffering in this life and that He has prepared an eternal life in which there shall be no suffering.

Philip Yancey has written a book entitled *Where Is God When It Hurts.* I would encourage anyone who is suffering to purchase and read this book (published by Zondervan, Grand Rapids, Michigan). In this book, chapter 8, entitled "Arms Too Short to Box with God," he wrote, "You are lying in a hospital bed, kept alive by tubes of plastic spilling from your arm and nose. A killer tornado has destroyed everything you own. All you've worked for—your house, car, savings account—has disappeared forever. Your family decimated, you have no visitors except some rather cranky neighbors. You are barely hanging on to life. You move through the usual stages of grief, your prayers, and questions tinged with bitterness. *If only God would visit me personally and give me some answers,* you say to yourself. *I want to believe Him, but how can I? What has happened contradicts everything I know about a loving*

Simply Speaking...

God. If I could just see Him once and hear Him explain why I must go through this hard time, then I could endure." What a great picture Yancey paints of many today. We may not have had all these things at once; however, many of us have experienced them at some time in our lives.

There was one who experienced a very similar scenario in his life: Job. Job was a man who followed God in every fiber of his being. On one occasion, Satan slipped into heaven with the angels. God responded with this question, "Where have you come from?" The reply from Satan was, "From roaming through the earth and going back and forth in it." (This could be translated, "I was seeking whom I might tempt and draw away from You, God.") God's response to Satan was, "Have you considered my servant Job? There is no one on earth like him; he is blameless and upright, a man who fears God and shuns evil." There is more back and forth between God and Satan, and the conversation comes down to a contest between whether Satan could make Job sin or not. You can read all about it in The Book of Job, chapter one. The first test came when Satan destroyed everything Job had, including his ten children. God had said that Job himself could not be harmed. After the fact that Job would not sin, Satan was permitted to strike Job with terrible boils and anything else Satan wanted to do to him except take his life. When even this did not work to cause Job to sin, three "friends" came to visit Job and challenged him. The belief was that Job had done something so terrible that God had brought these things upon him. Does this sound familiar? When we suffer, do we not often blame God first? Even Job's wife gave him some advice. In Job 2:9, she said, "Are you still holding on to your integrity? Curse God and die!" (NIV). Job's response was classic, "You are talking like a foolish woman. Shall we accept good from God, and not trouble?" What a question? We would do well to think about this question in our own lives. When all is going our way and we have what we want and are not suffering, we look at God as One who deserves our adoration. When things go wrong, however, the attitude often changes, and we seek to blame God for everything that is *wrong*.

Jeremiah was another who suffered. He is the author of the prophecy bearing his name and the book that follows appropriately named *Lamentations*. He suffered at every turn. His own people sought to kill him, and he was in great distress when his prophesy was not heeded and the Babylonian captivity occurred. David suffered when, because of his sin with Bathsheba, the child she bore him died shortly after birth. Ezekiel also suffered for the sins of God's people. Most of the prophets suffered, and many were killed by the people to whom they prophesied because the people did not want to hear what the prophets had to say.

The One who suffered the most was Jesus Christ. From the time of His birth to the end of His short life, He suffered. We know very little about His childhood experiences yet living under an oppressive occupation such as the Romans could not have been easy. The Old Testament, from Genesis through the prophets, speaks of the suffering the Messiah would undergo. The things He suffered at the hands of His own people are great, even the rejection by His own family. There was a time when they thought He was insane. He suffered the death of a criminal, that of crucifixion, when He had committed no crime. Perhaps Jesus had the thought, "Why should I have to undergo this suffering for people who are only going to spit on me and reject me?" We do know that He prayed while in the Garden of Gethsemane that He would not have to die.

While it would seem wonderful if we did not have to suffer and undergo pain, it is an unrealistic hope. Pain is not always a bad thing. It is used to alert us that something is "just not right in our bodies." If we never had a pain, we would never know that we were having a heart attack, or that we were touching a hot stove, or many other things that could do much harm. Therefore, pain is an important aspect of life.

As to just when enough is enough is not within our ability to say. Pain is different for everyone. Some can tolerate more pain than can others. As to how much pain each individual can tolerate is on a case-by-case basis. Suffice it to say that sometimes pain is a blessing while at other times it is a curse.

HOW, THEN, DOES THE CHRISTIAN VIEW PAIN AND SUFFERING?

The Christian sees pain and suffering, from a human viewpoint, the same as the non-Christian. However, from a spiritual perspective, we view pain and suffering as only a temporary condition. The time will come when *all* pain and suffering for the Christian shall be no more. Until that time comes, we should have a little better understanding as to how to address pain and suffering.

Peter, in I Peter 4:19 said, "So then, those who suffer according to God's will should submit themselves to their faithful Creator and continue to do good" (NIV). This, then, appears to be saying that there is suffering *according to God's will* and there is suffering that is *not* according to God's will. When Christians suffer because they are doing God's will, God will bless them. On those occasions when the Christian is suffering for what they did *on their own* or *outside* God's will, meaning sin, the suffering will come only because the will of God has been broken. This puts a new light on the sufferings of the Christian. We should be very careful to examine the *cause* of our suffering.

Simply Speaking...

James wrote on suffering in this manner, "Consider it pure joy, my brothers, whenever you face trials of many kinds, because you know that the testing of your faith develops perseverance" (James 1:2-3 NIV). Paul, in writing to the Church at Rome said, "Not only so, but we also rejoice in our sufferings, because we know that suffering produces perseverance" (Romans 5:3 NIV). In Colossians 1:24a, Paul wrote, "Now I rejoice in what was suffered for you" (NIV). We can easily see that there is some suffering, like some pain, that is a blessing.

Again, Paul, in Romans 8:17, says, "Now if we are children, then we are heirs—heirs of God and co-heirs with Christ, if indeed we share in His *sufferings* in order that we may also share in His glory" (NIV, emphasis mine). He continues in verse 18 by saying, "I consider that our present sufferings are not worth comparing with the glory that will be revealed in us" (NIV).

The other side of suffering is suffering for unrighteousness. Returning to I Peter 4:12-15, we read, "Dear friends, do not be surprised at the painful trial you are suffering, as though something strange were happening to you. But, rejoice that you participate in the sufferings of Christ, so that you may be overjoyed when His glory is revealed. If you are insulted because of the name of Christ, you are blessed, for the Spirit of glory and of God rests on you. If you suffer, it should not be as a murderer or thief or any other kind of a criminal, or even as a meddler" (NIV). Peter makes it clear that suffering can be for the wrong reason. Suffering outside of the will of God is never a good thing, and we cannot blame God for this suffering.

When we are tried or tested, we must meet the challenge with thanksgiving. These trials show of what material we are made. If we are strong in the Lord (as we should be), there is nothing that can remove us from the love of God in Christ (see Romans 8:37-39). Some have attempted to make this mean that once we are saved nothing can take us from that salvation. This was not Paul's intent here as he was telling us that there is nothing *outside of ourselves* that can remove us from that great love. Trials show us our strength and should strengthen us all the more if we do not succumb to the temptation of turning away from the God of love.

SUFFERING CAN BE EDUCATIONAL

Perhaps you are saying, "How can I *learn* from suffering?" There are many ways to learn from suffering. One thing we can learn from suffering is *patience*. Patience *is* a learned attribute. None of us is born with patience; it is something we acquire by being *tried* and through suffering. Many have gone to the "School of Hard Knocks" and we have learned to be patient in doing the Lord's will. We tend to learn more from our *mistakes* than we do from our triumphs. Often it takes being "burned" so that we learn that we do not put our hand on a *hot* stove. We can be warned not to do many things; however, for many it takes the suffering of being "burned" to learn a very valuable lesson.

After the experience of 9/11, people flocked to churches in record numbers. The country seemed to come together with the thought of major adversity. This "feeling," however, did not last long and soon it was back to normal for many. If we do not learn to put our priorities in the proper order, we will never learn from adversity. 9/11 was a wake-up call to our nation. There are those who want to "bury us," the same was said during the "Cold War," and although the names have changed, the desire remains the same. Whether it is national sufferings or personal, the end result may well be the same. Suffering can lead us to repentance and a renewed desire to serve the Lord more closely, or it can turn us away from Him as we attempt to *blame* God for our sufferings.

There are *blessings* that can come from sufferings. Aside from coming closer to the Lord, we can learn to have a stronger prayer life. Prayer is the manner in which we communicate with God, and He wants to hear from His family. Some *only* pray when there are trials in their lives. This is not the best time to get to know their Heavenly Father. There was a saying during World War II, "There are no atheists in foxholes!" I have heard of people on airplanes that have developed engine trouble, people on ships that have some problems and are in danger of sinking, and many other situations where death seems imminent, who immediately make all types of promises to God if only He would get them out of the immediate problem. God may or may not intervene in these and other situations. The problem is not with God; the problem is with the fact that too many begin a prayer time only when they seem to be on the heels of a disaster.

Another blessing that can come from suffering is compassion for others. How often do we see people of a community coming together when a child is lost or someone with Alzheimer's disease has "wandered away?" Compassion is something that Christians are to have for their fellow Christians no matter the circumstances. Where there is a need the church is commanded to assist. When a fellow Christian is suffering, it is our responsibility to be there to provide comfort.

Many other blessings can come from suffering. It is up to the individual or local church to see just how blessings can come from what may seem to be disasters.

GOD NEVER PROMISED A *ROSE GARDEN*

What if God removed all pain, suffering, and evil from the world? What would that leave us? If God were to remove all the *ills* from the world, He would also have to remove *free will!* We are too quick to claim our *rights in a free society*; how would we feel if ALL those rights were removed from us? Not just the "rights" afforded us by our Constitution but the rights as free will Christians. We, as humans, want "our cake and eat it too." We want God to be in control of *everything* except those things over which we want control. This simply would create anarchy and everyone's "rights" would trump everyone else's. Free will is the basis on which God created mankind. He wanted to create an entity that could choose whether to serve Him or not. It is too bad that Adam and Eve chose to serve themselves rather than God. That aside, we must understand that should God take away our *freedoms* we would not be happy. With those freedoms go responsibilities, and with those responsibilities go the desire to please God. We make choices in everything we do.

God *suffers* when His children suffer. Do you not "feel the pain" of your children? In much the same manner, God feels our pain. He understands just what it is to suffer. Remember how His Son, Jesus, suffered? I am not simply referring to the sufferings of the cross and the related beatings He took, rather, the spiritual sufferings He underwent. He was tempted as are we and found without sin (see Hebrews 4:15); therefore, He knows what we are facing in our temptations.

After the creation and fall of man, during the time of Noah, mankind's sin had grown to the point that God actually *repented* that He had ever made man. He sent rain and caused the waters to rise to flood the entire earth, and those who survived were Noah, his wife, their three sons

Simply Speaking. . .

and their wives, along with a pair of everything God had created all in the ark. God *suffers* over sin and strongly desires that we should not suffer because of our sins. He, therefore, created a means by which *He* could take our sins upon Himself and suffer in our stead.

Life is not all "peaches and cream" or a "bed of roses." The old saying, "Life is what you make it," is quite true. We can make things good for ourselves by *choosing* to do what is right or we can suffer by *choosing* to follow our own path. Life is, at best, difficult enough without making the wrong choices. Sometimes we make improper choices out of ignorance, meaning that we do not know which way is the right way. When we suffer for those choices, we can call them "mistakes." When, however, we make conscious wrong choices and suffer for them we deserve what we get. That may seem harsh, yet it is the simple truth. We should not derive any pleasure when we see people suffer, even when they bring it on themselves. The truth, however, is that there are times when we do like to see others suffer when they have made very wrong choices. This is not an attitude God would endorse, and we should not enjoy seeing others suffer.

A question arises, "What about *tough love?*" So called, "tough love," does not necessarily involve suffering in the classic view of suffering. There may be some perceived sufferings associated with "tough love," however, these are very temporary and the intended consequence is to make a change in character. This type of love is similar to the discipline or chastisement that God provides to those whom He loves (see Hebrews 12).

God has created a *cure* for our suffering. It is in the blood of Jesus Christ and can be administered through Christian baptism. God does not desire to see His children suffer and He has made it possible to be blessed when we do. James, in James 1:2, said, "Consider it pure joy, my brothers, whenever you face trials of many kinds" (NIV). It can be considered joy because we know that God will bless us in these trials.

CONCLUSION: Suffering has been a part of mankind since the fall in the Garden of Eden. We are all the products of suffering in that our mothers were made to suffer in childbirth. Suffering can be a blessing or a curse depending upon the *cause* or *motive* of our suffering.

The Good News is there will be a time when suffering shall end! When Christ returns to receive His Bride, the Church, there shall be no more suffering for those who are in Christ and taken to be with Him. For those, however, who do not know Him, the suffering will be just beginning. If you desire to escape eternal suffering and pain, I urge you to accept the suffering for Christ in this life so that you may be made perfect in the life to come.

CHAPTER TWENTY-TWO

WHAT ARE ELDERS AND DEACONS?

QUALIFICATIONS AND DUTIES

INTRODUCTION: Before we can adequately understand the offices of elder and deacon, we must first understand the *Church* they serve. Jesus said in Matthew 16:18, "And I tell you that you are Peter, and on this rock I will build my Church, and the gates of Hades will not overcome it" (NIV). The "Church" which Jesus was to build was based on the statement made by Peter in verse 16, "Simon Peter answered, 'You are the Christ, the Son of the living God" (NIV). The *fact* of that statement was the "rock" upon which the Church was to be built. Jesus said "I will build *my* Church." This simply means that the Church belongs to Jesus Christ and not to any person, living or dead. To use, then, a person's name to indicate what type of church it is, is not Scriptural and should be avoided at any cost.

The Church is "the body of Christ." This is evident in Ephesians 1:22-23, "And God placed all things under His (Christ's) feet and appointed Him to be head over everything for the church, which is *His body*, the fullness of Him who fills everything in every way" (NIV, emphasis mine). Also in Colossians 1:18, "And he is the head of the body, the church; He is the beginning of the firstborn from among the dead, so that in everything He might have the supremacy" (NIV). Likewise in Ephesians 4:12, Paul wrote, "to prepare God's people for works of service, so that the *body of Christ* may be built up" (NIV, emphasis mine). You may also want to see I Corinthians 12:12-31.

The foundation of the Church is seen in Acts 4:11, "He is the stone you builders rejected, which has become the capstone" (NIV) and in I Corinthians 3:11, "For no one can lay any foundation other than the one already laid, which is Jesus Christ" (NIV). See Ephesians 2:19-22 and I Peter 2:4-8 for more references to the "foundation" of the Church being Jesus Christ.

Perhaps it would be good to define the Church at this point. The Greek word for "Church" is *Ecclesia* which means "the called out." Peter, in I Peter 1:9 said, "But you are a chosen people, a royal priesthood, a holy nation, a people belonging to God, that you may declare the praises of Him who *called you out of darkness into His wonderful light*" (NIV, emphasis mine). The Church has been "called out" of the darkness of the world to be a shining light for Jesus, the founder. The church has been made holy, meaning set apart to a purpose.

"The Church of Christ upon the earth is essentially, intentionally and constitutionally one, consisting of all those in every place who profess their faith in Christ and obedience to Him in all things according to the Scriptures, and that manifest the same tempers and conduct, and of none else, because none else can be truly and properly called Christians." (Excerpt from the *Declaration and Address*, September 7, 1809, given by Thomas Campbell).

THE ELDERS

There are three Greek words which apply to the eldership and may be used interchangeably.

1. *Bishop* (Greek, *Episcopos*). This word literally means "overseer, guardian, supervisor, and superintendant. (See Acts 20:28; Philippians 1:1; I Timothy 3:1-2; Titus 1:7). There was always a plurality of "bishops" in each local Church in the New Testament. Never do we see any writer referring to a single "elder" in any Church. The term is only used in a singular sense when one is referring to himself as an elder (see II John 1; III John 1; and I Peter 5:1). In fact, there are ample Scripture references to show us that the term is always used in the plural. Some of these are Acts 20:7; Philippians 1:1; I Timothy 4:14; and James 5:14.

   The expressed function of the "bishops" is to *lead* the Church of God, not to push or pull it. The elders are to be the *spiritual overseers* of the Church and guide it in spiritual teachings along with guarding the Church against false teachers and false doctrines. The primary expressed function of the elders is to be men of God who can determine what is Scriptural and what is not. The function is decidedly NOT to be the "boss" (see I Peter 5:2-4).

2. Elder (Greek, *Presbuteros*). The meaning of this word is "one greater, higher, more important, and elder." In the sense that they are "more important," the concept is that they are not "more important" than any other Christian from a personal standpoint, rather a spiritual one. They hold an office in the Church that is "above" any other office. They are to be held to a higher degree of accountability

and will, indeed, be judged accordingly (see I Peter 5:4). Jesus said in Luke 12:48b, "From everyone who has been given much, much will be demanded; and from the one who has *been entrusted with much, much more will be asked"* (NIV, emphasis mine). This verse tells us that those who have been given more responsibility, such as elders, more is expected. Can you imagine allowing one to move directly from the "mailroom" to become the "chairman of the board" in any corporation?

By comparison, we can see that the word "elder(s)" is used interchangeably with the word "bishop(s)." In Titus 1:5, "elder" is used, whereas, in Titus 1:7 the word "bishop" is used referring to the same office. The same is true in Acts 20:17, "elder" and in Acts 20:27, "bishop." Finally, in I Peter 5:1, "elder" and in I Peter 5:2, the words, "serving as *overseer"* (bishop) are used.

3. Pastor (Greek *poimerr*). This word means "shepherd, protector, overseers of the Christian assembly." This term is representative of a shepherd caring for his sheep. A "pastor" was never used in connection with one who would be a paid "clergyman" of a congregation. The term is used in connection with the eldership and has been misused in our modern church society. We have adopted the term to be those who are staff members and paid to be "ministers" of the church. It is unfortunate that this term has come to mean this when, if it is applied correctly, will return the "pastoral" duties to the eldership where they rightly belong. The Church today has given too much of the work of the eldership to a paid person who also, in many cases, exercises authority over the local family of Christians.

QUALIFICATIONS FOR ELDERS

It would be beneficial here to read and study I Timothy 3:1-7 and Titus 1:5-9 to reach an understanding of these qualifications. These two passages of Scripture are the most definitive of all relating to these men and their responsibilities and qualifications. When a congregation fails to follow carefully these qualifications, as set forth by Paul for the eldership, the congregation, as well as those chosen, will be, in no small part, responsible for the "problems" which will inevitably arise. It is imperative, therefore, that the congregation "qualify" each man seeking this high office by the standards listed in I Timothy and Titus.

I Timothy 3:1 states, ""Here is a trustworthy saying: If anyone sets his heart on being an overseer (elder), he desires a noble task" (NIV). The office of elder is one of great responsibility and at the same time one of great reward. When a man desires to be an elder he is seeking the highest office within the Church. With this office goes awesome responsibility. However, if done properly, it also provides great rewards in this life, as well as in the life to come.

- I Timothy 3:2 says, "Now the overseer must be above reproach" and in Titus 1:6, Paul uses the word "blameless." Does this mean that an elder must be "perfect?" Absolutely not, however, it does mean that he must not have any past that will cause others to use against him. There may be people who have a past that would come back to "haunt" them, and Paul, in his first qualification, says that this cannot be. An elder must have a responsible character which no one will be able to use against him or the Church.

Simply Speaking. . .

- "The husband of but one wife," repeated in Titus 1:6. This is, most probably, the most abused quality of an elder. This has been used against any man who has gone through a divorce, and it does not mean that at all! The same standard has been applied to many a godly man who would serve the Lord as a minister (evangelist). This literally means, "A one-woman man." It does not mean that a man cannot have had another wife in his life; rather, it means that he is to have "one at a time." Since the practice of polygamy was prevalent at the time of Paul's writing, it was important that the concept of the sanctity of marriage be observed. I hasten to add that it is important that the local church adequately inspect the life of any man desiring the office of elder. It is simply not a Biblical command to disqualify a man who has met all the other qualifications to become an elder simply because he has been divorced and remarried.

  Some questions arise: Must a man be married to qualify? Must his wife be living? Would a widower qualify? Is a divorced man eligible? If he is married to a divorced woman and this is his first marriage, is it then acceptable? Are any of these questions valid? Who is to answer these questions? Since there are no definitive answers to these questions, we are left to the realm of opinion. Because there exists nothing other than opinion, who is to say, with authority, exactly what Paul meant? Perhaps we would do well not to be so dogmatic with respect to this qualification and not automatically disqualify someone who has all the other qualities, failing only in our *opinion* of the meaning of this one!

- "Temperate." Titus 1:8 uses the word, "self-controlled." This would mean self-possessed, poised, sensible, and able to exercise self-control, not one to "pop-off." It would indicate one who could remain "cool" under pressure and not be quick to act without spending time in prayer over a matter.
- "Respectable." This would go to reputation, both inside and outside the congregation. It is important that non-believers respect the eldership as individuals in their lives outside the work of the Church. This goes to "character" as does "temperate," which precedes it. The character of an elder should be above reproach and should speak well of the household of God.
- "Hospitable." This is a term used by Paul to both Timothy and Titus. These men would be those who are given to hospitality in that they thoroughly enjoyed fellowship with fellow Christians. They would love to share with others, be kind to strangers, and have an "open door" policy to guests. This would include a lack of selfishness, an interest in the needs of others (charitable), and an inner health.
- "Able to teach." In Titus, Paul stated it this way: "He must hold firmly to the trustworthy message as it has been taught, so that he can encourage others by sound doctrine and refute those who oppose it" (Titus 1:9 NIV). This simply means that the elders should be men who *know* the Word of God and can teach it to others as well as being able to stand up to false teachers and bring down false doctrines.
- "Not given to drunkenness." This admonition is not mentioned in Titus; however, it is an important issue. There is some controversy with respect to

this quality. Some believe that it is acceptable to use alcoholic beverages, if only in moderation, not becoming drunk in the process, while others believe that alcohol, in any form, is a sin. Paul's words here are, "not given to drunkenness." I am in no position to advise anyone that it is acceptable to drink alcoholic beverages at any time, nor am I in a position to say that it is *always* a sin. It would take one much more qualified than I to speak to this matter. I simply take Paul at his word here and say that elders are not to be drunkards.

- "Not violent but gentle." This would rule out the "wife-beater" or the "child-abuser." It would also rule out violence in any form with another person. Paul said that the elder was to be "gentle." It is increasingly difficult to find "gentle-men" any more. This quality means to be fair, reasonable, sensible, have a genuine concern for fairness, and able to get along with others. They must be sympathetic, gracious, forbearing, and considerate. This must be done, however, with no sense of appeasement.
- "Not quarrelsome." The elders must not be those who stir-up trouble, who lose their tempers easily, who are negative, insolent, angry, belligerent, etc. To be a well-qualified elder, one should have no negative qualities.
- "Not a lover of money." This does not mean that elders cannot be wealthy. It means exactly what it says: *not a lover of money*. Not all lovers of money are wealthy and not all wealthy men are lovers of money. One who would fall into this category of loving money would be those who would put the love of money ahead of their service to Christ and His Church. Money, and the love of it, can easily come between Christians and their service to the

Lord. When an elder is involved with a love affair with money, he is creating a very dangerous environment for himself and the Church which He serves.

He must manage his own family well and see that his children obey him with proper respect. "If anyone does not know how to manage his own family, how can he take care of God's Church?" The elder is to be "the head of the house," and that does not mean that he is "the boss." He is to be the responsible party for his home. He is responsible to God and to the Church. He is to be respected as such. He would handle his personal finances well and his other affairs wisely. He is to demonstrate a good administration of his own home so that he can administer the spiritual affairs of the Church.

The questions that arise are: "Must an elder have children?" "Must he have more than one child since the word 'children' is used here?" "Must the children be old enough to have accepted Christ?" "When do children cease to be children?" "Are they children only as long as they are at home; or do they cease to be children when they leave home and marry?" There, obviously, exist no Biblical answers to these questions. Again, we are in the realm of speculation and opinion. Just as there is no specific age requirement for the eldership (that they should have attained a certain age to be an elder), there is no answer to how many, if any, children he should have. Suffice it to say, the elder should have his family in subjection to the will of the Lord or he is unqualified to be an elder.

Having children is not always an option. There may well be circumstances in which a couple cannot have children. Would then, the option to adopt arise and should one expect said elder to adopt a child or children simply to meet this qualification? Having children is a gift from God and not the prerogative of man and, as such, is beyond the control of anyone. Should we, then, disqualify a man who possesses all the other qualities for eldership because he does not have children? My view is no! It is imperative, however, that should he have children, they should be well-mannered and well-behaved children and Christians if they have reached the age when they can discern the meaning of that great decision.

- "He must not be a recent convert." The reason for this admonition is simple and should be easily understood. An elder is to be the "defender of the faith." How could one be such if he is a new Christian? He is too spiritually weak to be in such a position of authority. He must be taught before he is capable of teaching. He must "crawl before he is able to walk." Since we are all "re-born," we must realize that as new converts we are "babes in Christ" and, as such, in need of moving from "milk" to "meat" of the Word. Paul continues with this quality by saying, "Lest he become conceited and fall under the same judgment as the devil." This is to say that if one becomes an elder too soon and becomes conceited, his conceit will cause him to fall and be lost as Satan is lost.
- "He must also have a good reputation with outsiders, so that he will not fall into disgrace and into the devil's trap." Here is the second mention in a row of the "devil." Paul is assuming that the Christian men are being made elders when they are not quite ready to be such. The fact that they are "Christian" and made an "elder" is clear. The fact that they can be lost is also abundantly clear. It is important that elders be above reproach. If they

come into the eldership with an unclean reputation in the community, they will not only be disgraced by the community, but will also bring disgrace to the Church for which Christ died and which He created. This is another example that Christians can be lost!

You will notice that all references to elders have been in the masculine gender. The reason for this is simple; all elders were, and should remain, male. There is no Biblical precedent for ordaining women to the eldership. All the qualifications are to men, and Paul was adamant as to the role of women in the Church. I have no problem with women serving in many capacities in the Church today, and I feel that in nearly all respects they should be considered equally; however, the pulpit ministry and the eldership are two places where women are not to be considered. I fully understand the argument that we are now living in the Twenty-first Century and that *things have changed*. This may well be; however, I follow the Biblical principal of not having women in the position of elder.

THE DEACONS

The office of deacon is one of great import and should not be entered into or taken lightly. The word deacon is transliterated into the English language from the Greek. The original Greek word is *Diakonos*, and it literally means "servant or minister." This is a more appropriate title for the paid clergy of today rather than *pastor*.

The first reference to deacons in the early Church is found in Acts 6. In this passage the number of followers of Christ was increasing rapidly, and the Grecian widows were complaining because their fellow believing Jewish widows were receiving the greater attention to their physical needs (food, etc.). The apostles chose to rectify the problem by advising the Church at Jerusalem to "choose seven men from among you who are known to be full of the Spirit and wisdom" (Acts 6:3 NIV). We have here the first qualifications for the office of *deacon*. Notice the first quality was that they be *full of the Spirit*. This is no accident as we see later in this chapter when Stephen, a deacon chosen by the Jerusalem Church, was preaching, and in Acts 6:8 we read, "Now Stephen, a man full of God's grace and power, did great wonders and miraculous signs among the people" (NIV). It was not long that jealousy arose among the Jews, and they sought to silence him. In verse 10 we read, "but they could not stand up against his *wisdom or the Spirit by which he spoke*" (NIV, emphasis mine). It is easily seen that this man, a deacon, was also a preacher and one who was endowed with Spiritual gifts. As Stephen "preached" to the Sanhedrin and the assembled crowd, his message was powerful enough to anger these people to the point that they seized him and stoned him to death (Acts 7). It was as he was being stoned that he looked up into heaven and saw Jesus standing at the right hand of God (Acts 7:56) and in his dying moments he prayed, "Lord Jesus, receive my spirit" and finally, "Lord, do not hold this sin against them. When he said this he fell asleep" (Acts 7:59 NIV).

We also see another *deacon* mentioned in the Book of Acts. His name was Philip, and this is not the same Philip who was an apostle. This Philip was one of the seven originally chosen as deacons by the Jerusalem Church. The Holy Spirit told Philip to go from Samaria, where he was *preaching*, to a desert road between Jerusalem and Gaza. It was there that he encountered an Ethiopian who was traveling home from Jerusalem. Philip was told by the Holy Spirit to stop the conveyance of this Ethiopian, which he did. After explaining the passage of Isaiah being read by the Ethiopian, Philip "then began with that very passage of

Scripture and told him the good news about Jesus" (Acts 8:35 NIV). Philip baptized this Ethiopian, and he (the Ethiopian) went on his way rejoicing (see Acts 8:39). It was at this point that Philip was removed from this place by the Holy Spirit and appeared in Azoutus traveling around and "preaching the gospel in all towns until he reached Caesarea" (Acts 8:40 NIV). It is obvious that Philip, a deacon, was also a preacher of the Gospel.

From these two examples of *deacons* in the Book of Acts we see that the office of "deacon" is one that is much more than that of "a helper to the elders" or "one who serves communion to the congregation." Neither is it a "stepping stone" for young men to the eldership. Being a deacon is not a position to learn how to be an elder. In fact, as we shall soon see, the office is a noble office in itself and one to be desired for the service that may be rendered.

Paul, in I Timothy 3:8-13, provides us with the qualifications for deacons. Many of them are the same as those for an elder, and we will only discuss the obvious different qualifications as listed here.

- Worthy of respect
- Not given to much wine. (A similar quality for elder in that an elder is not to be a drunkard.)
- Not pursuing dishonest gain. (Similar to that of "not a lover of money." Not one having a mercenary spirit.)
- They must keep hold of the deep truths of the faith with a clear conscience. This refers to having a deep knowledge of the Word of God and an ability to apply those truths to their own lives.
- They must first be tested; and then if there is nothing against them, let them serve as deacons. (A reference to character, much the same as an elder.)

Simply Speaking...

- A deacon must be the husband of but one wife. (The same principle applies here as to an elder. The added admonition is found in verse 11, "In the same way, their wives are to be women worthy of respect, not malicious talkers but temperate and trustworthy in everything." It is only fitting that the wife of the deacon be examined for her character.)
- The deacon must manage his home and his family in the same manner as an elder.

A deacon must have many of the same qualities as an elder, and it is important that we understand that there is very little difference in their relationship to God and the Church. The main difference is that the elders are to be responsible to God for the spiritual health of the church and that the deacons are to be assistants to these elders. The term "deacon" means servant, and this is the primary responsibility of a deacon.

The example in Acts shows them assisting with the food distribution to the widows in the Jerusalem Church. We also see that they were "preachers" or "evangelists." Deacons are, likewise, listed as men. With all due respect to the role of women in the Church, they are never shown to hold the office of a deacon. For those who wish to understand the reference in Romans 16:1, where Paul refers to Phoebe and a "servant" of the Church in Cenchrea and make this a proof text for women being ordained as "deaconesses," I believe that had Paul been so inclined he would have given a more definitive referral. I am in no position to argue the point, however, I feel that this role, as well as that of elder, is given to men.

There is no admonition that a deacon should not "be a new Christian" as exists for an elder. Therefore, we may agree that one who is younger in the faith can assume that office, remembering that he is to "keep hold of the deep truths of the faith with a clear conscience." It would not be wise to put a man into this office who is a brand new Christian who has not been taught these deep truths. We are to "let him be tested" and this would appear to be a testing of his faith.

CONCLUSION: With all the responsibility that goes with being an elder or a deacon we must not allow this to become a "popularity contest." There is far too much at stake to allow someone to become an elder or a deacon who is not properly qualified by the Scriptures. For far too many Churches, the only quality that matters is that the candidate has never been divorced, that he has been a member of the local congregation for a while, and that everyone likes him. This is a sad way to bring men into these offices. Many Churches have an "election" yearly to bring men into these offices with no regard to their Biblical qualities and allow them to serve for a "lifetime." Other Churches elect elders and deacons for a determined "term" and allow them to serve for that time and then require them to "rotate" off for (one year or more). I am not convinced that that is a Biblical manner in which to choose elders and deacons. It is, however, a better manner than "putting them in for life" and expecting God to work out the details. Surely, there is a better method than that!

I pray that God will give to each congregation within the Restoration movement an answer to the question of elders and deacons. We certainly need competent and qualified men to serve in these offices in this time.

CHAPTER TWENTY-THREE

WHAT ARE THE ROLES OF ELDERS AND DEACONS?

INTRODUCTION: The roles of elders and deacons are clearly defined in the New Testament and need to be fully understood in order to be a New Testament Church. These roles are often abused and misunderstood in the "government" of the Church. We shall attempt to briefly describe the roles of elders and deacons. It is not my intent to make this an exhaustive study, rather a simple definition of roles and responsibilities of each office.

THE ROLE OF ELDER

The word "elder" evokes many views in various denominational churches today. It is a role of leadership and responsibility as defined in the New Testament and does not refer to "an old person." There are various words used for elder in the New Testament. Some of these are: pastor, overseer, bishop, and shepherd. Each of these terms may be used interchangeably as they mean the very same thing. Those who have chosen to separate the position of elder into different offices are not being responsible to the original intent of the new Testament Church. In Titus 1:5, 7, Paul uses the words interchangeably as he wrote, "The reason I left you in Crete was that you might straighten out what was left unfinished and *appoint elders* in every town, as I directed you... Since an *overseer* is entrusted with God's work..." (NIV, emphasis mine).

BIBLICAL DEFINITION OF ELDERS

In Acts 20, the Apostle Paul called for the *elders* of the Church at Ephesus and gave them instructions. The words, elders (v. 17), overseers [bishops] (v. 28), and shepherds [pastors] (v. 28) appear in this passage to refer to the same men. At this time, Paul, seeing his impending death, called the elders of Ephesus to meet him at the seaport town of Miletus. It was here that he charged them with their responsibilities as noted above. The three Greek words used here are *presbuteroi* (elders), *poimaenoi* (shepherds, pastors), *episkopoi* (overseers, bishops). The first of these words, translated "elders," means "older ones who lead because of experience"—older in years and older in spiritual experience. The second word translated "shepherds/ pastors" means those who lead as in keeping a flock of sheep, being a protector of the flock. The third word translated "overseers/ bishops," means guides, caretakers, leaders, or those on watch. These words may be used interchangeably and are always used in the plural (I will discuss these terms in more detail). In fact, there is not one example of a single "elder" being an overseer of more than one church. Quite the opposite is true, in that these elders (plural) were always shepherds of a single Church. Never do we see Paul saying, "Make an elder (singular) to watch over many churches in an area." This idea came much later as the Church grew and the ideas of men entered the picture distorting the original intent.

In I Peter 5:1-2, Peter appeals to the *elders* in the Church "as a fellow *elder* to be *shepherds of God's flock that is under your care, serving as overseers*" (NIV, emphasis mine). The emphasis here in on elders, plural, and the fact that they were to be overseers over those who had been entrusted to their care. Peter continues in verses 2b-4 to say, "Not because you must, but because you are *willing*, as God wants you to be; not greedy for money, but eager to serve; not lording it over those entrusted to you, but being *examples* to the flock. And when the Chief Shepherd appears, you will receive the crown of glory that will never fade away" (NIV, emphasis mine). Peter spoke of himself as a "fellow elder." He did not use the word "apostle" which would seem to be more "important." Rather, he referred to himself as an *elder*.

John, in his three letters, refers to himself as an *elder*, and with this distinction he seems to be very content. He, too, could have referred to himself as *apostle*, yet he chose the designation, elder.

ELDERS AS SHEPHERDS

The fact that elders are referred to as shepherds is significant since Jesus often referred to himself as a "Shepherd." He used the parable of "The Lost Sheep," and made it clear that He was the Shepherd who went after the one that was lost. In John 10:11 Jesus said, "I am the Good Shepherd. The good shepherd lays down his life for the sheep" (NIV). In 10:14, He continued the theme and said, "I am the Good Shepherd, I know my sheep and my sheep know me. . ." In verse 16 He said, "I have other sheep that are not of this sheep pen. I must bring them also. They too will listen to my voice, and there shall be one flock and one shepherd" (NIV). (The reference to "other sheep" is obviously to the Gentiles who would later be brought into the

Light of the Gospel.) Hebrews 13:20 refers to Jesus as that "Great Shepherd of the sheep."

The position of "shepherd" was not a noble one. The shepherds were among the lowest of the low in terms of a profession at the time of Jesus. They often slept with, ate with, and remained with the sheep 24/7. There was little getting away, and "vacations" were not an option. They did not work a forty-hour week and go "home" when not attending the sheep. Sheep required constant vigilance and protection. They smelled very bad and were not the cleanest animals alive. The role of shepherd was one of great sacrifice. It is quite fitting that Jesus chose to refer to Himself as a "Shepherd."

The fact that elders are called "shepherds" means a life of sacrifice for the flock (Church). There will be times when an elder shall be called upon to do things he might not want to do. There are responsibilities of "protecting the flock" from those who would do it harm. An elder, then, must be prepared to make difficult decisions reached by being a godly man, and one who is very familiar with the Word of God (the Sword of the Spirit) and is capable of using that Word to defend the Church. He must also be a man given to prayer and able to call upon the aid of the Holy Spirit to assist him in such protection. "Shepherds" are to be responsible, first to themselves and then to the Church they serve (see Acts 20:17).

ELDERS AS PASTORS

This is much the same as "shepherds." The role of a "pastor" is NOT as it is used in most churches today. In most churches today the term "pastor" has been relegated to the "clergyman" or "minister" being the *paid* staff member(s) of a local body of believers. There is no such reference that this term should be applied to the person(s) who are paid by the local congregation in the New Testament. Many of the Restoration Movement churches have adopted that term and applied it to their staff members and have, subsequently, given the role of a pastor to that person(s). It is not the responsibility of a paid minister to take on the role of "pastor." Since the word applies to "elders," and elders only, we should re-evaluate our use of the term. Pastors are responsible for the "feeding" of the Church. (We will review the qualifications and responsibilities of elders later.) This feeding is to make certain that the Church is *properly* taught and able to determine the Truth from false doctrine.

There are many references in the writings of the New Testament regarding false teachers and false doctrines. In the event that the elders of the Church do not know the Truth they are in no position to distinguish the difference between Truth and lies (see Acts 20:28-31; Ephesians 4:11-16; Titus 1:9-11).

ELDERS AS "OVERSEERS" OR "BISHOPS"

Here, again, is a situation that has been distorted in the Church. The word "bishop" has been used to apply to one who is the "overseer" of many congregations. There are bishops who have been appointed by men to do exactly what Peter told them NOT to do (see I Peter 5:3). An "overseer" is simply one who "watches over or looks after the welfare of another" and was never used as one to have authority over a group of congregations. Neither was a "bishop" to have such authority. The work of an overseer or bishop is to *lead*. This leadership does involve some "authority." There can not be leaders without giving them authority. This authority is not to be used to "lord it over those who have been entrusted to you (bishops)" (I Peter

5:3); rather it is to use it wisely in the protection and edification of the Church.

Elders are *leaders* and as such must be men with leadership abilities. To have men in the position of elder who are incapable of leadership is useless. This is not a position for a novice; weak-minded man who does not know the Word and is incapable of leading, within the company of other elders, an elder is to lead a congregation into a greater relationship with the Lord.

QUALIFICATIONS FOR ELDERS

Paul, in writing to two of his young "sons in the faith," listed the qualifications for elders so that they would know what is required to be an elder as they went from place to place "appointing" elders in Churches. These qualifications will be taken from I Timothy 3 and Titus 1.

I Timothy 3:1-7

- The overseer must be above reproach
- The husband of but one wife
- Temperate
- Self-controlled
- Respectable
- Hospitable
- Able to teach
- Not given to drunkenness
- Not violent but gentle
- Not quarrelsome
- Not a lover of money
- He must oversee his own family well and see to it that his children obey him with the proper respect
- He must not be a recent convert
- He must have a good reputation with outsiders

From Titus 1:6-9

- An elder must be blameless
- The husband of but one wife, a man whose children believe and are not open to the charge of being wild and disobedient
- Since an overseer is entrusted with God's work, he must be blameless—not overbearing, not quick tempered, not given to drunkenness, not violent, not pursuing dishonest gain
- Rather he must be hospitable
- One who loves what is good
- Who is self-controlled, upright, holy and disciplined
- He must hold firmly to the trustworthy message as it has been taught, so that he can encourage others by sound doctrine and refute those who oppose it

These are the qualifications prescribed by the Apostle Paul to these two evangelists. These qualifications are not to be met in part, rather in whole. Paul does not give instruction to find men who meet *most* of these qualifications. You will notice that these qualifications are basically the same in both cases. This is to show the necessity for unity in the different Churches established by these two young men.

It is unfortunate that the New Testament Church that is seen through the Restoration Movement has abandoned the basis for these qualifications and many are willing to *settle for what they can get*. We have come a long way away from the spiritual leaders spoken of by Paul in I Timothy and Titus in many of our churches. Many churches have accepted men who are not qualified to be elders to the detriment of the local church. It can be seen in the lack of spiritual growth and in the fact that many churches are not prepared to defend the Faith against false teachers.

You will notice that I have used the masculine word *man* or *men* when referring to elders. The reason is simple: Paul spoke of elders as *men* not women. In fact, Paul did not consider women to be leaders of a church and advised that women should not speak in churches nor have authority over men (I Cor. 14:34-35). Many denominational churches today have ordained women as preachers, elders, and deacons: not so within the Restoration Movement, although the Christian Church (Disciples of Christ) has done so. We believe that the office of elder is still one which should be held by a male and is not open to women. While some may say, "That is an *old-fashioned* approach and is not fit for the twenty-first century," I believe that the Scripture is clear on this matter and it is not open to discussion. It may well be old-fashioned, however, it remains Scriptural and that is sufficient for me. (There is a chapter on "The Role of Women" later in this book.)

THE ROLE OF DEACON

The role of deacon is likewise defined in the New Testament by Paul in his letter to Timothy. The Greek word, *diakonos*, is translated "servant, helper, one who carries out the will of or purpose of another, one who ministers to the needs of others." The term is used in some New Testament Scriptures in a generic manner and used for anyone, male or female, who served the needs of others.

The term as used in certain other passages of Scripture is more of an "official" role, such as I Timothy 3:8, 12. Here the word is used for those who would hold the "office" of *deacon*. Those holding this office would be appointed by the local congregation for a specific purpose.

The first "deacons" were appointed by the Jerusalem Church to care for the Grecian Jewish widows who were being overlooked in the daily distribution of food in favor of the Hebraic Jewish widows. The apostles gathered the disciples together and told them that they (the apostles) needed to devote themselves to the ministry of the Word. With this in mind, the apostles advised the disciples (members of the church) to "choose seven men from among you who are known to be full of the [Holy] Spirit and wisdom" (Acts 6:3 NIV). The key to these men was that they were to be "full of the Spirit." The following verses of Acts 6 give the names of these seven men. A short time later Stephen, one of these seven *deacons*, was accused of blasphemy and put on trial. Beginning with chapter seven, Stephen's sermon is recorded, and the Jews rose up and stoned him to death. Look to verse 55, "But Stephen, *full of the Holy Spirit*, looked up to heaven and saw the glory of God, and Jesus standing at the right hand of God" (NIV, emphasis mine). It is clear that they were *evangelists/ preachers* and that they were godly men. The office of deacon preceded that of elder. It is unfortunate that there are some within the Restoration Movement who believe that the office of deacon is simply a "stepping stone" to becoming an elder. Many of these same people believe that deacons are to be "young men" while elders are to be "older." The office of deacon is one of service, and it is not one of lesser import than that of elder.

WHAT IS THE ROLE OF DEACON IN THE LOCAL CHURCH?

It is unfortunate that the Bible is not clearer as to the role of deacon. As seen earlier, the role of deacon is that of a *servant*. We may determine that as a servant, the deacon provides services other than spiritual. That is not to say that deacons are not spiritual leaders as well. We need only see the role of Stephen in Acts 6 and 7 and the role of Phillip in Acts 8 to see that these men were evangelists. Though these seven men mentioned in Acts 6:1-6 are not called by the title "deacon" yet, the example is there. The relationship between these seven men and elders in today's Church was the same. As any other person in a local church, the deacons work under the "oversight" of the elders. Deacons are to be the "physical arm" of the church. They are to conduct the "business" of the church so that the elders can devote themselves to the spiritual and pastoral care of the believers. The elders are to create the policy of the local church through study of the Scriptures and through prayer, and the deacons are the "servants" who assist the elders in the implementation of that policy.

Unfortunately, the elders and deacons have been used in the modern church as a "governing body" and have combined to create one unit to do all things relating to the church. This is unfortunate since that is NOT the design of the early Church or the intent of the Holy Spirit when He gave the qualifications of elders and deacons. The role of deacon is much more than "serving the Lord's Supper to the congregation" or simply being a "board member" with the same voting power as the elders. The roles of elder and deacon are different enough to have two separate "governing bodies," a board of elders and a board of deacons. The New Testament gives the elders the authority to "govern" the affairs of the Church and not the deacons. The role of deacon is one of support and assistance to the elders.

Since the role of elder is to be "overseer" and "pastor," the role of a deacon is to handle the more physical matters relating to the Church. There are matters of finance, the physical part of the building(s), and to see to it that the physical needs of the church are met, for example, those of the congregation who might need food or other things which can be supplied by the church.

Qualifications for deacon as given by the Apostle Paul in I Timothy 3:8-11 follows:

- Men worthy of respect
- Sincere
- Not indulging in much wine
- Not pursuing dishonest gain
- Must keep hold of the deep truths of the faith with a clear conscience
- Must first be tested; then if there is nothing against them, they may serve as deacons
- Wives must be women worthy of respect
- Must be the husband of but one wife
- Must manage his children and his household well

Paul concludes this list by saying, "Those who have served well gain an excellent standing and great assurance in their faith in Christ Jesus" (I Timothy 3:13 NIV). He does not here, nor anywhere else, say that "should they do well, they may one day be elders." This is an unfortunate view by many in the Church today. Deacons are to be commended for their "servant's hearts" and to be respected by the congregation for their work in the kingdom.

CONCLUSION: If we would follow the New Testament examples in the roles of elders and deacons and select men of faith and ability to hold these worthy offices, there would be much less strife within the Church. We must allow the Holy Spirit to assist in the selection of these who would serve God first and the Church secondly. It is not a popularity contest whereby we select those who we feel will "do a good job," nor is it a position for life. The tendency for many who hold office in the church to believe it is "theirs for life." While the Bible gives no "term limits" to either office, it should be understood that when an elder or deacon reaches a time when he is ineffective, for any reason, he should step down or be removed by the congregation. Many churches have established a rotating system for elders and deacons. They are "elected" for a certain term, and when that term expires, they must become inactive for a period of time. This is, most likely, a good principle by which to work. While there may be times when a particular elder or deacon is doing a great job, it is good to "take time off" to rest and re-charge his spiritual batteries. If one is taking his position seriously and spiritually he will need such a break because of the often exhausting nature of the position.

Pray that God will raise up spiritual men who *desire* the office of elder or deacon and who will do everything to glorify the Heavenly Father.

CHAPTER TWENTY-FOUR

WHAT IS THE ROLE OF WOMEN IN THE CHURCH?

INTRODUCTION: We, in the Restoration Movement (or at least, the conservative side of the Movement), have placed women at a decided disadvantage in their "roles" in the Church. We take Paul's words that "women should keep silent in the churches" and "that they should have no authority over men" to be literally what it says. Is this the way we should view the role of women in the twenty-first century, or should we re-think this question? To best understand the role of women in the Church today we must return to the Bible and the role women played in both the Old Testament and the First Century Church.

Women, in the Old Testament, were seen more as "property" than as wives. It is only after the establishment of the Church that we see a role reversal for women in religious history. The original view came as a result of the fact that woman was created from the rib of man and created *after* man. Genesis 2:21-24 tells us that woman was created form the side of Adam and he called her "woman for she was taken out of man." Eve, being the first woman, was to be a helper to Adam. Perhaps it is because of the event that

Simply Speaking...

would take place later in the Garden of Eden, namely, the temptation of Eve and her partaking of the forbidden fruit, that she fell lower in the grand scheme of things, perhaps not. This is only speculation. Rightly or wrongly, the place of woman in the Old Testament was not a good one. Women were looked upon as having no role in decisions, politics, or any other thing of concern. Their roles were to be the bearer of a man's children and perhaps to keep things in order at home. This was about the extent of their role in Old Testament society. There were some notable exceptions to this, namely, Deborah, Esther, Ruth, and a few others. Women were not counted in a census and were, for the most part, considered of lesser value than cattle or sheep.

One good example of this pattern is found in Genesis 12. Abram (Abraham) went to Egypt because of a famine in his land. As he went into Egypt, he told his wife Sarai (Sarah) that because of her great beauty, the Egyptians would likely kill him and take her. He devised a scheme to tell only a half-truth. While it was true that Sarai was his half-sister, she was also his wife; Abram told her to tell the Egyptians that she was only his sister and being seen by Pharaoh's officials, she was taken to be a wife of the Pharaoh. It was only after things went terribly wrong that Pharaoh told Abram to take his wife and "get out!" Abraham was willing to give up his wife to save his own skin.

MORE ON THE ROLE OF WOMEN IN THE OLD TESTAMENT

The example of Abram and Sarai as seen above is but one of many examples. Let us turn our attention to Lot, Abraham's nephew. When given the choice of places to live by Abraham (which rightly would have been Abraham's choice), Lot chose the fertile plains and gave Abraham the less suitable foothills for grazing his herds and flocks. The only problem with Lot's choice was that there were two cities on this plane which were called Sodom and Gomorrah. I am quite certain that you know what happened to them as a result of their wickedness. It was when the angels of the Lord came to Lot's house that the men of Sodom asked that Lot send these "men" out of his house so that they might have sex with them. Lot offered his daughters to the men instead. The daughters, who were virgins, were soundly rejected as the men of Sodom were only interested in having sex with other men. The point here is that women, in this case, Lot's own daughters were of little value as Lot offered his daughters to a mob for the purpose of their being raped by that mob. Later, we see Lot, his wife, and daughters fleeing Sodom because the wrath of God is about to be brought upon these two wicked cities. Lot's wife, after being told not to look back, turned to see what she had left behind and was instantly turned into a pillar of salt! There is no mention of Lot's grieving the loss of his wife since we see him, very soon, sleeping with his two daughters and making them pregnant.

David's lust for a woman whom he saw taking a bath (perhaps appropriately named Bathsheba) brought him great sorrow and created great sin in his life. He had her husband killed, committed adultery, lost a child, and suffered greatly because of his actions.

Esther is another prominently mentioned woman in the Old Testament. In fact, there is a Book which bears her name. It is the story of a woman whose influence saved her people from destruction.

The Book of Ruth is another great story of a woman whose first marriage ended in tragedy only to find love on the threshing floor. She was the grandmother of King David. Her story is a beautiful one and deserves our attention.

Simply Speaking...

There are many other examples of women, both good and bad, in the Old Testament playing a role in God's scheme of things. May we now move into the New Testament era?

THE ROLE OF WOMEN IN THE NEW TESTAMENT

Moving from the Old Testament into the new is simple since there is little change in the Gospel accounts. Viewing Mary, the mother of Jesus, we see that she was still under Old Testament law and, therefore, without many "rights." When it was determined that she was pregnant and betrothed (engaged) to Joseph, Joseph planned to divorce her as was prescribed in the Law of Moses. This was the lesser of two punishments since she could have been stoned to death for having sex with a man prior to marriage. It took a visit from the Angel Gabriel to convince Joseph that the child Mary was carrying was the Son of God. Mary had no special status even after the birth of Jesus and likely became a widow sometime after Jesus twelfth birthday since Joseph is not mentioned again in the Gospel accounts. In fact, Mary is mentioned only sparingly as the ministry of Jesus unfolds.

Other women are mentioned prominently in the Gospels including Mary Magdalene, Mary and Martha (sisters of Lazarus), Mary, the mother of James and John, etc. These women were some who attended to Jesus' earthly needs and were present at His death and intended to prepare His body for proper burial. The women, however, were not "leaders" in the early Church.

It is only after the writing of the Bible that we see women coming into some prominence. Paul, in writing about the role of women in the Church, is quite vocal as to their place. He, in I Corinthians 14:34-35, said this: ". . . women should remain silent in the churches. They are not allowed to speak, but must be in submission, as the Law says. If they want to inquire about something, they should ask their own husbands at home; for it is *disgraceful for a woman to speak in the church.*" (NIV, emphasis mine). This is a very difficult passage for us, today, to understand. It, along with others, has caused controversy among many scholars and churches today. Many "denominations" have ordained women as ministers, elders, deacons etc., and, if these verses are to be taken literally, this is not acceptable in the Lord's Church. How do we view these two verses from I Corinthians? They were written by the Apostle Paul who was divinely directed as were all the writers of the Bible. Let us look at another of Paul's writings along the same line.

Paul, also in I Corinthians, in reference to worship found in chapter eleven, makes several comments regarding women in worship. In verse 3 he wrote, "Now I want you to realize that the head of every man is Christ, *and the head of the woman is man*, and the head of Christ is God" (NIV, emphasis mine).

Paul continues his direction for women in the verses that follow: "Every man who prays or prophesies with his head covered dishonors his head. *And every woman who prays or prophesies with her head uncovered dishonors her head*—it is just as though her head were shaved. If a woman does not cover her head, she should have her hair cut off; and if it is a disgrace for a woman to have her hair cut or shaved off, she should cover her head. A man ought not to cover his head, since he is the image and glory of God; *but the woman is the glory of man. For man did not come from woman, but woman from man. Neither was man created for woman, but woman for man.* For this reason, and because of the angels, the woman ought to have a sign of authority on her head" (NIV, emphasis mine). WOW!

Simply Speaking...

Does that ever put women in their places? Let us take a further look at this passage of Scripture.

Before we discuss the woman having her head covered, let us look at the man having his head un-covered. In the Old Testament, a man was to cover his head when he prayed, showing respect for God. In the New Testament, it was a sign of disrespect for a man to cover his head when praying. The question is begged, "Why the difference?" The difference is simply a difference in *custom*. The custom of the Old Testament time and the custom of the New Testament time were different. Now let us move to verse 5 where Paul decrees that "every woman who prays or prophesies with her head uncovered dishonors her head. . ." What does the term "head" mean? There is some controversy regarding that term. Some believe that it refers to the husband of the woman, while others believe that it is her literal head that needs to be covered with some kind of external head covering, such as a shawl, scarf, etc. It was the custom of the day that women should wear a veil when in public and hence, the idea would be that a "loose" moral woman would be one who was "uncovered." A second explanation for the "covering" was the woman's long hair. The problem existing at Corinth was that women were having their hair cut and were therefore, "uncovering their head." A third explanation offered recently is that the term "uncovered" has to do with "loosed hair." This simply means that a woman should have long hair and that it should not be "piled-up" on her head, rather left flowing as a shawl would be.

None of these explanations are easy to accept. Perhaps it would be wise to accept the "traditional" explanation and say that the veil is the accepted method of head covering as was the practice of the time. A woman wearing a veil in ancient times was less likely to be "bothered" by a man. Were she to be un-veiled, however, she would be considered to be loose and "available" and more likely to be harassed. The veil was a sign that she was not a loose woman.

"*Every woman who prays or prophesies. . .*" What is this? Is it permissible to "pray or prophesy" in the public worship service? The same words are used here as were used in the previous account of "praying and prophesying" with respect to a man. This must mean that it is acceptable! In the Old Testament there were female prophets. Some of these women are: Miriam (the sister of Moses), Deborah (read about her in the Book of Judges), Huldah (lived during the reign of King Josiah, see II Kings 22:14; II Chronicles 34:22), and Noadiah (opposed Nehemiah's efforts to rebuild the wall in Jerusalem, see Nehemiah 6:14). These women were prophetesses and mentioned in the Bible for a reason. That reason being, God is telling us that women can be used by Him as can men.

Anna was a prophetess living in the Temple area when Jesus was brought by Joseph and Mary to the Temple for His circumcision at the age of eight days. She was a widow who lived in the Temple, longing to see the Messiah, and was rewarded for her faithfulness by seeing Jesus at this time (see Luke 2:36-38).

We also see in the New Testament, Phillip's virgin daughters who prophesied (see Acts 21:9). We find two other references to women (wives) being limited as to their participation in public worship (I Corinthians 14:34 and I Timothy 2:12). It is because of these references that we conclude that Paul was referring to the manner of dress for women in said public worship.

The question may then be asked, "If they (women) are properly dressed, does there remain a prohibition to their praying or prophesying?" Scholars have debated this question for a very long time. Hiding just under the surface is the bigger question, "Should the Restoration

Simply Speaking...

Movement Churches allow women to be preachers?" Prior to answering that question there are several more questions which must be addressed. One such question is, "How can we harmonize this passage, I Corinthians 11: 5 with Paul's comments in I Corinthians 14:34 and in I Timothy 2:12?" In this passage, Paul was referring to the disharmony which existed in the worship service. There was a great deal of discord in the Corinthian Church, and this was another example of such disharmony. It is the opinion of this writer that women were praying and prophesying in the "formal" worship services, although some of them were not in the proper dress by not having their heads properly covered.

Men were prohibited from having long hair since it was a sign to the Corinthian people that they were homo-sexual. With this in mind, it is easy to understand the prohibitions for such requirements. Paul is addressing people in a time when customs were different than they are today. Society can, and does, dictate certain "styles" of dress and decorum and as times change, we change our dress styles and hair styles. This is not a matter of "doctrine" or a matter of "faith." It is simply a matter of choice as to how we dress. The key to this would be dress "appropriately." Ladies, by your dress, you should not bring dishonor to yourselves or to your husbands who are your "heads" as described by Paul here in I Corinthians 11.

Another question to be asked is, "What does Paul mean in I Timothy 2: 12 when he says, 'I do not permit a woman to teach, or have authority over a man; she must be silent?'" The point here is that a woman is not permitted to *have authority over a man*. Paul continues in the next verses to explain the reason for such prohibition by saying, "For Adam was formed first, then Eve. And Adam was not the one deceived; it was the woman who was deceived and became a sinner." This indicates, as in I Corinthians 11, Paul taught that the woman was subject to the man because of the order of their creation. The key here, once again, is in the matter of "authority." While there are many women who are more capable of teaching the Scriptures than many men, the prohibition still exists: Women can have no *spiritual* authority over a man. Prophesying, as in the case of Phillip's daughters, or teaching, does not exercise such authority and are, therefore, permissible. As to women becoming elders, evangelists, etc, the prohibition exists.

I Corinthians 14:33b-35 says, as in the case of all the congregations of the saints, women should remain silent in the churches. They are not allowed to speak, but must be in submission, as the Law says. If they want to inquire about something, they should ask their own husbands at home; for it is *disgraceful for a woman to speak in the church*." Does this mean that Paul has changed his "tune" since the eleventh chapter of I Corinthians? After all, he is speaking of prophesying and tongues in this chapter! I cannot pretend to know the "mind" of the Apostle Paul; however, I believe, as previously stated, that it was a matter of the time during which he wrote these words. I fully understand that it was at the urging of the Holy Spirit and that "all Scripture is God-breathed." Having said that, I am in no way "correcting" the words of Paul. Although there are many who believe that the role of women in the churches is defined by these verses, I am not one of them.

If we view this passage in context, we see that Paul is making reference to *order in the worship service*. The fourteenth chapter opens with a dissertation of speaking in tongues and of prophesy, and the first twenty-five verses make reference to that situation at Corinth. It may be that Paul was referring to women not taking part in these activities. If this is the case, Paul would have been incorrect in chapter eleven. Since this in not the case, we must seek another explanation. A plausible explanation is that Paul's command to "keep silent" refers to their not being permitted to take part in the "final decisions" of the assembly about the legitimacy of the prophesies which were being given. "Speak" in twenty of the twenty-one appearances of this verb in this chapter, outside verses 34-35, refers directly to or by analogy to four very specific kinds of speech: tongues, their interpretation, prophesy or its evaluation. The first three of these are "Spiritual Gifts" dispensed by the Holy Spirit without regard to gender. An authoritative evaluation of prophesy, however, while requiring input from the whole congregation, would have ultimately been the responsibility of the leadership of the congregation, i.e., the elders. These elders were exclusively male. This view also explains the reason that this prohibition comes where it does in the text. The sequence of topics from verses 27-33 has been precisely: tongues, their interpretation, prophesy, and its evaluation, in that order.

As is the case in I Corinthians 11:2-16, the women who Paul silences are "wives." This would explain why they must not publicly challenge the church's prophesies but "ask their own husbands" at home (v. 35). To do otherwise might be to challenge their husbands in church in ways that would contradict their God-ordained submission to their husbands (see v. 34). The "Law" cannot refer to an Old Testament prohibition against women speaking in public worship since no such "Law" exists. Most likely, Paul refers to the "order of creation" as he did in chapter 11:8-9.

Paul brings the entire matter to a conclusion in verse 39, "Therefore, my brothers, be eager to prophesy, and do not forbid speaking in tongues. But everything should be done in a fitting and orderly way." With this in mind, let us view the section forbidding women to "speak" in the public worship in context of the whole. I Corinthians 12-14 deal with the use of Spiritual Gifts, and this admonition should be couched in that context.

I TIMOTHY 2:11-15

Paul, once again takes up the position of women in the churches. In this passage he says, "A woman should learn in quietness and full submission. I do not permit a woman to teach or have authority over a man; she must be silent. For Adam was formed first, then Eve. And Adam was not the one deceived; it was the woman who was deceived and became a sinner. But women will be saved through childbearing—if they continue in faith, love and holiness with propriety" (NIV).

Here is another difficult text to understand, especially in the twenty-first century. "Since woman was created after man and from man, she is subordinate to him." This is the argument that Paul puts forth here. God has placed man as a leader in worship in the public assembly, and women are prohibited to have "authority" over men. It is not wrong for women to teach the Word of God, but is wrong for them to teach in such a way that it assumes authority or superiority over men (see Titus 2:5). This is the only reason given in the Scripture as to why it is wrong.

Paul uses the argument that Adam was first created and then Eve. Due to this fact, man is not of woman; rather, woman is of man. In any public position relating to the Church, women are to assume a subordinate role to men. This position is not based upon some arbitrary statement of man, rather, it is a statement based upon the order of creation as God chose—the divine order of creation which formed woman as man's "helpmate."

Paul continues his argument by referring to the "fall." It was, after all, that woman was the first sinner, then the man. While it is true that both Adam and Eve sinned, it was the woman who was first tempted and bore the brunt of the punishment. Since Adam was "not the one deceived," Paul is indicating that Adam *followed* Eve into sin, presumably by his own choice. Adam followed Eve into sin "with his eyes fully open." She fell into Satan's deceit. Both were involved in the sin, but Eve allowed herself to be deluded. One would find it difficult to find a more vivid illustration of the difference between the male and female nature. Since there is this distinction between the sexes, then that distinction forms the basis for the argument and the reason for the instruction given. This great catastrophe in Eden forms the distinct beacon for all generations which followed. Because of the manner in which the "fall" occurred, the woman is always to be in subjection to her husband and never usurp authority over him. Even if he is weaker spiritually, she is to be in subjection to him when they are in public worship.

In verse 15, Paul refers to her salvation coming through "child-bearing." This involves more than simply "having children," and goes to the rearing and nurturing of those children. The domestic life of child rearing is in contrast with the taking authority over her husband.

Paul concludes this thought by saying, "If they continue in faith, love and holiness with propriety." We could add that if they continue in faith in God, love to humanity, and holiness of life, coupled with her modest behavior. Often women (and men) think that this is demeaning to women and that it assigns them to an inferior position. Nothing could be farther from the truth. What a great opportunity and responsibility for a woman to have than to rear her children in the care and nurture of a Christian home. She is designed with a different body and nature than man and, as such, she is better equipped for this purpose, while man is made to be the more physical of the two, and he is, by God's ordination, to be the "breadwinner."

The "theme" in this second chapter of I Timothy is *worship* just as it was in I Corinthians 14. The order given by Paul with respect to women in public worship is to keep order in worship and not to have chaos. That is not to say that women bring chaos in public worship, rather, that by their participation they could have a different view of things than their husbands and therefore bring shame to their husbands.

The prohibition of women *teaching* or *having authority over men* would not be foreign to either Jews or Greeks since they did not permit women to do either. Although in some parts of the Roman Empire a different view of the role of women was held, the prevailing attitude of Paul toward women would be the norm. One well known example of ancient standards was the assortment of "household codes," that is, lists of duties and relationships that were traditionally observed within families and in external society in ancient Greece. We do not know if these were still in existence at the time of Paul's writing, however, it is likely that some of same standards were present. Any deviation of these standards would be noted and used against the Christians. We can easily see this principle in Titus 2 when Paul refers to the "older women training the younger women." He says, "so that no one will malign the Word of God." It would seem that the role of women in Greco/Roman society was well established at the time of Paul's writings. Paul continues in verse 8, ". . . so that those who oppose you may be ashamed because they have nothing bad to say about us." He continues in verse 10, ". . . so that in every way they will make the teaching about God our Savior attractive." These references to the role of women by Paul to Titus appear to be in keeping with the traditions of the times.

We may take some ethical examples from Old Testament requirements regarding worship. The Law of Moses called upon the Jews to perform certain acts within their worship experience. These acts were not brought into the Church even though God did not change. We also see Paul referring to eating meat sacrificed to idols, something we are not concerned with today. In many cases, circumstances called for *different* responses and practices that in other circumstances would be considered important.

It is often difficult for readers of the Bible to understand certain practices, especially when they are not done within the modern society. Sometimes Biblical practices are meaningful in some circumstances and not in others. In fact, they may seem strange and even turn people away should they be repeated in certain situations other than the original intended ones. It is very important that one determine the original theological basis, the reason for any accompanying text, the purpose of the practice, and the changing circumstances that might require a fresh look at the practices involved to accomplish the same purpose and express the same Biblical truths.

This, in no way, is an attempt to interpret Scripture by culture or historical customs. Rather, the Bible stands alone and often against contemporary culture. We can, however, apply the intended use of Scripture if we understand how it was originally intended to be applied. This may assist us in determining the functional reasons why certain commands and practices were placed in the writings of the Bible, where they dealt with real life situations.

MANY QUESTIONS ABOUND

There are many questions which beg to be answered. Some of these might be:

1. Does the use of the verb *authenteo* in this context restrict women from having authority of any sort, or is a stronger meaning of controlling, dominating or assuming authority on their own better understood here? This would narrow the scope of restriction.

2. If a woman teaches a mixed group today (men and women), does it imply the same authority as it did in the time of Paul's writings?
3. Would a woman's teaching men be a part of a leadership team to which men are accountable be the same today as it was in Paul's time?
4. Was Paul's description of his apostolic practice ("I do not permit") a command for all time and circumstances, even though it was not expressed as an imperative?
5. In addressing our Biblically illiterate society, should we use the fact that Adam was first created, then Eve and the fact that Eve was the one deceived as being useful in understanding the prohibition for women to teach men or have a role in leadership?
6. Should we require women to refrain from teaching men or having a role in leadership? Should we also require women to have their heads covered in worship as did Paul in I Corinthians 11?

In answering any of these questions with an "I don't know!" or should there be any doubt, we should re-consider the prohibition for their using their Spirit-given gifts in the Church.

It is important here to redefine the two opposing views on this issue.

- There is no legitimate way to avoid concluding from I Timothy 2:11-15 that Paul did not allow women either to teach men or to have any kind of authority over them. Further, this prohibition was not confined to the socio-religious conditions at Ephesus. Therefore, any attempts to adjust it for Western or any other contemporary culture is expressly wrong.

- The other view would hold that Paul's statements were directed to specific circumstances at Ephesus and to the Church at Ephesus, such as the prominence of women in pagan religion and the victimization of women in the Church. It is wrong to apply it without adjustment to other circumstances.

The strength of the first view is in its focus on the words and grammar of the text. The weakness is its failure to pay proper attention to the larger context or take into account the problems of application. The strength of the second view is its awareness that the letter was written to address specific circumstances that are different from our own. Its weakness is in overemphasizing the background, perhaps to the point of distortion and straining the text.

Perhaps there is a third possible approach. Due to the nature of the times, Paul may well be giving Timothy instructions regarding the role of women, while carefully avoiding placing it into a "command for all times and places." These instructions are not limited to Ephesus but apply to the entire ancient world, both Jewish and pagan, that regarded it as immoral for women to go beyond certain public restrictions. Paul had a missionary purpose as seen in I Corinthians 9:20-23 (NIV), "To the Jews I became like a Jew, to win the Jews. To those under the Law, I became like one under the Law (though I myself am not under the Law), so as to win those not having the Law. To those not having the Law, I became like one not having the Law. To the weak I became weak, to win the weak. I have become all things to all men so that by all possible means I might save some. I do all this for the sake of the Gospel, that I may share in its blessings." By applying this approach to these passages, we should be able to understand Paul's missionary approach and purpose to our own social context rather than repeat the same restrictions that were appropriate then but could become a "stumbling block" to the people of our time and culture.

However this issue may be settled, the ideals of this passage, beginning with prayer and including peaceful holiness on the part of men and modesty on the part of women, should be pursued by all Christians today. In addition, men should not abuse or harshly dominate women, as has been the practice of some. Women should not neglect their pursuit of the gracious qualities as taught in I Timothy 2:9-15, as some have done. *No church should split over these issues.* We would do well to remember the words of Paul in Ephesians 4:3, "Make every effort to keep the unity of the Spirit through the bond of peace" (NIV).

Having made arguments both for and against the roles of women in today's assembly, may I now express my own opinion? I believe that there are many women who are more learned and better apt to teach than many men; however, there exists still the argument of *authority*. I believe that men are, in no way, superior to women and that women deserve the same respect if they are godly women as do godly men. Having said this, I believe that women are not to be elevated to the role of elder or evangelist in the New Testament Church today. There remains an issue, as Paul said, regarding the fact that "woman was created from man," and this, alone, would remain an argument for women not to have authority over man. This issue has created much controversy over the years, and many churches have resolved the issue by ordaining women as elders, ministers, etc. This may well be a "test of fellowship" for many of the Restoration Movement Churches, as it would be for this writer. I remain quite opposed to this practice. May we all continue to pray that God will give us guidance in this matter as well as all others.

CHAPTER TWENTY-FIVE

HOW SHOULD WE VIEW MARRIAGE, DIVORCE AND REMARRIAGE?

INTRODUCTION: As we come to one of the most divisive issues in the Church today, we are tempted to say, "God hates divorce," and be done with it. While this is true, as He said in Malachi 2:16, "I hate divorce . . ." (NIV), the answer is not as simple as that. God makes provisions for those who have been and are now stung by the situation. There are many "factors" in the discussion of divorce and many who are legalistic and say, "There are *no* legitimate grounds for divorce for any reason." There is another group who proclaim that there is only *one* Biblical ground for divorce and that is adultery," while other, more liberal thinkers believe that Paul allowed divorce for "abandonment by an unbeliever." The Church is sharply divided on this issue, and perhaps some of you reading this right now have a totally different view on the subject.

In this chapter we shall consider the place for marriage in the Bible; when, or if, divorce is allowed in the Bible; and when, or if, re-marriage is ever acceptable. We will search the Bible and see just what God has to say on these subjects. Some of the Scripture may be painful and cause us to "think" about our notions. It shall be the goal of this writer to remain as objective as possible while seeking the Biblical answers to these most pressing questions. While this will not be a definitive treatise, I pray that it shall be sufficient to push the reader to think about the attitudes that he or she may have held for many years and always to remember that we must view all matters through the lens of God's love and His grace.

MARRIAGE

Marriage is an institution ordained by God for the purpose of procreating. As an added "bonus," marriage allows two people (a man and a woman) to be united in love and affection for each other. Marriage "makes a house a home" and at the same time, provides a stable environment in which we rear our children.

Marriage finds its beginning in the beginning. Marriage was instituted in the Garden of Eden as God created woman from Adam and presented her to him to be his "wife." This occurred because there was found no "helper" for man from all the beings God had created. In Genesis, chapter two, we read about the formation of man and woman. Beginning with verse 21 we read, "So the Lord God caused the man to fall into a deep sleep; and while he was sleeping, He took one of the man's ribs and closed up the place with flesh. Then the Lord God made a woman from the rib He had taken out of the man, and He brought her to the man. The man said, 'This is now bone of my bones and flesh of my flesh; she shall be called woman, for she has been taken out of man.' For this reason a man will leave his father and mother and be united to his wife, and they will become one flesh" (Genesis 2:21-23 NIV). Since God created both man and woman and "united" them and "they became one flesh," God had intended that they remain together throughout their entire lives.

It was not until after the "fall" that man and woman recognized their nakedness and knew of their sin. As a result of the sins committed by Adam and Eve in the Garden of Eden, they were removed from the Garden and received the curse spoken of in Genesis 3:16-19. Adam named his wife "Eve" because she was to become the "mother of all the living."

Jesus' first recorded miracle was at a wedding feast where He turned the water into wine when the host had run out of wine for his guests. Jesus, by His mere presence at this wedding, must have sanctioned such a union. Jesus refers to Himself as the "Bridegroom" and the Church as the "Bride" in parables, and in the Revelation letter, the Church is viewed as the "Bride of the Lamb." There are many other references to marriage, both literally and spiritually, throughout the Bible.

Marriage is not something easy to maintain. Once upon a time, marriage was without conflict, anger, insecurity, insensitivity, or any other negative. The truth today, however, is that there are many things that work against a marriage being successful. There are external forces as well as internal forces pulling at the marriage. There are the strains of financial situations, the strains of rearing children, the strains of religious differences in many marriages, and many other difficulties. We rarely see marriages lasting "until death do us part." When marriage reaches the "breaking point," there is usually nothing that can be done to repair it. It is the *Humpty Dumpty Syndrome*. I believe the legal words are "irretrievably broken." It is at this point that a divorce usually follows. It is often something as simple as "drifting apart." One spouse will say to the other, "I just don't want to be married to you anymore." It may be that the bond of love has simply dissolved. Whatever the reason, there occurs a "split" in the marital relationship, and one or both parties are forever injured.

Marriage can (and should) be the most satisfying and happiest experience in anyone's life. When two people come together in the "bonds of matrimony" and have a beautiful wedding experience, it is so easy to see the radiant beauty of the bride and the happiness in the groom's face. For far too many, this day is quickly marred with the disappointments and realities of life together. The successful marriages are those in which two people can "agree to disagree." No two people will ever see "eye to eye" on *everything*. Since a marriage is made from the union of *two separate and unique individuals*, there are bound to be some disagreements. The key to survival is being willing to accept these differences and willing to do the most difficult work of getting past these differences and working together to accomplish a united *goal*. Far too many enter the marriage relationship with one hand tied behind the back of each. This is because the feeling exists that "if it doesn't work out, we can get a divorce." With this attitude, a marriage is likely doomed to failure.

The marriage principles as set forth in I Corinthians chapter seven are in harmony with all other Scriptures relating to marriage. Paul instructs the Corinthian Church (and us) that it is better not to marry. The reason for this is simple: There was a severe persecution of the Church at the time of this writing, and it was only to become worse. Paul wished for all of his readers to be unmarried because it was difficult enough to endure persecution alone; however, it was much more difficult if one had a family. Paul then gives instructions as to the sexual nature of marriage, concluding that each person in the marriage is responsible to the other with respect to their bodies. Paul speaks to sexual immorality and divorce in this chapter. He gives instruction as to how a marriage is to be and how one is to conduct oneself if planning to remain unmarried. We will discuss this chapter in I Corinthians more fully as we view divorce and remarriage.

Can marriages survive poor starts, or adultery, or financial problems, or any other such problems? The short answer is *yes, they can*. While it is possible for marriages to survive these devastating situations, most do not. It is very difficult to put a broken marriage back together once it has been broken. When the *trust issue* has been broken, there exists a most difficult road to travel. While, as I have just said, it is *possible*, it is not *probable*.

DIVORCE AND REMARRIAGE

Divorce is a very ugly word to many Christians today. It carries with it a sense of failure. It is, to many, an unpardonable sin which carries with it the penalty of spiritual death and a life of not being able to serve the Lord. Far too many Christians limit anyone's ability to serve the Church in any capacity, such as elder, deacon, minister, etc., should that person have been divorced. Some would even go so far as to place a black "D" on the chest of those who are divorced. As an example, this would be in keeping with Hawthorne's book, *The Scarlet Letter*, which was written about an adulteress in Colonial America. She was forced to wear a scarlet "A" on her dress signifying the fact that she was an adulteress. While our society is not quite so inclined, we are, in the Church of Jesus Christ, almost that way. It is very difficult for a divorced man in many of our churches to find a place where he can serve Christ if he has been divorced. Women are not exempt either. Many women are considered not worthy to teach children and are shunned by other married women because the latter think that the "divorced woman is after their man." While we are becoming more tolerant and understanding of God's Word and His great love for all Christians, there are still some who hold fast to this view.

There are many misunderstandings with respect to divorce and the Church. The first thing we need to consider is that neither Jesus nor Paul *ever* condemned anyone simply because they sinned. There are many who believe that they are being consistent with the teachings of the New Testament by insisting that others *keep the rules*. They have become more like the Pharisees than the Pharisees ever were. These people believe that they must live in a certain manner to receive the favor of God, and if anyone should deviate from the *Rule Book* that they have created for all Christians, those people are in a *"heap of trouble."* This mind-set was prevalent in the days of Jesus and is still as prevalent today. It is as *wrong* today as it was *wrong* then. Jesus and Paul were the two who most protested against this *performance-based* attitude during their ministries. Jesus reserved His harshest criticism for those who had such a mindset. The Pharisees were the most *religious* of their day, and Jesus labeled them "vipers" and "whitewashed sepulchers full of dead men's bones" (see Matthew 23:1-26). In such a manner, the Apostle Paul stood firmly against people who entered churches insisting that Christians should live a certain way before they could expect God to show them any *favor*. Should you desire to know more about Paul's attitude toward those with this mind-set, read his letter to the Galatians.

It is ironic, then, that many Christians would attempt to use the teachings of Jesus and Paul to scrutinize fellow Christians, who may be struggling to learn God's Word and His will for their lives, in an effort to make them do "what is right."

Secondly, the marriage commitment is to be held in the highest regard. I am disheartened when I hear of anyone getting a divorce. I don't like divorce. I do not like the potential damage it does to children, the strains it places on friendships, and how extended family members are adversely affected by it. The marriage commitment is a powerfully necessary ingredient for a church and for a society that want to stand for things that are good and right and pure.

Those who enter divorce proceedings lightly show shallow thinking and are putting themselves in the position of adopting a value system that is relativistic and self-serving. Divorce should be a decision only of last resort and should be accompanied by wise counsel and accountability.

I do not wish to be viewed as one who gives license or credence to people who are simply living for self-satisfaction. What I *do* want to prompt is a loving attitude toward those who are divorced. I want to encourage you to exert the maximum effort to save a dying marriage, even if the reason for the divorce is on Biblical grounds, but the marriage appears to remain irreparable. When Christians come to the end of an extremely difficult, even ungodly marriage, the last thing they need is for other Christians to feed them a diet of guilt and shame. Instead, let us be encouragers and full of kindness. Let us uphold them in love; let us be vessels of grace even as we continue to believe in the full Biblical principles.

Divorce was permitted by God as He gave Moses the Law and gave permission for a "Bill of Divorcement" to be presented to a wife who "displeased" her husband. She was then free to remarry; however, should her new husband also divorce her or die, she was not free to be remarried to her first husband.

As we come into the New Testament, divorce is viewed in an entirely different light. Jesus taught on divorce in His Sermon on the Mount found in Matthew 5:31-32: "It has been said, 'Anyone who divorces his wife must give her a certificate of divorce.' But I tell you that anyone who divorces his wife, except for marital unfaithfulness, causes her to become an adulteress, and anyone who marries the divorced woman commits adultery" (NIV). Jesus chose a very sensitive subject on which to comment. After teaching on murder and adultery, He taught on the subject of divorce. His words placed divorce in a whole new light, leaving only marital unfaithfulness as a cause for divorce.

What, then, do we do with Christians who find themselves in a marriage that is broken and headed for divorce? The first principle we must apply is *love*. We must not shun them, cause more pain, or in any way make them feel inferior. Our love for our brother and sister must remain strong as they navigate their way through a most painful experience. Secondly, we must be in an attitude of prayer for these two hurting souls. God expects that we should love them and pray for them. They need our prayerful support in these most difficult times. We cannot "take sides" in such a situation and must be there to comfort each as needed. It is not for any Christian to "make an assumption of guilt" on either party since none of us know what "goes on behind closed doors." God has made it quite clear that *He* is the only righteous Judge and that it is not within our scope of ability to judge anyone.

Those who are being divorced or have already undergone such are in need of even more from the Christian. Since the Church should be a place where Christians are admonished to "Carry each other's burdens, and in this way you will fulfill the law of Christ" (Galatians 6:2, NIV), we should not be a place where the divorced (or anyone else) should expect to be shunned. We should nurture the "hurting" from any ills, not treating them as "second class citizens."

MATTHEW 19; MARK 10

Jesus, in Matthew 19, (Mark also records this incident) once again, addressed the matter of divorce. He was asked by the Pharisees (in an effort to test Him) about the subject of divorce. It is important that we understand that in both Matthew's and Mark's accounts of this incident, we are told that it occurred "beyond the Jordan." This is important because Jesus was in the region where John the Baptizer had accused Herod Antipas and Herodias (his brother's wife) of being in an adulterous situation.

The question: "Is it lawful for a man to divorce his wife for any and every reason?" (Matthew 19:3b, NIV). Follows then a mini debate in which Jesus is asking a question of the Pharisees and they with yet another question, followed by Jesus reply. The disciples hearing the exchange asked (in private), "If this is the situation between a husband and a wife, is it better not to marry?" (Matthew 19:10, NIV).

Jesus was not giving a "new law" here; rather, He was reiterating the law already given by Moses. God had not "changed His mind" with respect to divorce. The moral laws of both the Old and New Testaments were continuous and identical because they grow and reflect the basic nature and character of God. Since God's nature had not changed from Moses to Jesus, God was not lax on the subject of divorce and remarriage.

What Jesus was saying was that Herod Antipas, and his wife Herodias had defied God's will concerning the sanctity of marriage. They had committed adultery. Jesus was not about to rescind John's preaching on the subject of their adultery because it was from God! When Jesus was alone with His disciples, He reiterated the words He had spoken earlier.

Please notice something here that many miss in Mark's account: "Whoever divorces his wife and marries another woman commits adultery against her" (Mark 10:11 NIV). Did you catch it? "Adultery" is what a man does "against" his first wife if he tosses her away for another. Has anyone ever told you that divorce may sometimes be a "necessary evil" to protect a woman and her children from abuse, alcoholism, or other terrible situations but that her remarriage would be adultery? That is *not* what Jesus said!

In Mark's account, divorce and remarriage are treated in more austere language than in Matthew's. Exceptional cases are not in view. Divorce—whether remarriage occurs or not—is adultery (i.e. unfaithfulness, covenant-breaking). Both the Old and New Testaments assume that the divorced person will remarry, and there is *no prohibition* from doing so. It must be understood that those second marriages are not immoral situations where a man and a woman are "living in adultery." People may adulterate, breach, or otherwise abuse their marriage covenants by breaking a "one-flesh" union. That said, they are not "living in sin" if they marry again. It is important to realize that their effective repentance from the sin of adultery they committed by breaking the marriage vows from the previous marriage plays an important role in making the new marriage work.

There is no Biblical precedent set for anyone to leave the second, third, or even fourth marriage in order to "set things right with God" thinking they should return to a failed first marriage. In fact, this practice is expressly forbidden by God in Deuteronomy 24:1-4. If you are in a second, third, or fourth marriage today, the call of God to you has nothing to do with getting out of your present relationship and getting back with the original partner. It does, however, have everything to do with making your current relationship work by keeping it as healthy and divorce-proof as possible.

LUKE 16:18

The subject of divorce and remarriage occurs in Luke's account of the life of Christ with minimal context and has none of the imperatives seen in Matthew and Mark. This account is couched in the other teachings of Jesus and may be, arguably, the most helpful statement on the subject made by Jesus. As we become less inclined to embrace Pharisaic legalisms and teachings and begin to exhibit the hearts of believers in Christ's teachings of love, who is to say that this simple statement is not one of the best? Jesus said, "Anyone who divorces his wife and marries another woman commits adultery, and the man who marries a divorced woman commits adultery" (Luke 16:18, NIV).

Why is this text potentially the most helpful of all? It is the most direct and unequivocal statement from Jesus to the effect that divorce is not a good thing, not part of the ideal will of God, and nothing to be happy about. It is, in fact, something more often than not to be repented of—repented of in the confidence that God is in the business of forgiving sin and healing sinners.

Adultery is not a sin of sex; it is a sin of covenant-breaking. It is, in many ways, worse than fornication because it involves the element of personal betrayal. As a marriage fails, it has been my experience as a counselor that everyone suffers. That being the case, can we not still believe that God is capable of providing forgiveness to all parties involved as He can do for all sins committed by anyone?

To conclude this section, I believe that there are ten elements on divorce and remarriage in Jesus' teaching. They follow:

First, Jesus affirmed and upheld what the Law of Moses says on divorce and remarriage. That is, He did not come to give "new laws" on the subject but to show us that righteousness always requires more than law. Laws are necessary to righteousness, but they are not sufficient for it to be realized. Hearts must be transformed by renewal that can come only from above, and transformation must show itself in how people who claim to love God live out the implications of their love for one another. This is the righteousness that both "exceeds that of the Scribes and Pharisees" and allows one to "enter the kingdom of heaven."

Second, Jesus acknowledged that divorce is a part of human experience. It does not exist in the human experience because of God's will but because of our own human weakness, sinfulness, and hardness of heart.

Third, Jesus reflected on the fact that law was designed to protect some of the most vulnerable victims of divorce. Women (and their children) were intended to have special protection against exploitation in the community of Israel. Again, however, human sinfulness allowed some in the community to evade the point of those protections and to perpetuate and even to expand harm to women in a male-dominated society.

Fourth, divorce is a failure to experience God's desire for human marital relationships. It exposes human sinfulness in dramatic fashion. It is not the divorce decree—which is nothing more than the legal acknowledgment of the death of a relationship—but whatever the man or woman has done to put the relationship to death that is sinful.

Fifth, the person who seeks and initiates the divorce—especially one who involves a third party in sexual infidelity—is guilty of "adultery against" his or her mate in the most flagrant manner. In fact, the harm "against" others seems almost never to end in such cases. Eventually, every life touched by any of the parties is likely to be hurt and wounded by what happens. Families of origin, children to the once-married pair, future mates—all will pay a price of some sort for the dissolution of a marriage.

Sixth, adultery is not an unpardonable sin. Can we really believe—regardless of the heartache, damaged lives, and lifelong consequences that are involved—that a sinner whose offense is divorce (i.e. covenant breaking, adultery) has no option but to live with his or her brokenness forever? Do the gospels reveal a Jesus who can heal blind eyes, forgive His own murderers, etc. but cannot (or will not) heal the broken life of someone who fails at marriage? Repentance is one's genuine remorse over whatever he or she contributed to the breakup of a marriage, and forgiveness is always the divine response to a penitent heart.

Seventh, repentance and forgiveness entail the possibility of healing, moving ahead with life, and experiencing the good things one had otherwise forfeited. In the case of a divorced person, this means that remarriage is an option to consider. For some, though, getting married again may be inappropriate. One may have discovered that he or she is not capable of sustaining the intimacy of marriage. There may well be other factors that would inhibit such a union, such as personality, lifestyle, or career, which would make it advisable for him or her to remain single following a divorce.

Eighth, remaining single after a divorce is neither a penance nor a penalty upon which forgiveness is contingent. Divorced persons have the option of experiencing God's gracious pardons, learning from the mistakes of a failed marriage, and receiving his final touch of spiritual healing through a new marital relationship. The message of the New Testament about every human failure is grace, pardon, and healing. Divorce is not a sin in its own special class that requires a lifelong penance of remaining celibate and compassionless.

Ninth, marriages subsequent to a divorce are real marriages. That is, anyone who has divorced and remarried is actually married to the new mate—not "living in adultery" with that person or "still married to his/ her first husband/ wife in the eyes of God." A civil divorce terminates a marriage. Anyone with a legal divorce has both the civil and divine right to marry again. In the Gospels, after all, Jesus talked with a woman who had been married to five different men, and at the time she met the Master, she was living with a man to whom she was not married (John 4:16-18). Her life was out of control; her solution was not to connect with her first husband somehow, but to allow Jesus to transform her and make her new.

Tenth, there is no biblical precedent for breaking up a second (or later) marriage in order to make right the mistakes made in the first. While Jesus made it clear that some marriages are broken without justification, He did not tell us how to "fix" them. Again, while saying that people who take marriage so lightly as to put away their wives in order to marry another are guilty of adultery by doing so, He did not specify what should happen to those new marriages. We must not presume to impose solutions that do not come from a clear word from Jesus on the matter.

A LOOK AT I CORINTHIANS 7

ISSUES INVOLVING BELIEVERS (I Corinthians 7:1-11)

Paul was faced with the same predicament we are in: taking the words of Jesus and applying them to the life situations of those for whom he cared deeply. Fortunately, for us, he had the special empowerment of the Holy Spirit to guide him. Paul, the "apostle to the Gentiles," took the words he had learned in a Jewish context and used them to answer a variety of questions we still face.

It is in the writings of Paul to the Church at Corinth where everything found in the Scripture about marriage, divorce, and remarriage come together for present-day believers. Paul shows his "pastoral side" as he deals with this most difficult topic. In I Corinthians 7, Paul deals with the difficult issues of celibacy, marriage, and the disruption of marriage due to divorce and death. What he says to these issues is invaluable to our instruction.

We must first understand that Paul is imminently qualified to teach of this subject. He was Jewish by birth, steeped in the rabbinic study of Torah, and clearly aware—as we shall soon see—of what Jesus had said about divorce and the Law of Moses. He was also aware of Roman culture and law, for he had grown up in the free city of Tarsus and was himself a Roman citizen. The dual circumstance of being rooted in the Holy Scriptures and struggling to honor its demands of holiness in a pagan society placed him in a position not unlike our own today. We know the Bible teaches the high value of marriage and family stability, yet we also live in a culture where marital commitments are taken far too lightly and divorces are too easily obtained.

Second, Paul became our teacher as a Christian ethicist in modeling how the teachings of Jesus on divorce should be applied. The goal he keeps before his readers is always reconciliation in the current relationship rather than rushing into a new one. In this regard he is very Jesus-like and very pastoral; whatever has led to the failure of one relationship may well lead to the failure of another, so it is preferable to resolve problems rather than merely to run from one set of problems into another. We have all seen it happen: someone changes job, mate, residence, church—but remains troubled, unhappy, and angry. (This is the old "grass is always greener" syndrome). We might get the impression that this person is dragging his or her trouble with them, no matter the new life in which he or she may surface. Paul is very realistic in acknowledging the fact that the ideal may not always be achieved and that some will pursue divorce in spite of Jesus' words and the apostle's counsel based on these words.

Third, one should notice that Paul does not try to give a set of inflexible rules for solving complex dilemmas in human relationships. He appeals to each believer's desire to honor Christ in a culture that is often hostile to faith. He clearly expects that desire to extend to one's behavior toward one's mate, one's larger family-by-blood, and his or her still larger family-by-faith.

In the first eleven verses of the seventh chapter, Paul addressed various marital situations where all parties involved are Christians. Paul has just completed a section (6:10-20) where he teaches the Church at Corinth about sexual immorality. Corinth was a very important Roman seaport city in Greece where there existed an abundance of brothels for sailors and temples devoted to pagan gods in which sexual activity was the order of the day. It is with this background that the Apostle Paul felt compelled to give clear and direct instruction as to what constituted proper sexual behavior for the people who had committed themselves to Christ.

Some of the Corinthian Christians appear to have taken the Christian rejection of *porneia* (Greek, meaning sexual immorality; root word for our pornography) to mean that celibacy was a morally superior lifestyle. It would appear that they had developed a slogan for such an idea. We can see that from verse one: "It is good for a man not to marry" (7:1 NIV). These are not Paul's words as has been erroneously concluded. Rather these were the words of those who had written to Paul in their letter which Paul is about to address. Paul's response is found in verse two, "But since there is so much immorality, each man should have his own wife, and each woman her own husband" (NIV). In a rather remarkable section, Paul teaches that not only do men have the authority over their wives bodies for sexual intimacies but also, women have the same authority over their husbands' bodies for the same. As a result, both husbands and wives must be equally considerate of one another with regard to conjugal rights, and they should only rarely—and then only by mutual consent—enter extended periods of sexual abstinence; otherwise, Satan might be able to entice them into sin by testing the limits of their self-control (vs. 3-5). Even so, abstinence by married couples is never a "command" and certainly was not a means to moral superiority—as some were contending in Corinth; at best it was only a "concession" to special circumstances (v. 6). Far from a command to all, the celibate life is a gift (Greek, *charisma*) to the few such as Paul (v. 7).

For our study of divorce and remarriage, there are certainly those who believe that a celibate life is the only option open to those who have been divorced for their infidelity to an innocent party or those who have ended their marriages for such reasons as incompatibility, mental cruelty, or failure to be a responsible parent. One is forced to wonder if those who interpret Scripture in such a way as to bind such a penalty believe God gives the gift of celibacy to all who pursue such divorces. If not, the conclusion would seem to be that celibacy for the rest of one's life is either a punishment for being divorced or a penance required for forgiveness. To the contrary, Paul takes up the matter of those divorced and their fate in order to give them explicit permission to remarry following divorce—a permission that some (perhaps the celibacy crowd) appear to have denied them (see 7:8-11).

Simply Speaking...

The word unmarried in verse 7a and 11a is translated from the Greek term *agamos*. It is formed by adding an alpha-prefix (i.e., as with our English "un-," "in-," or "a-," in words such as *un*yielding, *in*hospitable, or *a*theistic) to the word for marriage. Someone who is *agamos* is either someone who has never married or who once was married but now is not. The term is therefore broad enough to include single, widowed, and divorced persons. It should be understood to embrace all these categories, unless the context clearly restricts its meaning.

For the study of Paul's teaching on divorce and remarriage, it is important to realize that this encompassing term always includes *those who were divorced*. Since Paul has specific terms for a widowed person (Gr., *chera*, v. 8) or the never married person (Gr., *parthenos*, vs. 25, 28, 34, 36, 37, and 38), *agamos* is best understood here as referring to divorced persons (cf. vs. 8, 11, 32, and 34) and to widows and to never married persons by logical extension. That this is true seems undeniable from verse 11, where *agamos* is the word used of a woman who had separated from (*chorizo*=divorce) her husband.

If one were to argue that *agamos* does not include those divorced, he is forced to make the improbable claim that Paul wrote forty verses on marriage problems to a church in a notoriously decadent city and never felt the need to speak about the situation of divorced men and women. That would seem highly unlikely. To the contrary, these notoriously complex situations would surely be among those most troubling to a church trying to find its way to a clear path for modeling the Gospel in a wide-open city such as Corinth. In three references to those having divorced, the Apostle Paul treats three different situations. In the first instance (vs. 8-9), he counsels those already divorced to remain single. He does not require it, however, in view of the larger issue of sexual immorality. For those without the gift of celibacy, he not only permits but encourages marriage. "For it is better to marry than to be aflame with passion." In the second case (vs. 10-11), where a believer was married to another Christian but sensed significant jeopardy in that relationship, he echoed the words of Jesus. Neither husband nor wife were supposed to separate from each other; if either should do so, the obligation at that point was not to seek a new mate but to explore the possibilities for reconciliation.

Paul's guidance represents not only good theology but good counseling. A Christian whose marriage is in trouble should be reminded of the no-divorce ideal taught in Scripture and affirmed by Jesus. Paul was, however, a realist who knew that some marriages do break down and result in separation and divorce. He counseled against a move by either one of them to become involved in another marriage, and he was not secretive in his motive for doing so. He hoped that a time of "cooling off," conversation, intervention by concerned parties, and moderation of positions might lead to reconciliation. There is still a third case involving those divorced that will emerge later in the chapter at verses 27-28. This case specifically addresses anyone who might hear "but if she does separate, let her remain unmarried or else be reconciled to her husband" as a prohibition of remarriage, and it will be dealt with when we reach that section of the text in chapter seven.

ISSUES INVOLVING UNBELIEVERS (I Corinthians 7:12-16)

Paul now turns his attention "to the rest" of the Corinthian Church who were married to unbelievers. He has offered guidance to those who were considering divorce or who had already separated previously. One should not read his comment, "I say—I am not the Lord" as a disclaimer of confidence about his counsel but as an affirmation of his apostolic authority to give it. Near the end of the epistle, he will say this: "Anyone who claims to be a prophet, or to have spiritual powers, must acknowledge that what I am writing to you is a command of the Lord" (14:37, NIV). He had responded to the believer-believer marriage plight by quoting well-known words from Jesus. Now, by the authority he has been given by the Holy Spirit, he extended them to believer-unbeliever relationships as well. That extension would have a significant caveat.

The essence of Paul's instruction to any Christian whose mate was still an unbeliever was that he or she should continue in the marriage *if possible*. However, continuing the relationship was nothing Paul could mandate to a non-Christian, of course, and would depend altogether on whether the person "consents" to remain with the Christian mate (vs. 12-13). In other words, Paul is realistic about the prospects for saving such marriages. The Christian mate was now obligated to put the kingdom of God above all else, and that very determination would not be well-received by a husband or wife who was hostile to the new faith that had come to Corinth via Paul's ministry. In situations where Christians could remain in their mixed marriages, they had the potential to "make holy" (NRSV) or "sanctify" (NIV) the other adult and any children in the family (v. 14). These words do not mean, of course, that the saving faith of Christians would somehow transfer redeeming merit to other family members. The Greek word translated "make holy" or "sanctify" (*hagiazo=set apart, dedicate*) is best understood here to say that the best hope for reaching the non-Christian mates or children is through the faithful exhibition of Christ-presence in the home by a believer. Thus verse 16 says, "Wife, for all you know, you might save your husband. Husband, for all you know, you might save your wife." By logical extension, the same was to be assumed by fathers and mothers about their unbelieving children.

There was always the possibility that the unbelieving partner may *not* choose to remain in the relationship. What then? Verse 15 says, "But if the unbeliever leaves, let him do so. A believing man or woman is not bound in such circumstances; God has called us to live in peace" (NIV). Consistent with the Christian ethical principle stressed by Jesus in the Sermon on the Mount and underscored by Paul in Romans 12, the ideal would be to have harmony within the family. Reject divorce. Seek reconciliation. For the sake of all parties involved, continue to live together peacefully. However, when this ideal is not within reach, divorce may be the only path to peace. It behooves Church leaders not to create an atmosphere of guilt within those who can see no other way than to get a divorce. While it is true that some may resort to divorce too quickly and with too little regard for those who will suffer negative consequences that will come, it is not the Church leaders who are to be the judges of such situations.

A GENERAL PRINCIPLE (I Corinthians 7:12-24)

The next eight verses have nothing to do with the subject of marriage, divorce, and remarriage. They are a parenthetical comment on the reconciliation-peace principle Paul has just applied to mixed marriages and the counsel he will give to all Christians in dealing with marital conundrums generally. We will, therefore, skip this section in the interest of time and space. I urge you to read and study this section on your own.

APPLICATION OF THE PEACE PRINCIPLE (I Corinthians 7:25-28)

It is here that Paul introduced yet another group in addition to the four he had already named—"virgins." Technically, as with the widows of verse 8, they could have been included under the broader term for "unmarried." He, however, reserves this group for last because of the importance some at Corinth had attached to celibacy as the spiritually superior lifestyle for Christians living in a decadent environment.

There seemed to be the existing crisis of some nature. It may well have been the coming persecution of the Church and Paul wished that all Christians at Corinth to "remain as you are." If they were married, they were not to seek a divorce. If they were unmarried or virgins, they were to remain that way. Paul's response was not a command but a way of relieving them of the distress that would be placed on them. It seems to be Paul's theme that they should remain as they were until the present crisis was resolved.

TIME IS GROWING SHORT (I Corinthians 7:29-35)

As to just what Paul had in mind when he said, "The time is short," I do not presume to know, and it is not relevant to this study. For my purpose in trying to understand how this relates to the subject at hand, it is sufficient to say that Paul knew that the lives of his spiritual charges at Corinth were always in danger of embracing the immediate without due consideration of the long term. This is true of Christians in every generation. We call it "living in the moment" today.

The general thrust of Paul's plea is that the Christians always be anxious about their service to the Lord and always be attempting to please Him above all else. If we seek the kingdom of God first, He said that all the other things would be ours. We must learn where to place our priorities.

If one were to choose to begin a family at that time, an unmarried man would be inviting a host of "anxieties." Those anxieties would be less about the kingdom mission and more about "pleasing his wife." This would be dividing his loyalty and the same applied for the wife. Paul said all this as "counsel" rather than "command."

PAUL'S FINAL THOUGHTS (I Corinthians 7:36-39)

I truly believe that Paul's Corinthian readers would not be totally satisfied with Paul's response to their request. They, like so many today, had divided into "camps" with each group believing that they were "right." In his closing remarks, Paul leaves it up to the believer to set his or her own course with respect to whether to marry or not.
The only "new instruction" is found in verse 39b, "But if her husband dies, she is free to marry anyone she wishes, but he must belong to the Lord" (NIV). The widow is not bound to a life of celibacy any more than a divorcee or one who has never been married. The *only* restriction for the Christian widow is that her new husband be a Christian.

SUMMARY

In offering a summary of Paul's teaching regarding marriage and divorce in I Corinthians 7, we should not overlook the following items:

1. There is not a full-blown theology of marriage, family, human sexuality, etc., in Paul. He did not write as a would-be theologian or family counselor. For example, he says nothing about child-rearing—

except that church leaders should demonstrate their abilities to nurture the Church as God's spiritual family by showing themselves in faithfully rearing their own children. Paul wrote many letters answering questions and addressing problems. Some of these problems he faced had to do with marriage, divorce, and remarriage; we should take cues from his method of dealing with these same problems.
2. Marriage should not be required of anyone, and the single life (i.e., choosing never to marry or deciding to remain single after a death or divorce of a mate) should not be disparaged. Making unmarried persons the butt of jokes is not only unkind but may even pressure people into ill-advised marriages. Churches should embrace everyone and affirm single or married, Jew or Greek, slave and free, male and female, divorced and widowed are all included in their life and ministry. This is considerably more difficult than many Church leaders realize or are willing to admit.
3. Not only is the single life not to be disparaged, Paul taught that it has great practical value for certain things pertaining to the kingdom of God. Certain situations lend themselves to a ministry of a single person being more advantageous than married persons could accomplish.
4. Occasional Christian teachings or groups to the contrary notwithstanding, a celibate lifestyle is neither morally nor spiritually superior to marriage (see I Timothy 4:3).
5. Marriage is honorable and should be regarded as a holy relationship to be encouraged and nurtured by Christians. It is not a concession to human weakness but part of the plan in the Garden of Eden for

human happiness. The family unit not only prevents immorality and provides for procreation of the human race but provides for the intimacies between human adults, life's safest nurturing atmosphere for rearing children, and life's most secure laboratory for personal spiritual growth.

6. Divorce is not part of the divine ideal. To the contrary, divorce represents a departure from God's will and always attests to sin. Since the essence of marriage is covenanting between a man and a woman, the repudiation of one's marital vows either by sexual infidelity or refusal to live in constant concern for one's mate constitutes adultery (i.e., covenant-breaking). Therefore Paul quotes Jesus to the effect that neither the husband nor wife is ever to take the initiative to disrupt covenant love and faithfulness.

7. Though not ideal, divorce is sometimes appropriate for a Christian who is married to an unbeliever. While God would use the believer's presence in a family to bless that person's mate and any children born to them, that blessing must be received and cannot be forced. Since marriage is a voluntary covenant, the believer—who is always called to God's peace in his or her life—is no longer bound to the abusing non-Christian mate and not guilty of covenant-breaking.

8. Although divorce is not part of God's ideal for human life, it is nevertheless a part of the human experience. Paul acknowledges that divorce happens without ever diminishing the seriousness of covenant-breaking. Sometimes, as just noted, unbelieving partners refuse to live with their Christian mates and cause their marriages to fail. In other instances, marriages fail for a variety of reasons that

involve sin on the part of one or both adult partners in the relationship.
9. Whenever a Christian is involved in a divorce, it is typically wise for him or her to remain unmarried for a time in order to avoid the pitfall of an ill-advised relationship. Marriage formed on the "rebound" is usually doomed to failure. There should be a time of healing and renewal. If reconciliation becomes a viable option during that time of renewal, it can be pursued.
10. Paul accepts the fact that marriage is likely to occur in the lives of most people who divorce. Aside from the caveat already specified about seeking reconciliation when possible, divorced persons who remarry do not sin by doing so and should not be excluded from the life of the Church. Even in cases where special circumstances seem to make marriage inadvisable—whether one's first, second, or subsequent marriage—marriage is holy and not to be forbidden.
11. Without regard to the circumstance of one's divorce, the right of marriage is explicitly granted by the apostle (i.e., if you marry you have not sinned" v. 28, NIV) and may be essential to one's spiritual recovery from a failed marriage.
12. Paul does not envision an ecclestical court or its equivalent, to investigate, judge, or otherwise pry into the pain of one's marital past. Church leaders in our own time should urge fidelity within marriage, offer resources to assist struggling relationships, and support post-divorce reconciliation when possible.

SOME QUESTIONS THAT ARISE

While I do not presume to have all the answers to the questions I will pose here, I will do my best to provide answers that may assist the reader to develop a Biblical attitude toward divorce and to assist others in being more loving and accepting of self and family and friends who have been touched by divorce.

Aren't you afraid that someone reading this chapter could interpret what you have said as giving "permission" to leave a bad marriage that could be saved with prayer, effort, and help?

Yes! I cannot write this without fearing that someone might get this very idea. There are always people whose marriages are shaky and whose commitment to saving them is minimal. It would be very foolish of me to think that there might be the possibility that someone might take this as a "license" to break-up a marriage. While the intention for this writing is not that, I do hope that readers will take the message as a whole and not attempt to make it something it is not intended to be.

In offering the Gospel's message of the forgiveness of sin to sinners—no matter the nature of the sin—I certainly do not invite people to sin (see Roman 6:2). I simply offer the message of hope that it is God's "good news" to everyone. Should someone's heart be so hardened as to hear the Gospel as a license to sin, it is not the message that is at fault.

If someone has divorced for a trivial cause and then marries again, I believe that they are in an adulterous relationship. How can two people repent of being in an adulterous relationship and remain in it? Don't they have to end their relationship? I know that anyone who stole a car would have to give it back in order to show the "fruits of repentance, and I do not think that marriage is any different.

With all due respect to the question, I do *not* agree, and I did not say, "The couple is living in an adulterous relationship!" The concept of an "adulterous relationship" is not a Biblical one. Adultery *is* a sin and it *is* "the breaking of a covenant relationship between a husband and a wife," and, as such, must be condemned as any other sin would be condemned. I have said, and I firmly believe, that this sin is as any other sin and can be forgiven if there is true repentance. Causing a couple who are married after a divorce for *any* reason to be divorced is also a sin. Which sin is greater? In my view, they would be equal. There is no Biblical precedent for anyone to leave a spouse of a second, or more, marriage in an effort to remove the "adulterous relationship."

Secondly, the Bible does not demand what is impossible. A repentant murder does not have to restore the life to the body from whom he or she has robbed it. It is equally impossible to unscramble the eggs of a broken marriage. It certainly is not right or reasonable to suggest that a "solution" is a second divorce. That would be the classic illustration of "two wrongs do make a right." Repenting of adultery means feeling genuine remorse for anything one may have contributed to the failure of a past marriage and determining not to repeat those mistakes in the new one. The fruits of repentance in the new relationship would be love, patience, and a commitment by the renewing power of the Holy Spirit.

I have friends in churches who forbid remarriage to all divorced persons—even if the innocent party in a divorce caused by sexual infidelity—on the basis of Paul's statement about adultery in Romans 7:2-3. How do you interpret this text? And the question may be asked, "Why did you not use it in this chapter?"

While it is true that some Christians base their view that opposes marriage by anyone except for widows/ widowers on the basis of this text: "For example, by law a married woman is bound to her husband as long as he is alive, but if her husband dies, she is released from the law of marriage.

So then, if she marries another man while her husband is still alive, she is called an adulteress. But if her husband dies, she is released from that law and is not an adulteress, even though she marries another man" (NIV). From this statement, it is concluded that "anybody with a living former husband or wife" would be committing adultery to marry following a divorce.

I disagree with this interpretation for several reasons. First, it clearly contradicts what both Jesus and Paul taught in the passages studied earlier. Paul was not a careless thinker or writer and would not be guilty of such flagrant self-contradiction. Second, it is not correct that "a married woman is bound by the law to her husband as long as he lives"—regardless of any special circumstances that might arise. The Law of Moses explicitly identifies a number of situations under which divorce might and should occur. Paul knew the Torah and the prophets and was aware of these.

In Romans 7, Paul is *not* addressing issues of divorce and remarriage for his readers. He is making an argument about the relationship of his fellow-Jews to the Law of Moses and Christ (see v. 1). He illustrates his point by saying the covenant of marriage works the same way; that is, death breaks the marital bond. He concludes: "So, my brothers, you also died to the law through the body of Christ, that you might belong to another, to Him who was raised from the dead, in order that we might bear fruit to God" (NIV).

Just as the marital covenant binds two people to each other, so did God's covenant with the Jews bind them together—as bridegroom to bride, a metaphor used in the Old Testament.

What does God recognize as divorce? Are people who have gone through the court process of divorce somehow "still married in the eyes of God"? Do they remain married to each other until one of them becomes another person's sexual partner in a new marriage?

Two people are married when the civil law to which they are accountable says they are married.

From culture to culture, even from state to state within the United States, the statutes vary. In general, we may say that when an unmarried man and an unmarried woman freely choose to marry, comply with the appropriate statutes (e.g., secure a marriage license), and covenant before a legal authority (e.g., a minister or a justice of the peace), they are married. Within their legal union, they have certain rights and obligations. Similarly, two people are divorced when the civil law to which they are subject says they are divorced. No one who is divorced under the relevant laws of the time and place where he or she lives is somehow mystically linked in marriage to the former wife or husband. When they are divorced, they are divorced.

What about people whose marriage is in real trouble? Right now the only thing holding the marriage together is their fear of what divorce might do to their children—and, to some degree, their fear of what would happen to them in the church. Who would have to leave? Who would get the church's support? Maybe I should just tell them not to worry so much about getting divorced, since they can both remarry later and perhaps be happy then.

Wow! That would be a terrible way to interpret the thesis of this chapter. Divorce *is* a terrible thing. Just ask anyone who has ever been divorced. I make every attempt to convince people to remain married and seek reconciliation where possible; but I *never* advise them to remain married for "the kid's sake." I have seen too much psychological damage done to children whose parents remain together for them only. Having said that, divorce is not always the answer, and I would urge the warring couple to seek professional assistance and make *every effort* to repair the damage and remain together. There is also a lot of psychological damage done to children of divorced parents.

Don't tell people not to worry about divorce. *Do* encourage them not to get divorced without trying everything possible to find a way to honor the commitments they have made.

As for "taking sides" in a divorce, let me ask these questions: "Does that sound like God? Does it sound like the godly thing to do? Why could not a church's leadership promise a couple not to choose sides—to love Bill and Sue, to help them both get the assistance they need, and to remain spiritual family to them regardless of the outcome?"

The idea that the Church must "side" with either party is to bring in the world's view. It is the responsibility of the Church (Christians) and its leadership to remain the loving body for which Christ died. The Church is not the "judge" of these two hurting parties, and its responsibility is to be a spiritual haven for *all* sinners, no matter the sin.

There are many other questions that may be anticipated; since this is not intended to be a "book on divorce," I am going to leave these questions for others to answer. I trust that as you have read this chapter, you will have a greater ability to assist those who have been injured by a divorce.

CONCLUSION: Divorce does not have to be the end of anyone's spiritual life. It is not the "end of the line" any more than it is an unpardonable sin. God has and does forgive this sin in the same manner He forgives any other: That is through *repentance*. God does not expect someone to do *penance* as some would suggest. He does, however, require repentance. Nothing can be done to change the situation after the fact; yet, we can make every effort to reverse the situations in life that caused the divorce and work diligently never to allow it to happen again, especially if remarriage is involved.

As previously stated, nowhere in the Bible are we told that a divorced person who chooses to remarry is "living in adultery." People *commit* adultery; they do not *live in it*. This view says that a person must either reconcile to the first spouse or remain celibate for life. I do not find any of this teaching in Paul's letters or in the teachings of Jesus. Some very good people hold these views in all good conscience; you may have been taught this in your church, and you may well believe them as I did. I like to feel that I have become more enlightened by the reading of the Word, studying it, praying for insight, and by being led by the Holy Spirit. We are to be a people of love and forgiveness and a people who have been saved by the grace of God. Placing ourselves in a position to judge someone else's sins is usurping the prerogative of God, and there is no provision to do so.

God is in the business of forgiveness. Divorce, for all the bad things you may choose to say about it, and in spite of all you have been taught about it, is forgivable. We cannot shorten God's ability to forgive simply because we do not choose to do so. In spite of anyone's past, God offers them a future. It is not a *partial* future or a future shackled to your past. It is a future with the potential for every good thing He has ever dreamed for you. His forgiveness is complete and not partial, absolute and not contingent on your future penance of forfeiting natural human companionship.

May God bless you to read this chapter with understanding, to receive the fullness of God's grace for your pain (whether self- or other-inflicted), and to rejoice in moving forward as God's pardoned and blessed child.

CHAPTER TWENTY-SIX

WHAT ABOUT *JUDGMENT?*

INTRODUCTION: An often-asked question is, "Will there really be a judgment day?" The short answer is *yes*! Paul, in Romans 14:10-12 wrote, "You, then, why do you judge your brother? Or why do you look down on your brother? For we will all stand before God's judgment seat. It is written: 'As surely as I live,' says the Lord, 'every knee will bow before me; every tongue will confess to God.' So then, each of us will give an account of himself to God" (NIV). There are numerous passages of Scripture pointing to the day when God will call a halt to everything He has created. At that time Jesus Christ will return to retrieve His Church and the judgment will follow. Judgment is inevitable; there is no escaping the judgment of God no matter who we are, Christian or not. God has been pronouncing judgment on humans since the fall in Eden. He pronounced judgment on Adam and Eve, the people who desired to build a tower up to heaven and be in the presence of God, the people in the days of Noah, upon the cities of Sodom and Gomorrah, Egypt (just before the Exodus), Israel often when they failed to do His will, and many individuals in the Old Testament.

In the New Testament, there are references to judgment on individuals. We read of the judgment that came upon Ananias and Sapphira because they lied to the Holy Spirit (Acts 5), King Herod was stricken and died, being eaten by worms (Acts 12:21-23), are but two examples.

The city of Jerusalem was judged and destroyed by the Romans in A. D. 70 whereby many thousands of Jews were killed. We see God's judgment in many ways throughout history, sometimes doing the deed Himself, while at other times using others to execute His judgment. While these types of judgment are impressive and we should understand them, they are nothing compared to the *final judgment* when Christ returns.

WHAT WILL HAPPEN ON THAT *GREAT JUDGMENT DAY?*

As previously stated, this shall occur *after* the second coming of Jesus Christ. The first thing that will occur is the dead in Christ shall rise from the grave; then the living Christians shall be taken up into heaven (see I Thessalonians 4:13-18). Jesus said, in Revelation 22:12, "Behold I am coming soon! My reward is with me, and I will give to everyone according to what he has done" (NIV). It would appear that when Jesus comes, He would bring judgment and reward His own at the same time. Since it is true that *time* is not a factor with God, we cannot put a timetable on the events.

As the people of the world stand before God's throne of judgment, the righteous (sheep) will be separated from the goats (wicked). Jesus gives us the most definitive view of judgment in Matthew 25:31-46. Although this is a rather long quote, I feel that it is important enough to place it here rather than simply making reference to it. Jesus said the following:

"When the Son of Man comes in His glory, and with all the angels with Him, He will sit on the throne in heavenly glory. All the nations will be gathered before Him, and He will separate the people one from another as a shepherd separates the sheep from the goats. He will put the sheep on His right and the goats on His left. Then the King will say to those on His right, 'Come, you who are blessed by my Father; take your inheritance, the kingdom prepared for you since the creation of the world. For I was hungry and you gave me something to eat, I was thirsty and you gave me something to drink, I was a stranger and you invited me in, I needed clothes and you clothed me, I was sick and you looked after me, I was in prison and you came to visit me. Then the righteous will answer Him, 'Lord when did we see you hungry or thirsty and give you something to drink? When did we see you a stranger and invite you in, or needing clothes and clothe you? When did we see you sick or in prison and go and visit you?' The King will reply, 'I tell you the truth, whatever you did for one of the least of these brothers of mine, you did for me.' Then He will say to those on His left, 'Depart from me, you who are cursed, into the eternal fire prepared for the devil and his angels. For I was hungry and you gave me nothing to eat, I was thirsty and you gave me nothing to drink, I was a stranger and you did not invite me in, I needed clothes and you did not clothe me, I was sick and in prison and you did not look after me.' They will also answer, 'Lord, when did we see you hungry or thirsty, or a stranger or needing clothes or sick or in prison, and did not help you?' He will reply, 'I tell you the truth, whatever you did not do for one of the least of these, you did not do for me.' Then they will go away to eternal punishment, but the righteous to eternal life" (NIV).

This passage of Scripture spells out, in great detail, the events of judgment. The end result is everyone who has ever lived shall enter into his or her rewards: for the righteous, eternal rest, for the un-righteous, eternal damnation. There shall be no exceptions.

WHY ARE CHRISTIANS TO BE JUDGED?

The question is often asked, "Since I am a Christian and my sins have been forgiven, why do I need to be judged?" This is a very good question, and the answer is not clear in the New Testament. We know what Jesus said regarding judgment, that it would be a time when the "sheep" will be given their eternal reward. We are also told that judgment will be a time when we will give an account of what we have *said* on the Day of Judgment (see Matthew 12:36-37). Jesus also tells us regarding our judging others, "For in the same way you judge others, you will be judged, and with the same measure you use, it will be measured to you" (NIV). Christians must be very careful as to how they "judge" each other. In fact, Christians are in no position to judge anyone at any time. We can and should judge one's "actions" because we are told that we shall know one another by our fruits (Matthew 7:20).

Peter, in I Peter 4:17 wrote, "For it is time for judgment to begin with the family of God; and if it begins with us, what will the outcome be for those who do not obey the gospel of God?" The key word, *judgment*, here represents two different types of judgments. First, judgment means the sufferings and trials the Christians were undergoing. The preliminary judgment through which the Church was enduring is but a preview of the final judgment. God's judgment begins with the Church and from there it spreads to the unsaved. Secondly, the terrible trial that the Church was facing was bad; however, the "outcome" for those who did not obey the gospel would be far worse. If the righteous require this judgment, how much more then do the un-righteous? If it is true that the righteous must undergo this judgment to enter into heaven, what shall be the end of the un-righteous?

The Christian is judged *totally*. There will be nothing that we have ever said, thought, or done that will not be revealed in that time of judgment. Every aspect of our lives will be revealed. You might ask, "For what purpose are we judged when we are being prepared to enter heaven?" The purpose of *this* judgment is not to determine who shall be saved and who shall be lost. The purpose of this judgment is to separate the righteous from the wicked and to provide the degrees of reward and punishment. Just as it is true that some will have greater rewards in heaven, others will have greater degrees of punishment in hell. Therefore, those who die in the Lord will be rewarded according to their deeds (see Matthew 5:19; 6:19-21; 18:4; II Corinthians 9:6). The determining factor for our rewards will be our works in this life. It is for this reason and this reason alone that our deeds will be judged. It is not to reveal our sins because the Hebrews writer said in Hebrews 8:12, "For I will forgive their wickedness and will *remember their sins no more*" (NIV, emphasis mine). This is not a time to "embarrass" God's children by showing all our sins to the entire world; however, they will be revealed. This reference does not mean that God literally *forgets* our sins; rather He does not use them to *condemn* us. God's judgment is shown to be impartial. He shall accomplish this by revealing our works to all assembled. His *fairness* shall be made plain.

The concept of "rewards" is clearly seen in Jesus' parable of the "money" in Luke 19:11-26. This parable was spoken just prior to Jesus entrance into Jerusalem for the final time. Paul, in II Corinthians 5:10, wrote, "For we must all appear before the judgment seat of Christ, *that each one may receive what is due him for the things done in the body, whether good or bad*" (NIV, emphasis mine). The use of the word "we" indicates that Paul is referring to Christians as well as non-Christians. We shall receive that which is "due" us. The thing that is "due" all is condemnation; however, by the *grace of God* we are saved and shall not receive our "just punishment." Those, on the other hand, who are not children of God, shall receive *exactly* what is due them.

"How is it that if we are *justified by faith* we are *judged by our works*? I thought that *works* could not save us." This is a very good question; the *salvation* referred to in the Scripture is most assuredly by *grace*, and there is no "work" that anyone can do to *earn* that salvation (see Romans 3:23). Judgment, on the other hand, is different. We are judged by what we *do* or *do not* do (see II Cor. 5:10).

Revelation 20:11-15 gives a very vivid description of judgment. In that passage John saw the "Books" being opened, and he said in verse 12, "And I saw the dead, great and small, standing before the throne, and books were opened. Another book was opened, which is the book of life. *The dead were judged according to what they had done as recorded in the books*" (NIV, emphasis mine). This being true, there can be no other view than that as given here. We are judged by our deeds. John emphasizes this fact when he wrote, ". . . and each person was judged according to what he had done" (13b NIV). Eternal damnation then follows as death, Hades, and all whose names were not found in the Lamb's Book of Life were cast into the "lake of fire." The "books" that were opened are the recordings of the actions of every person who has ever lived on the face of the earth, *including* Christians. The "Book of Life" is reserved for those who have been saved by the Blood of the Lamb.

Since we are known by our "fruits" (works), we are not only judged in the final Judgment of God, we are judged in this life. As others see Christians live their lives, they make a determination as to just what kind of Christian they are (see Matthew 7:15-23).

James' letter is a great example of how our "works" are necessary to show our relationship with Christ. He wrote, "What good is it, my brothers, if a man claim to have faith but has no deeds? Can such faith save him?" (James 2:14 NIV). He continues in verse 18b, "Show me your faith without deeds, and I will show you my faith *by what I do*" (NIV, emphasis mine). Faith is worthless without our deeds that *show* the world that we are, indeed, Christians. He does not say, "We are saved by our works;" rather he says that when we are a child of God, we are going to *act like it*. We will tell and proclaim to the world that we are Christians by what we do! It is, then, these *works* that will be revealed in judgment and be the basis of our reward.

Paul, in writing to the Corinthian Church, touches on the concept of our deeds in chapter 3. He wrote, "By the grace God has given me, I laid a foundation as an expert builder, and someone else is building on it. However, each one should be careful how he builds. For no one can lay a foundation other than the one already laid, which is Jesus Christ. If any man builds on this foundation using gold, silver, costly stones, wood, hay or straw, his work will be shown for what it is, because the Day [judgment] will bring it to light. It will be revealed with fire, and the fire will test the quality of each man's work. If what he has built survives, he will *receive his reward*. If it is burned up, he will suffer loss; he himself will be saved, but only as one escaping through the flames" (I Corinthians 3:10-15 NIV, emphasis mine). Paul is showing that our works are important and that they will reflect the degree of reward we are to receive in heaven. He laid the foundation, that is, preaching the Gospel; others built upon that foundation and we are still building upon it today. Each of us, as Christians, is building upon the foundation that was laid by Paul. Christians, therefore, are urged to work with all our might that we might receive a great reward (see Colossians 3:23-25).

WHY ARE THE WICKED (UNBELIEVERS) BROUGHT TO JUDGMENT? ARE NOT THEIR FATES ALREADY SEALED?

The answer to the later part of the question is a simple, yes! Their fates are already sealed because they failed to accept Jesus Christ as their Savior or they abandoned their faith and, therefore, forfeited their salvation. We can easily see from John 3:18-21 where Jesus gives a partial list of those who will be lost. To those who are "ashamed of Jesus" in this life, He will also be ashamed of them when He returns (see Mark 8:38-39). In I Corinthians 6:9-10 Paul gives a list of those who will *not* inherit the kingdom of God. He wrote, "Do you not know that the wicked will not inherit the kingdom of God? Do not be deceived. Neither the sexually immoral not idolaters nor adulterers nor male prostitutes nor homosexual offenders nor thieves nor drunkards nor slanderers nor swindlers will inherit the kingdom of God" (NIV).

II Thessalonians 1:8 says, "He will punish those who do not *know God and do not obey the gospel of our Lord Jesus*" (NIV, emphasis mine). This is quite clear, for those who have not *obeyed* the gospel will not enter heaven and stand in judgment condemned.

The reason those who have not acted to obey the gospel are in judgment is to receive their just reward, eternal damnation! I know that there are those who dispute this in the "religious world" today, and they are not new. From the beginning of the Church, there were those who denied the resurrection of the dead (saved or lost) and denied any type of eternal punishment. They were wrong then, and they are wrong today. There shall be eternal rewards for those who are in Christ and eternal damnation for those who are not. It is as simple as that.

CONCLUSION: Judgment is not a pleasant thing about which to think. However, the *fact* that there will be a Judgment should make us more aware of the need to "work for the night is coming when man's work is done." There will come a time when there can be no more work done; at that time our fate is sealed, and our reward is prepared. Let us all strive to do our best for the Master and serve Him to our fullest.

CHAPTER TWENTY-SEVEN

WHAT ABOUT THE MILLENNIUM?

INTRODUCTION: There are four main views on the millennium. Each will be discussed briefly in this chapter. Our goal is to give an accurate description of these various views. You, the reader, must decide which you accept, if any of them. The millennium view that anyone holds is not a matter of salvation, and scholars on all sides are adamant as to their view. I hold a particular view as to the events of the millennium, and I feel that it is correct; however, I shall never make a "test of fellowship" out of such a view. Those who make such a "test of fellowship" with their view are wrong and should not do so. Since God did not give us a complete, definitive, "blow by blow" view of the events that will precede the Second Coming of Jesus Christ, we are left to speculate. Many very knowledgeable people hold a view other than mine, and I am in no position to proclaim that they are *wrong* and I am *right*. I would suggest that if you are interested more in the issue of the Millennium that you research other volumes which will give you a more definitive view than I shall in this work.

Perhaps we should define the word *millennium* as used in the Bible. The word literally means *one thousand years*. The word appears only in one place in the New Testament, in Revelation 20:1-7, and it refers to the "one thousand year" period when Christ is to reign. Herein is the controversy: When and how shall this occur? The question is not *if* but *when* this event shall take place. One major thing to consider here is how one views the events of the world during this time. With this in mind, we shall proceed to a study of the four views on the Millennium.

THE TRADITIONAL PREMILLENNIAL VIEW

This is a widely held view which asserts that the "millennial reign of Jesus Christ" shall occur *after* the Church is taken out of this world. By *traditional*, I mean a more classical or historical view. The word *pre-millennium* means "before the millennium." The basic belief of traditional pre-millennialism is that Christ will return, take out His Church, set up a kingdom on earth, and rule for *one thousand years* as an earthly king, ruling with the saints who have been raptured at His coming. This, they believe, will be the "first resurrection." The "tribulation" shall precede this "return of Christ" and shall be marked with the coming of the "anti-Christ" and the "Battle of Armageddon." At the end of this "battle," Christ shall return and bring an end to the hostilities. This view holds that most prophesies are literal and that many have yet to be fulfilled. At the end of the "one thousand years" Satan will be loosed for a short time and he will lead the unrighteous in a pitched battle, against Christ and His saints. Following this battle, won by Christ, the "second resurrection" shall occur. This resurrection shall be of those who are wicked from the beginning of time and of those who have not accepted Christ. This "second resurrection" shall usher in the Judgment and the final eternal state of these wicked souls.

THE DISPINSATIONAL PRE-MILLENNIAL VIEW

This view is a relatively new view created in the early nineteenth century in Great Brittan. Since this view is a "pre-millennial" view, it holds the basics that the traditional view would hold. The basic difference is in the fact that they divide the history of the world into five to seven different segments they call *dispensations.* This view holds that all the Old Testament prophesies regarding the "kingdom of God" were *intended* to be fulfilled in the earthly *kingdom* established by the Messiah. Since Jesus was the Messiah and since He did not *get the job done* the first time, there must be a *second attempt.* Jesus established the church because there was not sufficient belief in Him the first time He was here. The church is to *keep the concept of a kingdom alive* until He can return and establish the intended kingdom. *The church is simply a substitute for the coming "kingdom." God never intended for Israel to be* abandoned, and He intends to fulfill His resurrected Jewish kingdom. The current "church age" is but an interlude between God's relationship with His "chosen people," the Jews, and the coming program which will re-start when Christ returns. The "re-start" will begin with a "secret rapture" (the first resurrection) of all Christians on the earth, in which they be given their incorruptible bodies and be re-united with the deceased saints. This will precede Christ's *first "second coming."* The next order of events will be the Judgment and then a wedding feast in heaven which will last for seven years (see Revelation 19:9).

Why such a "secret rapture?" There are two reasons for such. First, God has no more use for the "church" on the earth. The second reason is because while the Church is

Simply Speaking...

enjoying a "wedding feast" with Christ (the Bridegroom), the earth is set to be under great tribulation, the greatest tribulation the world has ever known, and God mercifully takes the Church out of the world to prevent her suffering. It is during this time that the Jews are converted to Christ, Jewish style of worship is restored, the anti-Christ will be ushered in, the "Great Tribulation" and the Battle of Armageddon shall occur. At the height of the Battle of Armageddon, Christ returns (a third coming). This coming will not be secret, as every eye will see Him and He will be accompanied by the saints who have been with him the past seven years. It is then that He, with His angels, destroys the forces of Satan, and the Battle of Armageddon ends. After these events, there will be another judgment during which the unsaved are thrown into hell, the converts from the "Great Tribulation" shall be given their rewards, Satan will be bound and his influence shall cease. The second bodily resurrection will then occur, and the saints for the Old Testament shall enter the millennial kingdom. There will, then, be a second Judgment, separating the "sheep from the goats," ushering the "sheep" into the kingdom of God.

It is only *now* that the Millennium is begun. It shall be a literal kingdom in which Christ reigns from Jerusalem with the Jews being given a prominent role in this reign. At the end of this millennium, Satan will be released only to deceive many of those who had accepted Christ during the earthly reign. Those deceived by Satan will launch the Battle of Gog and Magog only to be destroyed by God. At this time the *final* resurrection and the *final* judgment shall occur. It is at this time that *eternity* begins.

This is the view espoused in the *Left Behind* series of books written in the past few years. It is also the view of many TV preachers who are so popular today. Hal Lindsey wrote *The Late Great Planet Earth* a number of years ago, and it holds this view.

Simply Speaking...

THE POST-MILLENNIAL VIEW

The word post-millennium literally means, *after the millennium*. In other words, this view is that the millennium will occur, and *after* that, the Second Coming of Christ will occur. This view was held by Alexander Campbell and others and teaches that the millennium occurs between the *first* and *second* comings of Jesus. The period of time allotted for this is one thousand years and is the time in which Satan will be bound and at the end he will be loosed for a "season." The primary view is that the beginning of the Church Age is one in which the Church prospered in converting sinners to Christianity. This view holds that a "gradual binding of Satan" occurs during this time. This is accomplished by obeying the words in the Great Commission of Christ as He left this earth. The postmillennialists hold that this is occurring at the *present* time and will eventually reach a time where the millennium is ushered in. Jesus does not return to the earth; however, He does reign in a spiritual sense, and the world shall be at peace and harmony will prevail, resulting in a virtual "paradise of earth." This millennial view holds that this is the "second part" of the Church Age. There shall come a time when Satan will be loosed again, and the millennium will be over. The postmillennialists view is one that does not hold to a literal "one thousand years." It is, rather, an indeterminate amount of time. At the end of the "loosening of Satan," which shows the horribleness of sin, Christ will return and claim His own, after which shall come the Judgment.

THE A-MILLENNIAL VIEW

The fourth, and final, view is *a-millennialism*. This view, being the oldest view of any, literally means *no millennium*. The title is not exactly accurate since it suggests that there shall be no millennium. While those who hold this view do not believe that the millennium is non-existent because they do and take their reference to such from Revelation 20:1-6 as do the other views. The basic difference between the "amills" and the other three is in the fact that they do not believe that Christ shall rule *from* the earth. This view holds that the prophesies cited in the Bible relating to the kingdom of God are spiritual in nature and not physical.

The a-millennial view is one that holds that Jesus set up His kingdom when He was here the first time. He established His Lordship through His death, burial, and resurrection, and the kingdom came of Pentecost. Since that time, Jesus "rules" from heaven in His Spiritual Kingdom which exists on earth. This "Spiritual Kingdom" is the Church. Satan was bound and restrained because of Christ's redeeming death on the cross, and the "first resurrection" has been occurring since Pentecost when penitent believers are immersed into Christ for the remission of sins. The "first resurrection," then, is the spiritual resurrection from the dead as one rises from the watery grave of baptism.

The "end time" for a-millennialists is quite simple. At the end of this time, Satan will be "loosed" for a period of time and there will be a severe spiritual attack on the Church. This attack will not be physical in nature, such as a military one, rather a spiritual one. Satan could care less for the physical lives of mankind. He is more interested in the eternal lives of those whom God has created. This great attack will include both Armageddon and Gog and Magog together, and it will not be limited to a "plane in Israel," rather it will be universal. In the midst of this "battle," Christ will return in the air, destroy Satan's forces, redeem the Church, and then sit in Judgment. After this the eternal rewards or punishments of all inhabitants of the earth, both the dead and those who are alive at His coming, shall begin.

It is the view of this writer that the last view, the "amillennial" view, is the one which is most correct. It more closely coincides with the prophesies of the entire Bible, especially with the Book of Revelation.

CONCLUSION

These four views may create some concern in the new Christian or for the reader who simply has not been exposed to such, if any, teaching on the matter. I include them in this work, simply to introduce you to the matter. It is not my intent to push anyone toward any view since it is not a "matter of salvation," and for those who attempt to make it such, I pray that they would cease.

CHAPTER TWENTY-EIGHT

WHAT ABOUT HEAVEN AND HELL?

INTRODUCTION: There is much talk in this post-modern society regarding eternity. Questions arise such as, "Is there a literal heaven and hell?" The answer is, in a word, *yes*! As certain as there is life and death, there exists a literal heaven and hell. While it would be much more politically correct not to believe in such a place as hell, it would not be biblical. Many denominations and others today deny the existence of hell. This denial does not make it so, however. One can deny anything, at any time, and this does not mean that it does not really exist. I may wish to deny certain historical events because it would make me *feel better* about them, yet this does not change the fact that these events occurred.

LET US BEGIN WITH HELL

The mere fact that there shall be a literal hell should not concern any Christian. Hell has not been created for those who wear the name of Christ. It has been created primarily for Satan and his angels. It shall also encompass all who refuse to accept Christ as Savior and those who have refused to follow His commands and be faithful to Him. This fact should frighten all who have not accepted Christ, but has no effect on His faithful.

For those who believe that Satan is already in torment, I would say, "*not true.*" Peter tells us that Satan is alive and well and roaming the earth. In I Peter 5:8, "Be self-controlled and alert. Your enemy, the devil, prowls around like a roaring lion looking for someone to devour." Since Peter wrote this to Christians with the direction of the Holy Spirit, he must have believed that Satan is among us. We cannot believe that Satan is already in hell and can do us no harm. He is certainly in our midst and seeking God's children to destroy. Peter admonishes us to be *alert*. We can only surmise from that term that we, as Christians, are also at risk. It is imperative that we be alert to Satan's deceitful practices and be careful not to fall for his lies. Never be of the mindset that Satan cannot bring harm to God's family. One need only to view the Book of Job to understand otherwise.

WHAT WILL HELL BE LIKE?

There are many descriptions of hell. It has been described as a "lake of fire," "burning brimstone," a "bottomless pit," "blackest darkness." There are other descriptions of hell in the Bible, and all of them refer to tremendously horrible things.

Although hell is described as an awful place, the worst aspect of hell is the *absence of God*. Some might say, "So what? I have no use for God now anyway!" While this is true for many, there are blessings bestowed upon the non-Christian as well as the Christian. The unbelievers share in the sunshine and the rain, as well as many other things that occur from being a human being. Hell, on the other hand, will have no such blessings. There will be a total darkness because God *is* Light. Without God, there is simply no light and this darkness will be worse than anything anyone can imagine. No one can begin to imagine the awfulness of hell and all the descriptions we can muster will not do it justice. If you have ever been in a cave such as Mammoth Cave and the lights are turned out, you can *feel* the darkness. The darkness of hell will be greater.

Four words in the King James Version of the Bible have been translated *hell*.

An Old Testament word, *Sheol*, literally meaning *grave*, or *pit*, has been erroneously translated. There are times when it refers to punishment; however, most often it refers to the grave. A New Testament Greek word, *Hades*, is synonymous with the Hebrew word *Sheol*. This word literally means "unseen, covered, or unseen world." The reference in the New Testament is to the "abode of the dead" not to the eternal place of punishment. A third word, *Tartarus*, is also a Greek word and is used only once in the New Testament, in II Peter 2:4. This reference says, "For if God did not spare angels when they sinned, but sent them to *hell* (Tartarus) putting them into gloomy dungeons to be held for judgment . . ." (NIV). We are not told and do not know whether this is a place in which these angels are kept *until* judgment. There are those who believe that this is the same place where the wicked dead are held as a division of Hades (see Jude 6). The final word translated as hell in the King James Version of the Bible is *Gehenna*. This is also a Greek word and refers to a valley near Jerusalem. This valley, at the time of Jesus, was a garbage dump, and a constant fire burned there to burn the trash. *Gehenna* is a combination of two Aramaic words, *Ge* meaning "valley" and *Hinnom* (likely the name of a man). It literally means the "Valley of Hinnom." This word appears twelve times in the New Testament and eleven of them by Jesus (see

Simply Speaking...

Matthew 5:22; 29-30; 10:28; 18:9; 23:15; 23:33; Mark 9:43, 45, 47; Luke 12:5). Each of the above references is to a place of punishment. James, the brother of Jesus, is the only other writer to use the word (see James 3:6). It would serve us well to understand the use of such a place as Gehenna.

A brief history of the Valley of Hinnom follows: In I Kings 11:1, we find Solomon erecting an idol of the god Molech to placate his *foreign* wives. Sometime later under subsequent kings of Judah, Ahaz, Manasseh, and Amon, the valley became a place of heathen worship (see II Chronicles 28:13; 33:1-9, 21-25). The Jews built a great idol dedicated to the worship of Molech and sacrificed babies there. The idol was a large hollow brazen figure with out-stretched hands. A red-hot fire was ignited inside the idol, and babies were placed upon the hands of Molech as a burnt offering to the god (see II Kings 16:24; 21:1-6). It was only when King Josiah came to power and had all the priests of Molech executed that this practice ceased (see II Chronicles 34:4-5 and II Kings 23:1-20).

The Valley of Hinnom subsequently became synonymous with judgment to be brought upon Judah (see Jeremiah 7:31-32). Consequently, when Jesus described hell, He used the Valley of Hinnom or *Gehenna*. This would be a graphic illustration for his hearers and a reminder of such a place as hell.

When we think of the *fire of hell,* we should understand the fear that it brings to mind. Anyone who has feelings in their bodies will understand the recoil of anyone who encounters fire. Receiving a burn by fire or great heat is an awful thing. We all have an awful fear of fire and being burned. Whether the "fires of hell" are literal or figurative we cannot say. We do know, however, that the *fear* of such is real. Hell will be a place of *eternal punishment and torment.* This should be sufficient evidence for anyone who is capable of thinking and understanding to have a great desire to avoid such a place. Is it any wonder that there are those in the "religious" world who desire to deny the existence of hell?

Hell has been described as the *second death*. Since most of us fear death (an unnecessary fear when we are Christian), we should have an abhorrence for this second death. The first death is only a temporary separation, while the second death will be eternal. If we are to fear any death, this is the one to fear.

DOES HELL REALLY EXIST?

The *fact* that hell will be a real place is well documented in the Bible. Not only did Jesus refer to it, but so did the apostles and other writers in the New Testament. If one believes in the existence of heaven and God, for that matter, one *must* know that there is a literal hell. Even should we remove what the Bible says from the equation, we would, of necessity, conclude the reasoning for such a place. Purely from a logical perspective, we would come to this conclusion. If we accept as factual the existence of heaven, we must conclude the existence of an opposite place. If we believe the third principle of *Physics* that states, "For every action there is an equal and opposite reaction," we must believe in the existence of hell.

From a *judicial* perspective, we must believe in the existence of hell. Does not the existence of *law* require a "punishment?" Were there no *fear* of punishment there would be no *fear* of the law. In other words, the law would have no *teeth*. Who would desire to obey the law if there were no fear of punishment?

If you believe the Bible as the inspired Word of God, you *must* accept the existence of an eternal hell. God does not make empty promises, and this is a promise we can all count on being kept by Him.

HOW LONG WILL HELL LAST?

We have been reciting the fact that heaven is eternal. That would mean that there shall be no end to it. Some would ask, "If there is fire, and we have a *body*, would it be too difficult to believe that the body would "burn-up" and that would be that?" The answer would be NO! The "body" which will be provided after the resurrection (this would include those resurrected for eternal punishment) will be a body that is prepared to last for eternity. It will not be a body that is the *same* as the one we currently inhabit. The flesh and blood body cannot inherit eternal life. Paul, in I Corinthians 15:42b-44 wrote, "The body that is sown perishable, it is raised imperishable; it is sown in dishonor, it is raised in glory; it is sown in weakness, it is raised in power; *it is sown a natural body, it is raised a spiritual body*" (NIV, emphasis mine). This body will never die, decay, nor be destroyed.

CONCLUSION: The bottom line is that hell has no end. It is eternal, and there will be no end of punishment and torment. What a horrible thought that anyone should spend an eternity without God. For this reason alone, all who claim Jesus Christ as Savior should have a burning desire to keep everyone from entering eternity without God.

WHAT, THEN, AND WHERE IS HEAVEN?

To take the latter first, we should know that the Hebrew language refers to *three* heavens. The first heaven is that which we can see when we "look up." In Genesis 1:6-8 we read, "And God said, 'Let there be an expanse between the waters to separate water from water.' So God made the expanse and separated the water under the expanse from the water above it. And it was so. God called the expanse 'sky.' And there was evening, and there was morning—the second day" (NIV). This "heaven" is what we would call the "atmosphere" and extends about twenty miles above the earth.

The *second* heaven would be the domain of the sun, moon, and stars or "outer space." The "heavenly bodies" which are in this "outer limit" of the creation are spoken of in Genesis 1:14, "And God said, 'Let there be lights in the expanse of the sky to separate the day from the night, and let them serve as signs to mark seasons and days and years'" (NIV). David refers to this part of creation in Psalm 8:3-4. Abraham was told to count the stars in the *heavens* in Genesis 15:5, and a warning is given in Leviticus 4:19 not to worship the "sun, moon and stars—all the heavenly array." These "heavenly bodies" are in the second heaven.

The *third* heaven is the one holding the interest of the Christian. This heaven is the *dwelling place of God*. Most think of heaven as the dwelling place of God, and, indeed, that is so. We must be careful not to limit God to one place since He is *Omnipresent*, meaning that He is "everywhere at once." When we attempt to limit God to time and space, as are we, we do Him a great disservice. God has no limits, and we are in no position to attempt to place limits on Him. Though the "dwelling place of God" is in heaven, we must understand that He is also "dwelling" within all who bear His name.

To understand the third heaven as the place where we will spend eternity with God is to understand the end result of our salvation. This "heaven" is the future home of the redeemed. It is a *real* place and cannot be considered as just a "spiritual dwelling" as some have said. There are those who believe and teach that heaven is a "created place on earth" and that we create our own heaven by what we do and think.

The Bible refers to heaven as various things: "a country" (Hebrews 11:16), "a city" (Hebrews 11:10, 11:16b), "new Jerusalem" (Rev. 21:2), "the Father's House" (John 14:2). Each of these references to heaven is symbolic and shall be briefly considered here.

A Country. When the writer of Hebrews refers to heaven as a "country," he is referring to our need for a place we can call our "home" wherein we can claim "citizenship." Paul, in writing to the Philippians, makes this claim: "But our citizenship is in heaven . . ." (Philippians 3:20 NIV). Since we are all *citizens* of one country or another, we can easily understand that analogy. Peter refers to heaven as the "eternal kingdom" in II Peter 1:11. We are citizens of this world, as the world knows citizenship; however, we are not citizens of this world in a spiritual sense. Someday, when Christ returns, we will take our rightful place as citizens of heaven. In the words of the song:

> This world is not my home; I'm just passing through.
> My treasures are laid up somewhere beyond the blue.
> The angels beckon me from Heaven's open door,
> And I can't feel at home in this world any more.

A City. Another description of heaven is that of a city principally "The New Jerusalem." Since the City of Jerusalem meant so much to the readers of the New Testament and especially the readers of the Revelation, we should not be surprised at this designation. Also, in Psalm 46:4-5, we read, "There is a river whose streams make glad the *city* of God, the Holy Place where the Most High dwells" (NIV). The Hebrews writer refers to the "city" in Hebrews 11:10 and 11:16, and John calls it "the Holy

City" in Revelation 21:2. In that same reference, John calls heaven the "new Jerusalem." (cf. Gal. 4:6; Hebrews 12:22; Revelation 3:12 and Galatians 4:21-31). To further understand the immense size of the "city," one has only to view Revelation 21 and 22. The *wall* of the city is described in Revelation 17 and 18, while the *gates* and *streets* are further described in Revelation 21. The *light* of the city will not be the sun or the moon. The "light" will emanate from the "glory of God" and "the Lamb is its lamp" (Rev. 21:23 NIV). To further understand the brilliant light that will light up all of heaven we need only look to the Bible for points of reference. At the birth of Jesus, we see a brilliant light called the "glory of the Lord" as described in Luke 2:9. We see another such illumination at the "transfiguration" as recorded in Mark 9:3 and yet another when the Apostle Paul (then known as Saul) encountered the Lord on the Damascus Road (Acts 9:3).

The Father's House. Jesus, in His discussion of His leaving His disciples provides comfort to them at the thought with the words recorded in John 14. In verse 2 He said, "In my *Father's house* are many rooms . . ." (NIV, emphasis mine). (Other translations render the word "rooms" as "mansions.") The original text would render the word "abiding places." In view of the fact that man is viewed as a wanderer or "nomad" with no place to call home, the thought of an "abiding place" would have brought comfort to Jesus' hearers. In heaven, Christians will have no need to wander, as we will abide with God forever. This is perhaps a better expression of heaven as a "home" since we can all relate to a place we call home. As Dorothy in *The Wizard of Oz* so perfectly said, "There is no place like home; there is no place like home." How true that is. "No matter where we may roam, there is no place like home." If it is true that "home is where the heart is," we should have no difficulty relating since our "hearts" are with the Eternal God and our dwelling place is with Him. The "Father's House" can remind us all of a place where love and comfort abound. For those who have had a difficult childhood or no place to call home, it may be impossible to relate to such a place. However, there can be no mistaking our Father's House as any other place than that of love and comfort.

WHAT WILL WE FIND IN HEAVEN?

There are many aspects of heaven that we frequently overlook. One is that it is a place of *rest*. In Revelation 14:13b John wrote, "'Yes,' says the Spirit, 'they will *rest* from their labor, for their deeds will follow them'" (NIV, emphasis mine). While we are told to work in the kingdom of God and labor diligently in His vineyard, we can know that in heaven we will find rest. Much of our "labor" in our Christian life is against sin and its effects (see Ephesians 6:10-15). The contrast between the *rest* of the righteous and the *torment* of the unrighteous is clear (see Luke 16:23). Since there shall be no temptation or sin in heaven, there will be no need for the labor against these forces of Satan.

Some of the things we will *not* find in heaven will be life's troubles. In Revelation 21:4 John wrote, "He (God) will wipe away every tear from their eyes. There will be no more death or mourning or crying or pain, for the old order of things has passed away" (NIV). Because these are all negative things associated with this life, we can be certain that they will no longer plague us. Paul said to the Church at Corinth, ". . . Death has been swallowed up in victory. Where, O death, is your victory? Where, O death, is your sting? The sting of death is sin and the power of sin is the law. But thanks be to God! He gives us the victory through our Lord Jesus Christ"

(I Cor. 15:54b-57 NIV). Death has been defeated, and there is no need to fear it. The great enemy of humankind has been defeated and no longer has hold of anyone who is in Christ.

This brings us to another important aspect of heaven, *abundant (full) life*. When God created Adam and Eve, He placed in the midst of the Garden of Eden a tree. He called this tree the *Tree of Life*. God told Adam and Eve that they were forbidden to eat from this tree, and when they sinned, we hear of this tree no more until it reappears in The Revelation. We find the "tree of Life" in heaven where the redeemed can *eat* from it throughout eternity (See Revelation 22:1-5).

Jesus said in John 10:10b, "I have come so that they may have life, and have it to the full" (NIV). We are promised full (abundant) life both in this world and in the world to come (heaven). This "life" is clearly seen in the writings of the New Testament. Those who are Christ's can claim a life like no other if only we would make that claim. We are promised the indwelling of the Holy Spirit Who is there to assist us in living out our lives for Him. In heaven, we can expect to have a most full life as He has promised.

One part of heaven that we often overlook is that it will involve *service*. You may say, "Wait a minute. Did you not just say that heaven would be a place of *rest?* What, then, is this service business?" Service can mean more than just *work*. Service is often used when we mean *worship*. I believe we will "serve" (worship) God in heaven as we see in Revelation 22:3b, ". . . and His servants will serve Him" (NIV) and in Revelation 7:15 ". . . and serve Him day and night in His temple." Our *desire* will be to serve Him because He has made all things possible for us by the death of His Son. Our desire to serve Him will be a most natural thing and have no aspect of "toil" or "labor" in it.

There will be *worship*. If you think you have seen worship in your church, believe me when I tell you, "You ain't seen nothin' yet!" There will be such a worship service in heaven the likes of which no one has ever seen or experienced. Revelation contains many references to the *worship* of God and the Lamb. There are fifteen references to worship in the Book of Revelation alone. When you add in the past tense, *worshipped*, there are nine more. Granted, some of these references are to worship of other than God, however, most are in reference to God. When we get to heaven, there is going to be a worship service involving millions, including all the saints and angels. What a day that will be!

LET US EXAMINE SOME OFTEN ASKED QUESTIONS REGARDING HEAVEN

One of the most often asked questions about heaven is, "Will we know each other in heaven?" Because we are not given a direct answer to this question, the answer is wide open to interpretation. There seems to be plenty of Scripture to indicate that we will know each other in heaven; however, it is not clear.

The argument *in favor* of knowing each other will follow. Those who hold this view often quote certain passages of Scripture as "proof texts." One of these texts is Luke 9:28-36 and Matthew 17:1-8, both of which refer to the "transfiguration" in which Jesus was seen with Moses and Elijah. The three disciples recognized these two deceased men, never having seen them in the flesh. Luke says that they appeared in "glorious splendor" as they discussed Jesus' coming sacrifice. In whatever "splendor" they might have appeared, they were definitely *recognized*. Another "proof text" is found in the parable of "Lazarus and the rich man." Once again, we turn to the Gospel of

Simply Speaking...

Luke. In Luke 16:19-31, we find a parable in which Jesus is teaching about the state after death. In this parable, the rich man, in torment in Hades, is able to *recognize* Lazarus in "Abraham's bosom" (Paradise).

On the other side of the question, there are those who do not believe that we will recognize each other in heaven. Two questions are raised on this side, "What about loved ones who are not there? Would this not lead to sadness?" There is no definitive answer to these questions and proponents who believe that we will recognize each other in heaven simply say, "God will not allow such feelings in heaven. We will not be concerned with those who are not there." A "proof text" for those who do not believe we will recognize each other is found in Matthew 22. Here the Sadducees, who believed in no resurrection, attempted to trap Jesus with the question of a widow who married all the brothers of her first husband; each subsequently died, and then she died. The question was, "Now then, at the resurrection, whose wife shall she be of the seven, since all of them were married to her?" Jesus answer is a very interesting one. He said, "You are in error because you do not know the Scriptures or the power of God. At the resurrection people will neither marry nor give in marriage; they will be like the angels in heaven" (Matthew 22:29-30 NIV). The answer raises more questions in the minds of many. The main part of the answer is that there will be no *gender* in heaven as there will be no need of male and female. "If this is true, then, how will we recognize anyone since we know each other as male and female?" The primary answer is that we will be changed form a corruptible body into an incorruptible one with the emphasis on the *spiritual*. We are currently a spirit living in a fleshly body whereas then we will be a spirit living in a spiritual body.

The bottom line is that there exist arguments for each view. It is up to the reader to determine just which argument he or she accepts. None of this has any bearing on our eternal salvation.

Another question often asked, "What kind of body will we have?" We alluded to the answer at the close of the previous answer, and we will expand upon that answer. The *spiritual* or *glorified* body that will house our spirits is often spoken of in Scripture. Paul, in I Corinthians 15, gives a most definitive view of this new body. Beginning with verse 35 and continuing through the balance of the chapter, he speaks at length regarding the incorruptible body. Paul refers to the bodies of animals, birds, and fish, reminding his readers that not all flesh is the same. He then refers to the "splendor" of the heavenly bodies and declares that not all are the same.

In verses 42-43 Paul writes, "So will it be with the resurrection of the dead. The body that is sown is perishable, it is raised imperishable; it is sown in dishonor, it is raised in glory; it is sown in weakness, it is raised in power; it is sown a *natural* body, it is raised a *spiritual* body" (NIV, emphasis mine). Paul continues by describing the differences in the spiritual body and the physical.

John, in I John 3:2b says, ". . . But we know that when He appears, we shall be like Him, for we shall see Him as He is" (NIV). John also writes in The Revelation, "They will see His face and His name will be on their foreheads" (Rev. 22:4 NIV). This tells us that we shall have a spiritual body and it will be *like* that of Jesus. That being the case, what kind of body did Jesus have? Jesus' resurrected body was one of a spiritual nature, no longer that of flesh as He had at the time of His crucifixion and burial. Jesus' resurrected body was similar to, however different from, His earthly physical body. While He was recognized by some, others did not immediately recognize Him. When Jesus appeared to Mary Magdalene, she did not recognize Him even when He spoke to her. It was not until He called her

Simply Speaking...

---

by name that she recognized Him. We know that Jesus was able to *appear* in a room through closed and locked doors and just as easily disappear (see Luke 24:13-32, 36; Mark 16:12).

A third question that arises is, ""What about those who will not be there?" Though some believe that everyone will be in heaven, the Scriptures teach us otherwise. Paul warns the Galatian Church in Galatians 5:19-21 against living in the sinful nature. He said, "The acts of the sinful nature are obvious: sexual immorality, impurity and debauchery; idolatry and witchcraft; hatred, discord and jealousy, fits of rage, selfish ambition, dissensions, factions, and envy; drunkenness, orgies and the like. I warn you, as I did before, that those who live like this will not inherit the kingdom of God" (NIV). In II Thessalonians 1:8-9, Paul warns this Church about the coming wrath of Jesus when He returns. Paul writes, "He will punish those who do not know God and do not obey the gospel of our Lord Jesus. They will be punished with everlasting destruction and shut out from the presence of the Lord and from the majesty of His power" (NIV) (see Revelation 21:8, 27). From these passages, it is clear that *not everyone will* inherit eternal salvation.

"What if those who are absent are friends and/ or a family member?" We previously spoke to this question; however, it begs more explanation. The Bible is very clear that in order to achieve heaven we *must* follow the way of Christ. For those who do not, we say, "They have no promise of heaven." Since we are not the Judge, it is impossible for us to make a definitive statement regarding anyone's salvation other than that which is in the Word of God. I am reasonably certain that there are family members, friends, and acquaintances of mine who will not be in heaven. Will I be saddened by their not being there? The answer is *no*. The reason is clearly stated in Revelation where John writes that there will be no tears, sadness, or sorrow. If I am aware of their absence, it will not matter because I will be comforted in the presence of God. I do not know how this will happen, only that it will. The sad fact is that there are people dying every day who do not know Christ as their Savior. Our goal should be to bring the *good news* of salvation to all we know and make every effort to bring them into the family of God.

Another question that often is asked is, "Will I go directly to heaven when I die or will I have an intermediate state?" The answer lies in one's definition of heaven. That is not a "cop out" as I will explain. If by heaven one believes that we reach our *final* reward immediately after death, the answer is no. If the answer is a place called *Paradise* by Jesus as He was hanging on the cross, the answer is yes. The *heaven* to which we (Christians) go immediately after death is a created place in which disembodied spirits await the Second Coming of Jesus. This is an *intermediate state* but not the *final state* or our final heaven. This is made plain when Jesus said to the thief on the cross, "I tell you the truth, today you will be with me in *paradise*" (Luke 23:43 NIV, emphasis mine). Did Jesus ascend into the final heaven after His death? No! He went to the place where the righteous dead await His final resurrection and return. It was to this paradise He went and took with Him the thief.

Paul refers to this "paradise" in II Corinthians 12:1-4 when he refers to being caught up into the "third heaven," and later he refers to this experience as "paradise." Since, as previously mentioned, the Jews believed in three heavens, Paul is using this term to refer to the place where God dwells.

The word "paradise" is used only three times in the New Testament: the two previously mentioned and again in Revelation 2:7 where Jesus is speaking to the Church at Ephesus and says, "'He who has an ear, let him hear what the Spirit has to say to the churches. To him who overcomes, I will give the right to eat from the tree of life, which is in the *paradise* of God'" (NIV, emphasis mine).

My simple answer to the question is that we will spend the remaining time between our death and the return of the Lord in a blissful state of paradise which will be very much like the final heaven which will be ours after the second coming and the judgment. This fact is further seen when we look at I Thessalonians 4:13-18. Paul explained to the Church at Thessalonica the events of the coming of Christ. In this passage, Paul told the Church that they need not fear the fate of the dead. He makes it clear that they will be the *first* to be brought up to be with Him. These "dead in Christ" will precede those who are alive at the time of His coming. Since the dead will be *raised* first, the question arises, "If they are already in heaven, from which *grave* shall they be raised?" The answer is paradise or Hades, meaning the abode of the righteous dead.

CONCLUSION: Because there is so much room for speculation as to the events and place of heaven, there are many answers to these and other questions. The most important thing to remember is to *be prepared* to go to heaven, no matter when or where it may be. Remember the words of Jesus as He said, "Do not be afraid of what you are about to suffer. I tell you, the devil will put some of you in prison to test you, and you will suffer persecution for ten days, be faithful, even to the point of death and I will give you the crown of life" (Revelation 2:10 NIV).

LaVergne, TN USA
14 June 2010
186061LV00001B/10/P